# *Modernism and the Ordinary*

# *Modernism and the Ordinary*

Liesl Olson

OXFORD
UNIVERSITY PRESS
2009

OXFORD
UNIVERSITY PRESS

Oxford University Press, Inc., publishes works that further
Oxford University's objective of excellence
in research, scholarship, and education.

Oxford New York
Auckland Cape Town Dar es Salaam Hong Kong Karachi
Kuala Lumpur Madrid Melbourne Mexico City Nairobi
New Delhi Shanghai Taipei Toronto

With offices in
Argentina Austria Brazil Chile Czech Republic France Greece
Guatemala Hungary Italy Japan Poland Portugal Singapore
South Korea Switzerland Thailand Turkey Ukraine Vietnam



Published by Oxford University Press, Inc.
198 Madison Avenue, New York, New York 10016

www.oup.com



Library of Congress Cataloging-in-Publication Data
Olson, Liesl.
Modernism and the ordinary / Liesl Olson.
p. cm.
Includes bibliographical references.
ISBN 978-0-19-536812-3
1. Modernism (Literature) 2. Realism in literature. 3. Literature,
Modern—20th century—History and criticism. 4. Literature,
Modern—19th century—History and criticism. I. Title.
PN56.M54O47 2009
809.'9112—dc22 2008035628

1 3 5 7 9 8 6 4 2
Printed in the United States of America
on acid-free paper

For my family

The aspects of things that are most important for us are hidden because of their simplicity and familiarity. (One is unable to notice something—because it is always before one's eyes.)

—Ludwig Wittgenstein, *Philosophical Investigations* §129

Perhaps
The truth depends on a walk around a lake . . .

—Wallace Stevens

# Acknowledgments

This book began at Columbia University in New York City and was finished at the University of Chicago. I am indebted to many wonderful people at both institutions—and beyond—who read and responded to the manuscript at various stages in its development. My deepest gratitude goes to Sarah Cole, whose generosity and intelligence are dazzling. As a mentor and a friend, Sarah has sustained me through the many years it has taken to write a first book. I thank Kevin Dettmar as well for his excitement about the project from start to finish. His perspective on all things—"the very life we're living, which is so excellent"—has deeply shaped my own. At the crucial beginning so long ago, Ursula Heise inspired me and made sure that the book would be ambitious and comprehensive; I am very grateful to her. I also thank Pericles Lewis for his detailed review of the manuscript; his suggestions have greatly improved my argument. Special thanks also go to Michael Seidel for his sage wisdom about all things Joycean; to Nick Dames for expanding my knowledge of the everyday and the nineteenth-century novel; to Jonathan Levin for contributing to my ideas about Gertrude Stein and William James; to Jim Shapiro for his professional advice; to Jonathan Arac for the clarifying discussions that arose out of his seminar; and to Martin Puchner for helping me think about the general sweep of my introductory chapter.

At Chicago I have learned a great deal from being part of the Program in Poetry and Poetics, an especially dynamic community. One of my intellectual models is Bob von Hallberg. I am tremendously thankful for his interest in my work and his encouragement. Members of the Poetry and Poetics Workshop helped to sharpen my thinking about Wallace Stevens in ways that range from helping me to hear the music of a particular line to tracing the shape of his career. I especially want to thank two terrific friends who stand apart as poets and are, together, one of the best things about my life in Chicago: Suzanne Buffam and Chicu Reddy. They spent time with chapters of this book when it was most needed. I am grateful to a number of people here and elsewhere who have offered me advice and who have helped me think outside of my own field. In particular I thank Crisi Benford, Rebecca Berne, David Bevington, Judith Goldman, Oren Izenberg, Alison James, Sarah Kareem, James Lilley, Nancy Luxon, Ann Mikkelsen, Jeff Rees, Lisa Ruddick, Olga Sezneva, and Richard Strier. I also want to thank the teachers who first inspired me. From "my younger and more vulnerable years," Mark Fudemberg stands out; and from my time at Stanford, Michael Tratner, Jody Maxmin, and Alexander Nemerov.

Over the years I have benefited from a variety of grants and fellowships and the generosity of libraries and foundations. I would like to thank the Whiting Foundation for a year of support, the Henry Huntington Library for an idyllic summer of work in the Stevens archives, and Columbia University for five years as a President's Fellow and a dissertation fellowship. I also thank the Manuscript Division of the New York Public Library. In the Special Collections Research Center at the University of Chicago, David Pavelich is a librarian above all others. His incredible knowledge of the poetry archives and his lack of pretension have been extremely welcome. Parts of this book have been published previously as articles, and I thank the editors of the following journals for granting me permission to use this material: *Journal of Modern Literature, Twentieth-Century Literature,* and the *Wallace Stevens Journal.*

Many close friends have been crucial to me as I wrote this book. At Columbia, Sarah Gracombe read and commented on every chapter in early versions. Her insights always raised the most important questions. I wish also to thank Nadia Colburn, whose friendship I value and whose commitment to writing and raising children I truly admire. Special thanks goes to Allison Wade for her deep friendship over many years. I am privileged to have her artwork grace the cover of this book. My gratitude also goes to Linsay Firman for her lovely perspective on all things; to Mark Levine and Emily Wilson for letting me treat them as family; to Matty Lane for his hilarity; and to Kim Gilmore for just knowing me so well. Two friends are impossible to thank enough: Brian Soucek, who makes "working" seem like one long, interesting conversation; and Megan Quigley, to whom I will say it again—from the window table at Queen's Lane to venturing beyond the aisle chairs at the NYPL, it is truly wonderful to be in this together.

Finally, I wish to thank—and give thanks for—my entire, expanding family, especially John Everett McGuire and Teddy Olson McGuire. I work in the security of my father's sheer optimism ("you're an Olson!") and my mother's belief that every day deserves attention, and maybe a chocolate. My family makes everything possible. This book is dedicated to them.

# Contents


| | | |
|---|---|---|
| | Abbreviations | xiii |
| | Introduction | 3 |
| | *The Paradox of the Ordinary* | 3 |
| | *Everyday Life Theory* | 12 |
| | *The Nineteenth Century and the Everyday* | 17 |
| | *Ordinary Life and Modern War* | 27 |
| ONE | Joyce and the Realism of the Ordinary | 33 |
| | *Ibsen and Epiphany* | 37 |
| | *The Lists of* Ulysses | 45 |
| TWO | Virginia Woolf and the "Cotton Wool of Daily Life" | 57 |
| | *Poetry versus Prose* | 60 |
| | Mrs. Dalloway | 66 |
| | *Facts and Things* | 77 |
| THREE | Gertrude Stein, William James, and Habit in the Shadow of War | 89 |
| | *Habit: "The enormous fly-wheel of society"* | 91 |
| | *"Suspended in Tme"* | 101 |
| | *A "perfectly ordinary couple living an ordinary life"* | 106 |
| FOUR | Wallace Stevens's Commonplace | 115 |
| | *The Normal Poet* | 118 |
| | *"An Ordinary Evening in New Haven"* | 137 |
| | Conclusion: *Beginnings and Endings: Proust's Temporality and the Everyday* | 149 |
| | Notes | 163 |
| | Bibliography | 175 |
| | Index | 191 |

# Abbreviations

The following frequently cited works are referred to parenthetically with these abbreviations. See the bibliography for complete textual information.

| | |
|---|---|
| *JL* 1–3 | James Joyce, *The Letters of James Joyce,* Vols. 1–3 |
| *SH* | James Joyce, *Stephen Hero* |
| *Portrait* | James Joyce, *A Portrait of the Artist as a Young Man* |
| *U* | James Joyce, *Ulysses* |
| *WL* 1–6 | Virginia Woolf, *The Letters of Virginia Woolf,* Vols. 1–6 |
| *WD* 1–5 | Virginia Woolf, *The Diary of Virginia Woolf,* Vols. 1–5 |
| *MD* | Virginia Woolf, *Mrs. Dalloway* |
| *TTL* | Virginia Woolf, *To the Lighthouse* |
| *Lectures* | Gertrude Stein, *Lectures in America* |
| *WWJ* | William James, *Writings of William James* |
| *CP* | Wallace Stevens, *Collected Poems* |
| *SL* | Wallace Stevens, *Collected Letters of Wallace Stevens* |
| *NA* | Wallace Stevens, *The Necessary Angel* |
| *OP* | Wallace Stevens, *Opus Posthumous* |

# *Modernism and the Ordinary*

# Introduction

## The Paradox of the Ordinary

Literary modernism takes ordinary experience as its central subject. Yet the predominance of ordinariness has often been overlooked, largely because critics have overwhelmingly considered literary modernism as a movement away from the conventions of nineteenth-century realism and toward an aesthetic of self-conscious interiority. This line of thinking emphasizes how modernists sought to shed the heavy furniture of the realist and naturalist novel in order to render inner perception, the "atoms as they fall upon the mind in the order in which they fall," in Virginia Woolf's famous words ("Modern Fiction," 160). On this account, the most famous moments of literary modernism are moments of transcendent understanding; most modernists describe something of this kind: Woolf's "moment of being," James Joyce's "epiphany," Ezra Pound's "magic moment," Walter Benjamin's "shock," T. S. Eliot's "still point of the turning world," or Marcel Proust's explosion of memory, triggered by such events as the taste of the madeleine. These extraordinary moments magnify an awareness of the self, a coming into being of the individual, and an opening up of interior states of knowing. The modernist preoccupation with the extremities of self-consciousness, located most strikingly in such moments as these, has been praised and criticized but only rarely challenged.[1] One argument of this book is that this conception fundamentally obscures modernism's commitment to the ordinary, to experiences that are *not* heightened. The ordinary sometimes may be internalized, but it is never transcendent; it is what Wallace Stevens describes as "round and round, the merely going round, / Until merely going round is a final good" (*CP* 405). The ordinary is not always transformed into something else, into something beyond our everyday world; the ordinary indeed may endure in and of itself, as a "final good."

The modernist proclivity to dwell in the regularity of the ordinary often emerges out of a response to what is represented as the hollowness of modern life, the loss of abstract ideals in which to believe, and the difficulty of really knowing another person. Ordinary experience, in this sense, resembles Wittgenstein's conception of ordinary language. Wittgenstein does not suggest that ordinary language is something other than what we know it to be, nor that words have some purer, more abstract meaning detached from our usage; "but ordinary language is all right," as he states in *The Blue and Brown Books* (28). The meaning of what we say, according to Wittgenstein, lies in *how* we say it, in the grammar of language. Wittgenstein's *ordinary* consists of the language that we actually use when communicating with each other. "A word hasn't got a meaning given to it, as it were, by a power independent of us, so that there could be a kind of scientific investigation into what the word really means," Wittgenstein writes. "A word has the meaning someone has given to it" (28). Ordinary experience, similarly, can be understood as the things we do every day, meaningful in their usefulness.

The common logic about modernism, however, is that this state of beingness, what Heidegger calls "ready-to-hand," must be radically shaken up; it must be re-seen or seen anew. "Modernism," writes Rita Felski, "with its roughened verbal textures and often startling juxtapositions, can inject a sense of strangeness and surprise into its portrayal of the most commonplace phenomena. It makes the familiar seem newly uncanny, jolting us out of atrophied perceptions" ("Everyday," 608). The Russian Formalists called this technique *ostranenie*, or defamiliarization—art's ability to upset habitual modes of perception. In "Art as Technique" (1917), Victor Shklovsky claims that all art aims to undermine habit in habit's broadest sense, as both an affective experience of the world (perceiving the world in habitual ways) and as a way of organizing one's life. In his most famous passage, Shklovsky argues that art recovers what habit obscures: "Habitualization devours works, clothes, furniture, one's wife, and the fear of war. . . . And art exists that one may recover the sensation of life; it exists to make one feel things, to make the stone *stony*" (4). Shklovsky does not denounce ordinary objects in and of themselves; he questions how we sense and order the ordinary world. Art's heightened attention to the everyday, therefore, may ultimately sanctify the ordinary rather than cause a rupture with it. It is exactly these two modes of defamiliarization that the ordinariness of modernism resists.

Shklovsky was nineteen when he wrote "Art as Technique," the same age as Samuel Beckett when he wrote his 1930 essay on how habit and memory function in Proust's work. Not surprisingly, a critique of the ordinary—and bourgeois convention in particular—often originates in the questioning outlook of youth. Being suspicious of the ordinary might even be regarded as a commonplace condition of youth itself. But this kind of critique is not always sustained. That is, for many literary modernists, the ordinary possesses particular values at various times, including the values of stability, efficiency, and comfort. The representation of the ordinary *as* ordinary counterbalances the understanding of it as something that demands aesthetic defamiliarization. Beckett's body of work, for instance, displays an attraction to the physical and the concrete, in the solid immanence of both objects and repeated habits, despite his sharp awareness that habits can also have a deadening quality. Many other modernist works are marked by a pull toward the overlooked, forgotten, and insignificant elements of experience, and the representation of them as such. Ordinary experience, to modify Wittgenstein, can be all right.

The aesthetic of the everyday that characterizes modernism may seem to share something with an aesthetic that is resolutely postmodern, one that composer and writer John Cage summed up when he said that his "intention is to affirm this life, not to bring order out of chaos nor to suggest improvements in creation, but simply to wake up to the very life we're living, which is so excellent" (Cage 95). But my argument revises postmodern accounts of modernism as a period when writers turned away from the everyday or represented it in entirely negative terms. The modernist works that I address do not attempt to "bring order out of chaos" in the mode of "The Waste Land." The structure behind *Ulysses* or the "pattern" that Woolf sees beneath what she calls "the cotton wool of daily life" is always counter-balanced by a valued interest in the diffuse and messy particularities of that life. Moreover, modernist writers do not always "affirm" the ordinary—in Cage's sense—but they are always interested in how it operates. This said, modernism is still generally committed to modes of realism and coherence that could be called an aesthetic order. Modernism is not so "sunk in banality" as to have lost the power of aesthetic interest, as much postmodern art has done, according to the distinctions made by Arthur Danto in his exploration of what defines contemporary art (*Transfiguration,* vi). But modernist writing does take an enormous aesthetic risk.

Valuing the ordinary takes on three specific manifestations in the literary texts explored in this study, although the ordinary has not always been so distinctly categorized—the ordinary's theoretical appeal, in fact, derives from the capaciousness with which it can be invoked.[2] First, the ordinary is an affective experience of the world characterized by inattention or absentmindedness rather than Shklovsky's heightened *ostranenie.* This kind of ordinariness allows for a reader's own affective disinterest: the great risk that modernist literature takes is to *bore* its readers, pulling us into the very ordinariness that the text represents and embodies. Inattentive reading is not a mode that would seem to suit high modernist texts, with their complicated stylistic structures that demand to be systematically studied. But there is no doubt that a modernist novel such as Gertrude Stein's *Mrs. Reynolds* or Joyce's *Ulysses* allows a reader to lapse and tire, to feel a "negative emotion" like boredom rather than grand passion.[3] Thus reading, like countless other activities, might in fact be ordinary, depending upon the kind of attention we pay to it.

Second, the ordinary also consists of activities and things that are most frequently characterized by our inattention to them. This definition considers the ordinary as a *genre:* unheroic events and overlooked things, neither crucial moments of plot development nor temporal points that signify accomplishment. The ordinary can include mass-produced objects or the everyday errand, an event that is not always an Event. When Proust's narrator trips on uneven paving stones in the last volume of *In Search of Lost Time,* the moment cannot be called ordinary: it is conspicuous and pivotal, for both the narrator and our understanding of the novel's structure and meaning. In contrast to a moment like this one, the insignificance of events and objects that flood Joyce's *Ulysses* calls attention both to the material thingness of what we encounter when we enter a room or walk down the street, and to the overwhelming wealth of information about these things available to the modern individual. While early Joyce critics (and first-time readers of Joyce) frequently look to Joyce's "mythical method" or moments of "epiphany" as readerly guides to signify what is most important in the text, more recent critics have explored how Joyce constantly works to ironize the epiphanic. Joyce attempts to equalize events and objects in an environment chock-full of everyday *stuff.*

Third, the ordinary can be a mode of organizing life and representing it; it is a *style,* best represented by the routine, and aesthetic forms such as the list, or linguistic repetition, both of which attempt to embody the ordinary, to perform it. In "Portraits and Repetitions" (1934), Stein defends the innovative style of her portraits by explaining that her use of repetition is an attempt to get at "the rhythm of anybody's personality" (174). Rather than embrace a narrative structure of beginning, middle, and end—rather than tell a story—Stein's portraits re-create the "existence," as she calls it, of an individual. Routine and habit, enacted by linguistic repetition, become more important than heightened or chronologically ordered events. And in this sense, what characterizes an ordinary style is its openness: modernist literary forms are remarkable for the ways that they turn back upon themselves, for their refusal to move toward a teleological end.

These three principal aspects of the ordinary are interdependent. For instance, valued in opposition to other kinds of experience, the ordinary in its second manifestation as a genre nonetheless eludes qualitative defining: it is marked by its nonimportance; it is not worth noticing.[4] To say *this is ordinary* is to give significance to what is insignificant. Although many literary modernists may allude to the ordinary (it becomes a catchword for Woolf), actually representing it in fiction is a tricky task. If the ordinary is the nonrepresented, the overlooked, then the writer's objective is paradoxical: How does a writer replicate what is overlooked, if the nature of literary representation is to *look* closely at its subject? Modernist styles aim to embody this difficulty. To represent events and objects of common quality, Joyce's language of lists in *Ulysses* attempts to catalog and contain the ordinary's wide-ranging scope. This feature mimics the making of *Ulysses* and ultimately, its sheer size: Joyce edited and enlarged the novel by one third in proof (Ellmann, *Joyce,* 527). Chapter 1 of this book examines how *Ulysses* drowns what could be most important in a flood of insignificant stuff; "encyclopedic," as Joyce called *Ulysses,* the novel wants to contain it all.

But the proliferation of lists in *Ulysses* should be considered in light of its novelistic progenitors, from the timetables and balance sheets of *Robinson Crusoe* to the almanac of occupations in *Bouvard and Pécuchet.*[5] Joyce's catalogs of course also parody the epic catalogs of Homer, whose myth-making is a model for Joyce. In this sense, the inclusive impulse is not a particularly modern feature of the novel, though the varied ideological aims of modernist writers certainly reshape the way narrative inclusion functions. Along these lines, in chapter 2, I discuss how Woolf's theory about the modern novel illuminates her attraction and resistance to the narrative effect of "facts" in fiction. Despite Woolf's disparaging of Edwardian materialism (specifically the novels of Arnold Bennett, H. G. Wells, and John Galsworthy), she does not entirely reject their materialist techniques, striving instead to render a tactile, textured world in which her characters might be rooted in the urban landscape of London, or in the certainties of family genealogy, or in the historical specificity of post–World War I England. Woolf's emphasis on "facts" emerges out of her experimentation with how to create a palpable sense of what constitutes a person's life. In this context, I look closely at *Mrs. Dalloway,* a novel grounded in Woolf's desire to render the ordinary as an affective experience, what she called "moments of non-being," of prosaic, ongoing life.

The political valences of this nonheroic mode of experience, in both Joyce's and Woolf's works, suggest that to deflate heightened experience is not always to refuse revolutionary impulses or to embrace the status quo. Modernist epiphany is often initiated by a banal moment; the "vulgarity of speech," as Stephen Dedalus explains, can elicit a "sudden spiritual manifestation" (*SH* 210). But the return to ordinary experience is inevitable, if not part of the epiphanic moment itself. Ordinary life becomes the context in which epiphany is subsumed, reconsidered, and assessed in light of its continuity or its ability to actually change one's previous behavior. That is, the ordinary is often more politically efficacious than the moment of shock. As Peter Bürger has explained, aesthetic shock "is aimed for as a stimulus to change one's conduct of life," but the affective experience of being jolted out of the ordinary does not always offer a clear sense of *how* or *what* one is meant to change (*Theory of the Avant-Garde,* 80).

Consider briefly Rainer Maria Rilke's poem, "Archaic Torso of Apollo," in which the beauty of a Greek statue deeply affects the beholder, penetrating him with its radiant light. Despite the fact that the statue is missing a head (and therefore eyes), the statue's "gaze / now turned to low, / gleams in all its power." The statue has the capacity to perceive, if not judge, the person who studies it. The poem famously ends:

> denn da ist keine Stelle,
> die dich nicht sieht. Du mußt dein Leben ändern.
> [. . . for here there is no place
> that does not see you. You must change your life.]
> (60)

One effect of these lines is to suggest that humans are incomplete and must be transfigured, although part of the statue's "power" (and the poem's power) is the openness of this transfiguration. On this point (though not in direct response to Rilke's poem), Bürger notes that the idea of aesthetic shock can be dangerously nonspecific:

> Even a possible breaking through the aesthetic immanence does not insure that the recipient's change of behavior is given a particular direction. . . . On the contrary, one has to ask oneself whether the provocation does not strengthen existing attitudes because it provides them with an occasion to manifest themselves. A further difficulty inheres in the aesthetics of shock, and that is the impossibility to make permanent this kind of effect. Nothing loses its effectiveness more quickly than shock; by its very nature, it is a unique experience. (80)

Shock cannot have a permanent effect in and of itself. It is similar to Walter Pater's "moment," which may not actually give form to anything, but leaves the individual passive, waiting for the next heightened moment.[6] A return to the world of ordinary experience gives form to shock and integrates shock into a world where things happen, for better or worse, through legal institutions, social systems, and the biological necessities of living. The modernists were interested in how ordinary, individual lives were inflected by these all-too-familiar constraints. It was these negotiations between self and the world that Woolf was referring to when she spoke of the "cotton wool of daily life" or "non-being," in reference to substantial parts of the day that are not lived consciously and thus are not remembered. Proust refers to inescapable routine as "La Habitude," a feminine goddess stripped of political valence. Habit is neither "good" nor "bad" but is indispensable and ritualistic—the trigger by which the paradise of the past is recovered but to which the individual must inevitably return.

Along these lines, the "shock" of modern wartime is sometimes represented as strangely repetitious, even boring, both for those far removed from the fighting and for soldiers at the front. War gains force as a major theme in this book, not as the opposite of the ordinary, but as a sociopolitical context that highlights the pervasiveness of the ordinary's affective dimension even amid unprecedented historical events. Though war is never an ordinary event, war nonetheless can be ordinary in the first sense: it can be dull. In some instances, the ordinary consumes and absorbs a wartime fear of what will happen next. In *Mrs. Reynolds* and *Wars I Have Seen,* which I examine in chapter 3, Gertrude Stein describes a couple who retreat to the comfortable repetitions of home life during the violence of World War II. In this case, the politics of the ordinary become troubling, an aggressive retreat to the way living used to be. The couple's pacifism and refusal to acknowledge the logic of war—to an extent, defiantly—also emerge as dangerously escapist. Stein's depiction of habit reveals the unsettling ramifications of assuming that certain modes of behavior are "ordinary" when ordinary experience during wartime is actually sharply stratified along class lines. As Raymond Williams explains in his *Keywords* (1983), the word "ordinary," in the seventeenth century, took on negative connotations involving ideas of social superiority and inferiority; subsequently, "ordinary people" might mean both the uneducated masses ("What ordinary people believe") but also a sensible, decent, regular group of individuals who follow a "standard" mode of behavior (225–26). Stein assumes the latter definition in her portrait of an ordinary couple. However, Stein's "ordinary" may be simply those fortunate people who have options. Other modernist writers are also preoccupied with ordinary experience partly because they *can* be. In this way, the valuation of the ordinary emerges as an intrinsically bourgeois endeavor, a critical examination of middle-class behaviors and attitudes.

In making things new, the Modernists erase the possibility of habit.

In chapter 4, I discuss Wallace Stevens's acute awareness of his distance from the events of World War II, captured by his frequent references to the "weather of war," a phrase suggesting that the war was as omnipresent and routine as the daily weather report. The war—as well as other social, political, and economic issues of his time (including the Great Depression)—never directly threatened Stevens's way of life, though he was more mindful of politics than many critics have maintained. Stevens's idea of the "commonplace" in fact emerged from his attempt to write a more directly political poetry. His approach to the ordinary finds a philosophical counterpart in the pragmatist philosophy of William James, which I discuss in chapter 3 in conjunction with Stein's depiction of habit. James's overarching optimism about ordinary experience also squares with Stevens's work. Stevens was introduced to Jamesian pragmatism and the philosophy of George Santayana while he was a student at Harvard, where both James and Santayana were professors. Stevens's interpretation of pragmatist principles is linked closely with a distinct affirmation of the ordinary, a point that has not been emphasized in critical discussions regarding Stevens and his relationship to pragmatism.[7] This affirmation is essential to understanding Stevens's work, as it distinguishes him from W. B. Yeats, Eliot, and Pound, who were more skeptical of the ordinary's redeeming power.

One way to think about pragmatism's legacy, as Stanley Cavell has done, is to situate pragmatism as a way of thinking that affirms the ordinary specifically as a guard or resistance to philosophical skepticism. Cavell considers the ordinary language theory of Wittgenstein and J. L. Austin together with the pragmatism of Emerson and Thoreau in his long-standing exploration of what he has called "the problematic of the day, the everyday, the near, the low, the common" (*New Yet Unapproachable,* 36). Cavell's philosophical project takes into account the limitations of the ordinary—specifically ordinary language—while nonetheless affirming the ordinary against the idea that limitation somehow diminishes the quality or purpose of human life.[8] Wallace Stevens's long poem "An Ordinary Evening in New Haven" is animated by a similar tension between limitation and satisfaction, in which the centrality of ordinary experience becomes more important than conceptions of the imagination or divinity.

There are other writers whose work plays a role in defining the primacy of the ordinary during the modernist period: Beckett and Proust are in many ways this book's counterbalancing guides, especially as Proust's work is *read* by Beckett, whose interest in habit serves as this study's chronological endpoint. Beckett's disdain for the everyday may seem a far cry from Proust's aesthetic appreciation of the domestic and habitual, but both writers are simultaneously compelled and repelled by the banalities of modern life, and both are drawn to stylistic practices through which they might embody the everyday, especially its temporal dimension. Although *In Search of Lost Time* was written beforethe other major modernist texts in this study, it serves as the subject of this book's conclusion, largely because the work itself takes up the relationship between the ordinary and teleological endings. Proust examines the role of habit in resisting temporal flux and in negotiating the desire to see one's life in narrative terms with a beginning, a middle, and an end. *In Search of Lost Time* amplifies and distends its narrative to fit the temporality of the everyday while recognizing the fundamental incompatibility of the everyday with narrative form. This animating tension underlies my analysis of narrative more generally in each chapter, and returns this project to its genesis: the paradox of representing the unrepresented.

I treat European and American modernism as developing in concert, largely as a result of the dynamic interactions among so many of modernism's key figures on both sides of the Atlantic. Geographical difference becomes significant in some cases, however; for instance, the value that Stevens places on the ordinary cannot be understood apart from his isolation in Hartford, Connecticut, and his distance from international politics. Moreover, the function of ordinary experience becomes radically reconfigured when a war is being waged in one's own backyard. Stein was obsessed with the difference between "daily island life" in England and Paris and America, and she suggested that only in Europe existed traditions sufficiently entrenched to enable continual, uninterrupted habits, even during a time of war. But no overarching paradigm expresses a consistent geographical difference between how European and American literary modernists treat ordinary experience, and even Stein's claims seem limited in their generality. Taking Pater as an important proto-modernist figure who repudiated habit in favor of raw, sensory experience, on the one hand, and William James as an influential proponent of habit as a means of "success," on the other, it is possible to suggest a range of views about ordinary experience but reductive to say that these views are peculiarly "British" or "American." Even if Pater and James have become distinctly tied to their respective British and American literary cultures, their influence has certainly spread beyond these geographical borders.

However, there are important comparisons to be made among a range of philosophies of everyday life, especially as some strains of thought conflict and overlap. A case in point is the relationship between James and Henri Bergson, the French philosopher whose work, like James's, had a profound impact on literary modernism, catalyzing Proust's *In Search of Lost Time,* and deeply influencing the work of Woolf, Eliot, and Joyce. The exchange of ideas between James and Bergson (they met several times and corresponded) constitutes a loose influence and alliance that marks the modernism I address. Moreover, James's and

Bergson's philosophies might be viewed as paradigms in which habits are valued for their practical use and efficiency.[9] Their general acceptance of the everyday stands in contrast to the everyday life theory as articulated in France in the 1950s and 1960s, foremost by the work of the Marxist sociologist Henri Lefebvre, whose work has been rediscovered recently, especially in the field of cultural studies.[10] Lefebvre argues that the conditions of everyday life are driven largely by a capitalist culture in which actions have become mechanical, alienating, and soul-destroying. He advocates for the everyday to be redeemed, aesthetically and politically, an idea that has influenced many other theorists, including Michel de Certeau, Maurice Blanchot, Roland Barthes, and situationists such as Raoul Vaneigem and Guy Debord. Lefebvre seeks to transform the everyday through spontaneity and rebellion, arguing for nothing less than a cultural revolution beginning with how individuals lead their everyday lives.

## Everyday Life Theory

In his pioneering work *Everyday Life and the Modern World* (1968), an abridgment of the three-volume *Critique of Everyday Life* (1946–82), Lefebvre argues that *la vie quotidienne* cannot be defined or located. Everyday life eludes metaphor and "evades the grip of forms" (182). The everyday is not something we notice in any definitive manifestations. Lefebvre writes:

> The quotidian is what is humble and solid, what is taken for granted and that of which all the parts follow each other in such a regular, unvarying succession that those concerned have no call to question their sequence; thus it is undated and (apparently) insignificant; though it occupies and preoccupies it is practically untellable, and it is the ethics underlying routine and the aesthetics of familiar settings. (24)

Lefebvre's theory of the ordinary marks it as something that could incorporate a limitless variety of activities, in the sense that the everyday is pervasive and yet cannot be located in a set of practices. The everyday includes temporal rhythms and repetitions, typified by inattention. Specific behaviors are not the criteria by which the everyday is defined.

The limitlessness of Lefebvre's everyday becomes its most compelling quality, largely because it locates potentially subversive and political power within almost all facets of human experience. Although many modernist texts do in fact locate the everyday in precise details, actions, and images, modernist writers acknowledge and respond to the difficulty of representing the everyday, as it is both everywhere and nowhere, overlooked and yet a subject that deserves attention. The significance of Lefebvre's theory lies in his characterization of the everyday's paradoxical nature, a feature that animates many of literary modernism's experiments with form.

However, the everyday described by Lefebvre differs historically from the everyday of literary modernism, a point that this book emphasizes. In drawing upon a range of ideas from everyday life theory, I have taken into account the fact that Lefebvre's theoretical model (and those influenced by it) has a stronger link to the literature of the same period, such as that produced by Jean-Paul Sartre, Alain Robbe-Grillet, and George Perec. These writers approach the everyday very differently than did their nineteenth-century and modernist predecessors. Profoundly influenced by a consumerist ideology imported from the United States after the Second World War, many French writers of the 1950s and 1960s addressed the rapidly changing domestic life of their country, as washing machines, refrigerators, telephones, and automobiles changed the way that daily life functioned. As Lefebvre notes, the writers of his era assume a critical stance toward the urge to satisfy all desires with material objects, noting a "sense of unrest that pervades everyday life" (*Everyday,* 80). The literature of this period, while deeply influenced by the modernist preoccupation with everyday life, registers very specific economic and cultural shifts in France after the Second World War.[11] Alice Kaplan has suggested that French writers and intellectuals were "caught between their own Marxist sympathies and the reality of frantic cultural Americanization at the moment when France was losing its colonial empire" ("Puzzle Man," 797). According to Kristin Ross in *Fast Cars, Clean Bodies* (1995), the "colonization of everyday life" (a catchphrase used by Lefebvre and his later devotees, the situationists) should be understood literally as the continuation of the structures of imperialism within the everyday, as new values of American technology and consumerism promoted cleanliness, speed, efficiency, and interior isolation in French everyday life. Barthes' *Mythologies* (1957) might be read as a product of these times, as Barthes unravels the "signification" behind recent features of modern French living: *Elle* magazine, Greta Garbo, travel literature, cookery. Everyday habits are the very expression of certain values—markedly capitalistic—and manifest the ways in which these values control even the smallest aspects of bourgeois life in postwar France.

For historical and cultural reasons, then, I do not draw extensively upon Lefebvre's theoretical ideas. Furthermore, his work—which has gone in and out of favor since *Dialectical Materialism* appeared in 1939—is overall too broad for my purposes. Incredibly prolific, Lefebvre has always had a following in the social sciences, especially his *Production of Space* (1974), but only since the rise of cultural studies has *Critique of Everyday Life* become more widely known in literary fields. Not until 2006 was the last volume of *Critique,* subtitled *From Modernity to Modernism (Towards a Metaphilosophy of Daily Life),* made available in English translation. Under the aegis of Lefebvre, the everyday has now become an elastic theoretical concept deployed for diverse, sometimes inconsistent aims, which tempers the usefulness of his theory of the everyday to particular works of modernist literature. For instance, in the last chapter of the first volume of *Critique,* titled "Notes Written One Sunday in the French Countryside," Lefebvre draws upon the research he did during the Second World War, on the history of peasant society in the Pyrenees, in particular the history of medieval society. Lefebvre's return to a pre-industrial past illustrates the expansiveness of his conception of the everyday. Lefebvre imagines a rural utopia in which people live according to the rhythms of the seasons and the communal "festival." His humanist nostalgia for this way of life foresees the ways in which cultural studies often turns to the everyday as something more "real" than worlds constructed by literary texts, whose everyday relevance has been supplanted by more popular forms of entertainment. That is, no matter where the everyday is seemingly located—in the past (for Lefebvre) or in popular culture—the everyday is the realm of the authentic, quite in contrast with the assumptions behind other critical analyses of the everyday, such as Barthes' *Mythologies.*

Perhaps the most important difference between everyday life theory and how modernist writers understand the everyday is the Marxist framework that underlies the work of Lefebvre and others influenced by him. One of Lefebvre's assumptions is that people are estranged from themselves and from each other under the conditions of capitalist production. The objects that crowd an individual's days and occupy his or her thoughts, moreover, are a sign of capitalism's hold upon even the smallest details of modern life.[12] Ultimately, Lefebvre is interested in how material things reveal overarching economic structures. Although he claims that "a system of everyday life does not exist," he nonetheless establishes his theory of the everyday upon a Marxist system through which he argues that "a revolution [will take] place when and only when, in such a society, people can no longer lead their everyday lives" (*Everyday,* 86, 32). And in this sense, Lefebvre's theory reveals a contradiction between a desire to systematize the everyday and an acknowledgment of its essential openness. On this point, it could be argued that the movement from the everyday in literature to the everyday as a theoretical subject occurs when literature gives up on it. That is, theorists like Lefebvre begin to write about the everyday when it becomes a question of whether the novel or postmodern writing more generally can represent the everyday through the conventions of realism.[13] Although modernism may call into question how the everyday can be represented, everyday life theory fundamentally emphasizes the impossibility of its representation.

Michel de Certeau modifies Lefebvre's notion of the everyday by suggesting that the everyday might resist the status quo but can never have any true systematic political power. The only distinctive quality of De Certeau's everyday is its ubiquity. And while an awareness of the everyday as everywhere, according to De Certeau, will not likely bring about a revolution of everyday life, small "tactics" have the ability to oppose, in Michel Foucault's terms, an apparatus of social discipline and surveillance. In *The Practice of Everyday Life* (1984), De Certeau writes:

> Many everyday practices (talking, reading, moving about, shopping, cooking, etc.) are tactical in character. And so are, more generally, many "ways of operating": victories of the "weak" over the "strong" (whether the strength be that of powerful people or the violence of things or of an imposed order, etc.), clever tricks, knowing how to get away with things, "hunter's cunning," maneuvers, polymorphic simulations, joyful discoveries, poetic as well as warlike. (xix)

Quietly powerful, everyday habits resound with individual agency in a system that controls choice. Contrasting Barthes with Lefebvre and De Certeau calls attention to the dual function of the everyday's deployment: both life-denying and liberating, both conventional and transgressive.[14]

In his 1958 essay"Culture Is Ordinary," Raymond Williams offers an understanding of the ordinary that differs from what was emerging in France around the same time, if only because Williams, who sees the everyday as manifested in the British working class, does not altogether disparage the ordinary nor demand that it undergo a radical transformation. Williams emphasizes that "culture" should not be associated with highbrow affectation nor solely with bourgeois leisure:

> Culture is ordinary: that is the first fact. Every human society has its own shape, its own purposes, its own meanings. Every human society expresses these, in institutions, and in arts and learning. The making of a society is the finding of common meanings and directions, and its growth is an active debate and amendment under the pressures of experience, contact, and discovery, writing themselves into the land. (4)

Williams's broad definition of culture assumes that everyday behaviors shape both the physical landscape of people's lives (e.g., the actual layout of cities and towns) and the literature produced by a particular society. His notion of change is gradual, like Fernand Braudel's "longue durée," or even the "daily island life" that Stein coins in "What is English Literature" to describe the fabric of culture in England from Chaucer through the twentieth century. For Williams, the ordinariness of English culture stems from the strength of its working classes, with entrenched customs and pleasures that are not easily disrupted, and which stand apart from highbrow society.[15] Stein's "daily island life" is similarly resistant to change, providing the country with the stability essential to literary production.

Stein's notion of everyday life, however, stems from her personal love of domestic habit and an instinct to locate the ordinary in the particular experience of women. This association between the ordinary and the feminine has a long history: as Naomi Schor has argued, for instance, the "detail" is one stylistic feature of the ordinary that has always been associated with women, in both the literary and visual arts. Denounced by neoclassicists (Sir Joshua Reynolds, in particular), and ambiguously embraced by idealists such as Hegel, the "detail" participates in a "larger semantic framework," Schor argues, "bounded on the one side by the ornamental, with its traditional connotations of effeminacy and decadence, and on the other, by the everyday, whose 'prosiness' is rooted in the domestic sphere of social life presided over by women" (*Reading in Detail,* 4). Schor suggests, however, that the paradoxical importance of the insignificant "detail" was eventually claimed and valorized in modern and contemporary culture (largely, through Freudian analysis, in which every detail needs to be given a meaning, and every detail needs to be given). It is thus no longer possible to say that the insignificant detail is a feminine style, or that the ordinary belongs to the realm of women.[16] Indeed, what is striking if we look at everyday life theorists like Lefebvre, De Certeau, and the situationists is the way that they self-identify with the everyday, often assuming their own subjectivity as everyone else's, taking as their ideal figure the rootless urban man. Michel de Certeau dedicates *The Practice of Everyday Life* to someone like Leopold Bloom: "To the ordinary man. To a common hero, an ubiquitous character, walking in countless thousands on the streets" (v). Lefebvre opens *Everyday Life and the Modern World* (1968) by suggesting that *Ulysses* achieves something for which his work also strives: "Joyce's narrative rescues, one after the other, each facet of the quotidian from anonymity" (2). The life of urban, pedestrian, alienated modern *man*—originating in Baudelaire and represented by George Simmel's metropolis and Benjamin's arcades—constitutes the everyday for these theorists.

This understanding of the everyday obviously assumes a cultural homogeneity, and a masculinity, which is called into question by the fact that women's experience of the everyday is often represented as essentially different from men's, and that modernism also takes place within the spaces of the home.[17] Although Lefebvre acknowledges that everyday life "weighs heaviest on women" in that they "are the subjects of everyday life and its victims or objects and substitutes," he also assumes that women are not aware of the everydayness that they embody; "they are incapable of understanding it" (*Everyday Life,* 73). Lefebvre disparages women who try to avoid the everydayness that defines them, as if it were women's inexorable fate to generate the modern phenomenon on which Lefebvre's theories are sustained (92). Assessing Lefebvre, Laurie Langbauer writes: "According to the old logic that women cannot understand something because they embody it, the contradictions of the everyday, which make it opaque to everyone, make it particularly so to women" ("Cultural Studies," 51). What becomes clear in looking at modernist representations of everyday life is that individuals can be both enmeshed in the everyday and conscious of it at the same time. Although the writers I consider often treat ordinary experience as differentiated by gender, the ability to scrutinize one's experiences is certainly available to both men and women. Rita Felski has even suggested, counter to Lefebvre, that while women have historically embodied the everyday, they now possess a heightened consciousness of how the everyday operates. Specifically in regard to everyday *time,* Felski suggests, the conflicting demands of both work and home for women encourage clockwatching, or obsessing about appointments and deadlines ("Invention," 20). This contemporary reality is already evident in the literature of high modernism, as modernism's everyday consists of both public and private, urban and domestic realms, and the frequently disjointed movements in between.

## The Nineteenth Century and the Everyday

> Is everything in narrative significant, and if not, if insignificant stretches subsist in the narrative syntagm, what is ultimately, so to speak, the significance of this insignificance?
> —Roland Barthes, "The Reality Effect"

The desire to replicate ordinary experience is not exclusive to modernism. The more obvious assumption—one that many critics of the novel have sustained—is that the nineteenth-century novel is the exemplary chronicler of ordinary life, rooted in the realism of the domestic and the natural. Ian Watt's well-known study of the rise of the novel, beginning in the eighteenth century with Daniel Defoe, Samuel Richardson, and Henry Fielding, claims that the novel, as a new form, moved toward representing a kind of idiosyncratic individualism, away from the universals and ideals of classical literature. One of the novel's key elements in rendering a realistic portrait of an individual, according to Watt, is a detailed depiction of everyday life, including an accurate depiction of time and an intimacy with the texture of physical experience (*Rise of the Novel,* 9–30). Franco

Moretti's work builds from this premise that the everyday is the special province of the novel, especially in the nineteenth century when the novel had a wider circulation and influence than it did before or after.[18] The everyday experiences of an expanding bourgeois culture, according to this theory of the novel, become the material *stuff* of nineteenth-century fiction.

My project, not in opposition to this trajectory, undertakes to show how the modernist novel treats the everyday with a new centrality, putting pressure on the notion of a coherent individual subject, and reconfiguring (but not rejecting) representations of temporality and material culture as crucial to a representation of character. The understanding of "plot" in many modernist novels sometimes shifts from the course of a lifetime to the experience of one day, or a brief period of time, and thus "everydayness" takes on an expanded, amplified meaning. Moretti claims that the nineteenth-century novel's "only narrative invention" was "filler"—descriptive, realist moments (the opposite of turning points) from which modernism, he argues, broke to develop other narrative forms ("Serious," 379). But the twentieth century did not abandon the filler: an entire modernist novel might be filled with extremely minute details of everyday life, foregrounding the paradox of how the insignificance of the ordinary is examined with a wide-angle lens. Modernism makes the filler autonomous. Conversely, a classic framework of time for the Victorian novel—six months to two years—is dramatically lengthened by modernists such as Proust or Woolf or, a bit later, Anthony Powell. The time allotted to solve a problem, finish a project, or see courtship through to marriage becomes time in which no central experience can necessarily mark what the novel is "about." Like the novel of just one day, time tracked over the course of a lifetime (or longer) deflates the importance of event and outcome.

In looking at how ordinary experience becomes central to modernist literature, I return at various points to the relationship between modernism and realism. In *Mimesis: The Representation of Reality in Western Literature,* Eric Auerbach advances two key points about modern realism's relationship to previous realist modes. First, Auerbach assumes a direct correlation between historical events and literary styles, linking "multiple consciousness" in Joyce, Proust, and Woolf, for instance, with the decades of the First World War and after, marked by the "widening of man's horizon" (485). Modern realism, he writes, "has ever developed in increasingly rich forms, in keeping with the constantly changing and expanding reality of modern life" (489). The ordinary becomes especially important in the twentieth century, Auerbach suggests, as a result of the growing belief in the unique value of each human life: a combination of the Christian sense that each life is modeled on Christ's, the Jewish sense of the inherent seriousness of each life, and the classical need to depict the visible reality of this world extensively.[19] Woolf's *To the Lighthouse* is, for Auerbach, a fine example of modern realism's emphasis on the ordinary that has emerged from much older realist modes: the externalized, explicit realism of Homer—in whose stories all narrative action occurs in the foregrounded present—and the limited externalization of Old Testament stories, whose key moments are shaped within domestic and commonplace settings. Describing the prose of *To the Lighthouse,* Auerbach suggests that Woolf achieves "a more genuine, a deeper, and indeed a more real reality" through the oscillation of interior and exterior points of view, a movement that is symptomatic of the conditions of modern life (477). My argument, in comparison, does not emphasize an evolution of realism but rather notes the ways in which modernism's focus fundamentally changed as writers became obsessed with, and amplified, the banal. The work of Dante or Dickens does not seem less "real" to us now because we are familiar with newer stylistic modes. Auerbach implicitly agrees with this observation, given that his study of Western literature venerates the realism of Homer, Dante, Cervantes, Shakespeare, Molière and others. My point is that modernist writers focused upon a different aspect of "real life," a pervasive quotidian that was deeply affected by the First World War but not necessarily caused by it.

Second, Auerbach believes that there is an ethical imperative to realism; a representation of one ordinary life may help us to understand the lives of many other people. Auerbach is immensely and admirably idealistic. Like George Eliot, he believes that we all are linked by certain characteristics of our shared humanity. I also assume a strong link between different cultures and periods, rooted in a common experience of the everyday, but it is dangerous to lodge the everyday in one or another set of spaces, practices, or social classes. Essentially, ordinary experience might be defined not only by *what* we do (a genre of events) but also by *how* we do it (an affective experience of the world). As Rita Felski and Ben Highmore have both suggested, it is useful to think of the everyday as a relational concept. "It makes much more sense," Felksi argues, "to think of the everyday as a way of experiencing the world rather than as a circumscribed set of activities within the world," as "a lived process of routinization that all individuals experience" ("Invention," 31). In this sense, the ways in which various modernist writers treat the ordinary are deeply connected, even though their representations of ordinary life are located in different behaviors and environments, from the carnivalesque energy of Dublin streets to the gloomy interiors of New Haven.

In marking a distinction between the modernist novel and literary forms that preceded it, one of the most dramatic shifts in the development of realism, of course, also arises at the level of language. Watt argues that the novel was the first form to employ language to record what really exists, "that the function of language is much more largely referential in the novel than in other literary forms" (*Rise of the Novel,* 30). Many modernists explicitly question the notion of language as faithfully referential, and their linguistic experiments resulted in works that have been compared to poetic verse. In his introduction to Djuna Barnes's *Nightwood,* T. S. Eliot disparages novelistic prose that is "no more alive than that of a competent newspaper writer or government official" and contrasts it with the prose of *Nightwood,* which, he says, combines the "musical pattern" of poetry with a "prose rhythm that is prose style" (xii). Eliot's characterization of Barnes's novel is analogous to how many readers responded to Woolf's *The Waves.* Woolf herself called her work"purebred prose" that managed to "strike one or two sparks" of poetry (*WL* 4:381). Indeed, the everyday is not limited to the form of the novel: the nature of ordinary experience itself is not structured like a particular genre of art, much less a narrative with a clear beginning, middle, and end. Particularly as the genres of the novel and the lyric become less distinct, a dominant strain of modernist poetry also foregrounds the pleasures of the everyday in opposition to a romantic idealism and poetic language of the past.

Consider a long passage from George Gissing's *New Grub Street* (1891), a scene in which three young writers discuss their ambitions to write a novel. Biffen, the bohemian "realist," describes his work, titled "Mr. Bailey, Grocer," in terms that distinguish the literary values of the nineteenth century from more radical modes of expression. Biffen is the nineteenth-century novel's protomodernist:

> What I really aim at is an absolute realism in the sphere of the ignobly decent. The field as I understand it, is a new one; I don't know any writer who has treated ordinary vulgar life with fidelity and seriousness. Zola writes deliberate tragedies; his vilest figures become heroic from the place they fill in a strongly imagined drama. I want to deal with the essentially unheroic, with the day-to-day life of that vast majority of people who are at the mercy of paltry circumstance. Dickens understood the possibility of such work, but his tendency to melodrama on the one hand, and his humour on the other, prevented him from thinking of it. An instance, now. As I came along Regent's Park half an hour ago a man and a girl were walking close in front of me, love-making; I passed them slowly and heard a good deal of their talk—it was part of the situation that they should pay no heed to a stranger's proximity. Now such a love scene as that has absolutely never been written down; it was entirely decent, yet vulgar to the *n*th power. Dickens would have made it ludicrous—a gross injustice. Other men who deal with low-class life would perhaps have preferred idealising it—an absurdity. For my own part, I am going to reproduce it verbatim, without one single impertinent suggestion of any point of view save that of honest reporting. The result will be something unutterably

> tedious. Precisely. That is the stamp of the ignobly decent life. If it were anything but tedious it would be untrue. I speak, of course, of its effect upon the ordinary reader. (132–33)

Biffen's novel, when finished, receives critical praise but not commercial success. Readers do not tolerate the "unheroic" story of an ordinary grocer, but demand plot, the turning of events, something more than a "decent" and "tedious" realism. *Nothing happens* in Biffen's novel, a point that emphasizes what makes modernism's fascination with ordinary experience quite different from—and riskier than—the nineteenth century's interest in it. Many readers are bored by modernist literature, for plotlessness is modernism's great revolution.

However crude, this distinction between inaction and action is the greatest narrative divide between the modernist novel and its predecessors. When Biffen speaks of the effect of his novel upon the "ordinary reader," he foresees a modernist difficulty: nobody will want to read through a novel in which nothing happens. And though important events do take place in modernist novels (probably more than in Biffen's novel), certain coincidences and distinct plot patterns (marriage and inheritance plots, for example) are especially prevalent in the nineteenth-century novel. Plot here is frequently just the opposite of the ordinary; the unusual, the extraordinary, is what calls for narrative articulation. If nothing happens, then there is no story and nothing to tell. From the Middle French *nouvelle,* the English word "novel" implies just this sense of something new, a novelty. Diminishing the importance of plot, literary modernism privileges the ordinary first and foremost. The ordinary serves not merely as a backdrop to represent an objective reality, what Barthes calls "the reality effect," but as the central subject of the work itself. Yet, as Barthes points out, almost every Western narrative, regardless of historical period, possesses a certain number of "useless details"—pure description seemingly unrelated to the functional sequence of events ("Reality Effect," 142). George Eliot's Victorian classic *Middlemarch* might qualify as an example—a novel that accumulates detail, sprawling with notations of the minor. Barthes suggests that this kind of description has been an aesthetic convention and, more important, is "justified" by "the laws of literature: its 'meaning' exists, it depends on conformity not to the model but to the cultural rules of representation" (145). In this sense, Eliot's detailed descriptions of provincial life in a Midlands community during the years before the First Reform Bill—what she calls "this particular web"—often includes material that does not advance the plot of the novel or even embellish character, but rather underwrites an intractable belief in "the real" (*Middlemarch,* 116). The realism of modernist novels such as *Mrs. Dalloway* and *Ulysses,* in comparison, questions and foregrounds language's ability to signify an objective reality while nonetheless fixating on the problems of representing the details of the everyday, thus amplifying our sense of the everyday's presence.

Gissing's Biffen laments the novelist's incapacity to depict "a man and a girl" in Regent's Park, "love-making." Of course, pedestrian scenes—snatches of strangers' conversations—are exactly what a modernist like Woolf picks up in *Mrs. Dalloway*.[20] When Peter Walsh overhears a conversation between Rezia and Septimus in Regents Park, he thinks: "And that is being young . . . To be having an awful scene—the poor girl looked absolutely desperate—in the middle of the morning" (*MD* 77). Peter, of course, misreads the couple, seeing them only with a limited understanding of their lives (they reflect his own past with Clarissa). He is a mere bystander in the park. By tactically exposing Peter's inability to recognize the horror of Septimus's shell shock, Woolf keeps in check the notion of one totalizing reality. The shifts of perspective in the novel generate moments of casual dramatic irony. Peter is not judged for his limited point of view, per se, but the novel does not allow for the sentimentality with which Gissing's Biffen is all too familiar.

Multiple points of view—and everyday environments—constitute features of modern realism's ethical system identified by Auerbach in his chapter on Woolf. From Auerbach, an ethics of the everyday emerges in two ways. First, there is an inherent value in representing experiences that are often overlooked—passed over, for instance, by an omniscient perspective. Second, modernist works demonstrate how the subjective realm is where ethical choices are made. More explicitly than Auerbach, Charles Taylor presses the second point in arguing for the centrality of the ordinary as a mark of modernity. His ambitious *Sources of the Self: The Making of Modern Identity* (1989) argues that a modern sense of inwardness serves as the basis of moral judgment, as the foundation from which our evaluative discriminations emerge. In contrast to Georg Lukács or Fredric Jameson, Taylor does not understand modern inwardness as a dangerous retreat from a sociopolitical reality, but instead as a redefinition of individual ethics. The turn inward, for Taylor, occurs hand in hand with a turn toward the ordinary, in the sense that ordinary life defines what is "good to be," distinct from civic law, which defines "what is right to do" (3). Auerbach assumes a similar ethical imperative behind Woolf's representation of the everyday: the inwardness of modern writing makes visible "below the surface conflicts" what is shared by different cultures and different people (*Mimesis*, 488).

Woolf elicits our sympathy for characters by virtue of the small detail, a method learned from the great nineteenth-century writers whom she admired, especially George Eliot. No doubt Dorothea Brooke, for instance, foreshadows a woman like Clarissa Dalloway: the "determining acts of [Dorothea's] life," as the last page of *Middlemarch* reveals, are swallowed up by the everyday; "the effect of her being on those around her was incalculably diffusive" (682). Dorothea's effect is too minor to be registered, but her "unhistoric acts" nonetheless contribute to the "growing good of the world," Eliot assures us in the novel's tentative last paragraph. This is an idea that Clarissa Dalloway also upholds. The connectedness among human beings, as diffuse as "a mist between the people she knew best," Woolf writes, constitutes Clarissa's substitute for religion or what is "good" (10). Moreover, Woolf's feminist concern with how to represent a woman's life echoes Eliot's emphasis on the overlooked. In this sense, both Eliot and Woolf champion a feminine aesthetic of the detail against ideals of neoclassicism in which the detail is shunned as an impediment to the sublime.[21] In chapter 17 of *Adam Bede* (1859), titled "In Which the Story Pauses a Little," Eliot describes her early artistic aim in representing the everyday, a passage that serves as a striking precedent for Woolf's "Mr. Bennett and Mrs. Brown":

> It is for this rare, precious quality of truthfulness that I delight in many Dutch paintings, which lofty-minded people despise. I find a source of delicious sympathy in these faithful pictures of a monotonous homely existence, which has been the fate of so many more among my fellow-mortals than a life of pomp or of absolute indigence, of tragic suffering or of world-stirring action. I turn, without shrinking, from cloud-borne angels, from prophets, sibyls, and heroic warriors, to an old woman bending over her flower-pot, or eating her solitary dinner, while the noonday light, softened, perhaps by a screen of leaves, falls on her mob-cap, and just touches the rim of her spinning-wheel, and her stone jug, and all those cheap common things which are the precious necessaries of life to hers. (179)

Eliot finds her authentic model of ordinary life in a Dutch painting of a working-woman, much as Woolf imagines the common life of Mrs. Brown, an overworked charwoman traveling in a carriage from Richmond to Waterloo. Foreseeing some of the same issues that Woolf considers, Eliot gives the everyday a class consciousness, a bourgeois sensibility. The everyday is neither "a life of pomp or of absolute indigence" nor a life of destitution, but comprises a middle ground of work and leisure. Dutch realist paintings appeal to Eliot's sensibility primarily because they shun the flawless, idealized images of neoclassicism.[22] Indeed, Eliot here implicitly responds to Hegel's description of seventeenth-century Dutch paintings in his conceptualization of "The Ideal as Such" (*Aesthetics,* 153–74). Though the pleasure of daily activities attracts Hegel to these paintings—"in their taverns, at weddings and dances, at feasting and drinking, everything goes on merrily and jovially"—Hegel ultimately argues that there are "higher, more ideal, materials for art than the representation of such joy and bourgeois excellence" (169–71). The spirit that animates Hegel's "ideal" may be represented by "sensual" activities that any ordinary person can recognize, but these activities in themselves "are always inherently insignificant details," subsumed into a larger, higher vision (171). Hegel essentially sublimates the detail, as Naomi Schor has argued, like a neoclassicist, a "prisoner of aesthetic principles of a bygone era" (*Reading in Detail,* 29). In contrast, both Eliot and Woolf dwell on the detail not as synecdoche for some larger ideal, but as a source of realism, a display of how to represent the unrepresented, particularly the lives of women.

Scenes of everyday life, however, are not without a particular ideology—Dutch paintings can express anxiety about consumption, or a disdainful moralism, or an unabashed enjoyment of prosperity. This point is important when thinking about the ways in which ordinary actions, as well, are a product of a particular way of life and can sequester an individual from experiences that lie outside of one's scope. Pieter Bruegel'spainting "Landscape with the Fall of Icarus," for example, powerfully illustrates the limitations and dangers of going about one's business. The painting represents what gets overlooked when we are engaged in our own everyday necessities. In the foreground, a man plows a field, unaware of the boy who has just fallen from the sky. The boy's white legs are visible in the sea, but only if we are looking for them. As W. H. Auden understood in his poem about this painting, "Musée des Beaux-Arts" (1938), habits—even the necessary habits of work, like plowing—can blind us to others' suffering:

> About suffering they were never wrong,
> The Old Masters: how well they understood
> Its human position; how it takes place
> While someone else is eating or opening a window or just walking dully along
> (*Selected Poems,* 79)

To be self-absorbed—just eating or walking—is immensely human but also potentially dangerous. Here and elsewhere, Auden recognizes one of the most unsettling conflicts of the twentieth century, heightened by the horrors of two world wars, between an individual's ethical commitment to a civic world and his or her own personal needs and satisfactions.[23]

Stevens, whom Auden criticized for dwelling in personal or purely imaginative matters at the expense of political commitment, also draws on Dutch paintings in "Notes toward a Supreme Fiction," citing the paintings of the Dutch baroque painter Franz Hals. Stevens emphasizes the physical, and in particular, the inaccessibility of the abstract:

> Not to be realized because not to
> Be seen, not to be loved nor hated because
> Not to be realized. Weather by Franz Hals
>
> Brushed up by brushy winds in brushy clouds,
> Wetted by blue, colder for white. . . .
> (*CP* 385)

Pleasure in the weather does not transcend the body. In Stevens's work, the weather emerges as a recurrent metaphor expressing "one of the unphilosophical realities," as he explained, that we are "physical beings in a physical world" (*SL* 348–49). As Stevens writes in perhaps the most famous lines from "Esthétique du Mal," "the greatest poverty is not to live / In a physical world" (*CP* 325). It makes sense that Stevens did not collect many avant-garde works of art. Though Stevens's favorite painter was Paul Klee (he also admired Georges Rouault and Joan Miró), his own art collection was dominated by landscapes, portraits, and bowls of fruit—works that reveal a love of physical and tangible things and, most important, of figures within a context.[24] Against these images we could contrast Marcel Duchamp's gleaming white urinal, a work titled "Fountain" (1917) with which Stevens was familiar (he met Duchamp in 1915). "Fountain" is an ordinary object that has been radically decontextualized, a work of art that "shocks" a viewer in the sense that Victor Shklovsky believes all art should. Whereas Duchamp aimed to transfigure the ordinary, many writers of the period sought to represent the ordinary *as ordinary,* even while they questioned the possibility of successfully doing so.

Stevens celebrates the power of the imagination, an attitude generally associated with romantic poets whose experience of the natural world may spark a deep revelation—to "see into the life of things," as William Wordsworth writes in "Tintern Abbey" (*Selected Poems,* 109). But Stevens consistently differentiates his notion of the imagination from a "romantic" sensibility, emphasizing that the modern imagination must lead to discoveries free from sentimentality. Though Stevens does not deny his romantic precursors—he is especially indebted to John Keats—he contends that the imagination, properly understood, is bound up with the commonplace. In "Imagination as Value" (1948), he writes:

> We must somehow cleanse the imagination of the romantic. . . . The imagination is one of the great human powers. The romantic belittles it. The imagination is

> liberty of the mind. The romantic is a failure to make use of that liberty. It is to the imagination what sentimentality is to feeling. (*OP* 138)

Having critiqued this version of the "romantic," Stevens then reappropriates the term "romantic" to describe both his own work and the work of other poets whom he admires. In his controversial preface to William Carlos Williams's *Collected Poems 1921–1931* (1934), Stevens frames Williams as an "anti-poetic" romantic poet, suggesting that the romantic poet of today closely observes but does not idealize the world:

> All poets are, to some extent, romantic poets. . . . What, then, is a romantic poet now-a-days? He happens to be one who still dwells in an ivory tower, but who insists that life there would be intolerable except for the fact that one has, from the top, such an exceptional view of the public dump and the advertising signs of Snider's Catsup, Ivory Soap and Chevrolet Cars; he is the hermit who dwells alone with the sun and moon, but insists on taking a rotten newspaper. (*OP* 214)

Stevens might here be describing Joyce's *Ulysses* or some of his own poems, including "The Man on the Dump" (1942), which revels in the refuse of a day's closing:

> . . . So the sun,
> And so the moon, both come, and the janitor's poems
> Of every day, the wrapper on the can of pears,
> The cat in the paper-bag, the corset, the box
> From Esthonia: the tiger chest, for tea. (*CP* 201)

The imagination imbues the lowly with the exotic, but this act of the imagination is creative rather than visionary, playful rather than idealistic. Stevens also distinguishes Marianne Moore and T. S. Eliot as poets who espouse a romantic vision, classifying his American modernist peers according to his own ethos, whether they liked it or not.[25] Indeed, the essay serves as a defense of modern romanticism: "A thing is romantic when it is strange, unexpected, intense, superlative, extreme, unique, etc.," Stevens writes, adding, "It must also be living" (*OP* 221). His definition, of course, sounds something like his definition of a "supreme fiction," which "must be abstract," "must change," and "must give pleasure." (Stevens thought of adding a fourth section titled "It must be human.") Stevens strives for an ideal, or a supreme fiction, but recognizes the essential primacy of the experiential.

"No ideas but in things," William Carlos Williams enthusiastically declares in *Paterson*, a statement that voices a major aesthetic of literary modernism and certainly applies to the modernist novel as well as to Williams's poetry.[26] The modernist attention to ordinary experiences and ordinary things calls into question a well-known literary trajectory articulated by Lionel Trilling in his 1964 essay "The Fate of Pleasure: Wordsworth to Dostoevsky." Drawing on Dostoevsky's *Notes from Underground*, Trilling suggests that modernist literature renounces what Wordsworth and Keats celebrate as everyday joy or pleasure. Modern man—represented by Dostoevsky's miserable clerk—hates what he refers to as "'the sublime and the beautiful'" (104). Trilling writes: "The energy, the conspicuousness, and the wit of modern literature derive from its enterprise of violence against the specious good of whatever 'pleasure' may be offered to us by the universe or by our general culture in its quotidian aspects" (109). Though Trilling's observation might well apply to Dostoevsky's novel, the pleasure of the quotidian is rarely renounced by modernist writers. Everyday habits, or what Wordsworth calls in his Preface to *Lyrical Ballads* (a passage that Trilling cites) "the grand elementary principle of pleasure," the principle by which man "knows, and feels and lives and moves," do not fall away, are not suddenly abandoned by modernity (94). Rather, Wordsworth's celebration of "incidents and situations from common life" is often amplified by modernist texts, insofar as a frank clarity replaces the sentimentalized idealism found in romantic poetry, and as Auden hoped in his famous poem "Lullaby" (1940), we "find our mortal world enough" (*Selected Poems*, 51).

## Ordinary Life and Modern War

> It thereby follows that the novel exists not as a critique,
> but as a *culture of everyday life*.
> —Franco Moretti, *The Way of the World*

Franco Moretti has argued that the classical *Bildungsroman*, "though born declaring that it can and wants to talk about everything," avoids talking about revolution and war (*Way*, 52). Rather, a kind of "hetero-directed" form of life comes into being in the novel, consisting of the various activities of daily life (54). Though this theory holds true for a novel such as *Ulysses*, the unprecedented violence of two world wars put new pressures on the novel of everyday life and challenged older modes of literary expression. To position Thomas Mann's *Buddenbrooks* (1901) against *The Magic Mountain* (1924) serves as a case in point: the late-nineteenth-century novel of bourgeois family life (in which nothing really *happens*, but devolves) makes way for a novel about epidemic sickness and the seeming inevitability of war, which provides the novel's tragic conclusion. In *The Magic Mountain*, World War I puts an end to Hans Castorp's mountain retreat of repetition and routine, and certainly to the episodic customs depicted in *Buddenbrooks.* In his preface to *The Magic Mountain,* Mann describes how World War I created a deep historical "chasm," a sentiment later echoed by Woolf in her essays. How, these modernists ask, does ordinary experience continue? What happens to routine and habit when a violent disruption like world war intrudes?

Moretti's claim about the novel and its natural proclivity for the everyday holds true in relation to the modernist novel but in a strangely new way. In *Mrs. Dalloway* (1925), for instance, Woolf presents the altered climate of London during a day in June after World War I; in *To the Lighthouse* (1927), the war's devastating effects on the Ramsay family are enacted in the ordinary housework of two women. Woolf depicts war by depicting the everyday. Her novels, in fact, depict the everyday *in spite of* the war, so that the war's devastations are pervasively felt. While the war emerges directly through Septimus's flashbacks, Woolf's characterization of Septimus hinges on his relationship to ordinary actions and ordinary things. Similarly in her World War II texts, Stein refuses to treat the war through extremities of experience; both texts avoid relating chaotic or disturbing events, or even a climax. Only the repetition of the everyday remains during the war, and a hope that at least the everyday might continue.

Many modernists fixate on this tension between the war and everyday life; the "before and after" of the war emerges as a major modernist subject. The last two chapters of Stein's *The Autobiography of Alice B. Toklas* (1933), for instance, are titled "The War" and "After the War, 1919–1932."[27] Stein returns to the war again and again in her nonfiction and in her exegetical essays. In "Composition as Explanation," a lecture delivered to undergraduates at Oxford and Cambridge in 1926, she writes:

> This then was the period that brings me to the period of the beginning of 1914. Everything being alike everything naturally would be simply different and war came and everything being alike and everything being simply different brings everything being simply different brings it to romanticism. (520)

Stein suggests, in her typically elliptical way, that romanticism characterized the war years 1914–1918, but that modernity originated from the conflict between a peaceful, homogenous state and something "different" during the war. The nature of artistic "composition" thus changed in response to "the thing seen." Stein also suggests that World War I influenced people's ability to recognize otherwise overlooked or misunderstood works of art; war, she says in her essay "What Is English Literature" (1935), "advanced a general recognition of the expression of the contemporary composition by almost thirty years" (521). Stein does not specify the nature of this change, but she assumes a major shift in artistic modes of representation, expression, and reception.[28] Stein similarly claims that the peace and repetition of "daily island life" in England inspired writing on a prolific scale before World War I. While she playfully mocks England's provinciality and sense of self-contained greatness, she also admires the assurance and ease with which writers worked:

> And the daily life had always been worth writing about and so they always wrote a great deal. What else could they do. Granted that they lived this daily island life and realised it every day and were shut in every day with all of that daily island life every day what could they do but say it every day and as they said it every day they wrote it every day practically every day. (35)

Repeated seven times in this passage, the words "every day" signify both the frequency of the writing process and a conventional subject matter for writers. Writing itself becomes an everyday habit, disrupted by the onset of war.

Woolf's claims about life before World War I follow a similar line of reasoning; her comparison between "before and after" the war figures into her larger argument about the shape of modernist fiction. The postwar world, she believes, demands fresh novelistic forms; the traditional (or Edwardian) novel belongs to an age of limited artistic consciousness. In her late essay "The Leaning Tower" (1940), Woolf writes: "War then we can say, speaking roughly, did not affect either the writer or his vision of human life in the nineteenth century" (136). Woolf argues that British novelists before World War I had "immunity from war," despite the fact that war seems to have dominated English history. But World War I changed this easy flow of daily life and simultaneous writing about it: "Then suddenly, like a chasm in a smooth road, the war came" (136). Woolf situates World War I as the event that forced writers to face social problems, class divides, and economic crises; it caused the ivory tower of privileged creativity to become a "leaning tower," from which writers are now precariously perched. And while Woolf acknowledges that her "rough" history is much too simple (and even warns against propounding such large theories at all), her general sense of the war's effect on writers has been well supported by many critical studies about modernism and war.[29]

Terrence Des Pres' powerful documentary work *The Survivor: An Anatomy of Life in the Death Camps* (1976) describes a major departure, in the wake of World War II, from literature's classic representation of the active "hero": a movement away from the extraordinary and toward the everyday. In his first chapter,

"The Survivor in Fiction," Des Pres describes how the heroes of Western literature and religion traditionally have been those characters who risk their lives; "we reserve our reverence and highest praise for action which culminates in death" (5). However, this myth was radically undercut by the experience of those who bore witness to life in Nazi death camps, characterized by fixed activities and ritualized habits, where death has little dignity and "to die is in no way a triumph" (6). Drawing on such works as Albert Camus' *The Plague* (1947), Bernard Malamud's *The Fixer* (1966), and Aleksandr Solzhenitsyn's *One Day in the Life of Ivan Denisovich* (1962), Des Pres suggests that in the post–World War II age we have altered our notion of a hero as a risk taker or death seeker; literature must account for the value of the individual sustaining him or herself day to day. "Life goes on, if only through routine and habit," Des Pres explains, describing a survivor's perception of living, for life has no purpose beyond survival itself (81). Des Pres' trajectory provides one way of thinking historically about how our Western notion of the hero has changed in the wake of unprecedented crimes against humanity, a movement that had its start in the First World War's dramatic shattering of the Meliorist myth of progress, as Paul Fussell documents in his seminal work *The Great War and Modern Memory* (1975), and Ernest Hemingway sums up in a famous sentence from *A Farewell to Arms* (1929): "I was always embarrassed by the words sacred, glorious, and sacrifice and the expression in vain" (184). Giorgio Agamben's concept of *homo sacer* similarly traces the Western notion of "sacred life" from classical Greece to the Nazi death camps, where death could not be called heroic or "sacrificial," but was banal and methodical.[30] An affirmation of ordinary life—what Charles Taylor calls "the life of production and reproduction, of work and the family"—involves a polemical stance against both Platonic idealism and a warrior ethic, originally the dominant distinctions of our civilization. "The key point," Taylor argues, is that "the higher is to be found not outside of but as a manner of living ordinary life" (*Sources,* 23). Taylor's sweeping claims find manifestation in nineteenth and twentieth century works of art, and indeed art and literature are essential to Taylor's overall argument.[31] The texts that constitute the heart of this project represent this great shift in understanding about the nature of heroic experience and the language we use to describe it, as so many writers turned to what Stevens calls "what will suffice" (*CP* 240).

Ordinary experience during the wars of the twentieth century as represented by many literary modernists does not disappear as a way to reveal character or personality but assumes the function of registering the war's effects on individual lives at home. T. S. Eliot's "typist" and "young man carbuncular" in *The Waste Land,* for instance, eat "food in tins" in a sordid, cramped apartment; their indifference and sexual failure in some ways suggest a postwar failure of domestic life. While certainly some modernists depict the war as it was fought on the front lines, an ethos of detachment and distance also emerges as a way to represent forcefully inexplicable violence. In several of her late essays (including "The Leaning Tower"), Woolf criticizes the young writers of the 1930s who tried to represent the "actual," as she calls it—the raw facts of the modern age. Stevens reacts similarly to the pressures of the 1930s and 1940s in America, when many poets and critics were invested in more explicitly political work. Stanley Burnshaw's 1935 review of Stevens's poetry in the *New Masses* spurred Stevens to write a group of quasi-political poems in which he essentially tried to "isolate" poetry—to show how it must both respond to and retain some autonomy in the face of social upheaval.[32] As he stated on the front flap of the dust jacket for *The Man with the Blue Guitar and Other Poems* (1937), Stevens's intention was "to emphasize the opposition between things as they are and things imagined; in short, to isolate poetry" (*OP* 233). Whereas Woolf—unlike Stevens—is unmistakably a political writer, one whose pacifism and feminism animate a work like *Three Guineas* (1938), she finds fault with writers whose "realism" is charged by the desire to shock.

When asked what he did during the First World War, the story goes, Joyce replied, "I wrote *Ulysses*" (Budgen, *Joyce,* 196). We should not, however, understand this statement to mean that Joyce was entirely apolitical or that *Ulysses* does not engage with the war being waged as it was being written. *Ulysses*'s treatment of the ordinary has deep political resonances. As the work of Dominic Manganiello has shown, Joyce had a lively if ironic interest in current events and political developments, and this is reflected in his works: the second chapter of *Ulysses,* "Nestor," serves as one obvious example.[33] With the schema subject "History," "Nestor" opens with a classroom discussion of Pyrrhic battle, and proceeds to show Stephen's dissatisfaction with the traditional rhetoric of the headmaster Deasy, whose notion of heroic battle is emblematized by the portraits of British horses on the walls of his study. The students of Deasy's school, in 1904, are being trained in this rhetoric, which will lead them to the battlefields in 1914, when they are old enough to enlist. The chapter is steeped in descriptions that rumble with the reality of war. In fact, Stephen's reaction to Deasy resembles the sentiments of Hemingway's Lieutenant Henry. In response to Deasy's notion of English economic imperialism ("We are a generous people but we must also be just"), Stephen cautions: "I fear those big words . . . which make us so unhappy" (*U* 31). Joyce's version of the everyday attempts to deflate such grandiose views, as well as the idealism of romantic poetry from which Joyce emerged as a young poet. Finding his early model in the dramas of Henrik Ibsen, Joyce depicts the everyday against heavily symbolic or inflated revelations, working toward a kind of realism in *Ulysses* that celebrates coincidence rather than fixed paradigms of meaning. With its crucial theme of parallax—a reckoning of the observer and the point of observation—*Ulysses* regards the everyday as consequential, but also as a matter of a reader's own construal of the weight or triviality of ordinary events. This readerly choice is obviously the paradox of my own project, as I look closely at the very moments in modernist literature that are seemingly unimportant. I hope to make these moments not only worth noticing, but to lay claim to the endurance of the ordinary—untransformed, pervasive, and difficult to represent—as an essential feature of modernist literature.

# Chapter One

## Joyce and the Realism of the Ordinary

> In realism you are down to facts on which the world is based: that sudden reality which smashed romanticism into a pulp. What makes most people's lives unhappy is some disappointed romanticism, some unrealizable or misconceived ideal. In fact you may say that idealism is the ruin of man, and if we lived down to fact, as primitive man had to do, we would be better off. That is what we were made for. Nature is quite unromantic. It is we who put romance into her, which is a false attitude, an egotism, absurd like all egotisms. In *Ulysses* I tried to keep close to fact.
>
> —James Joyce to Arthur Power

To explore how the ordinary functions in literary modernism without examining *Ulysses* would be like describing the weather outside without noting the temperature. A novel obsessed with "facts" about the banal, vulgar, and routine elements of experience, *Ulysses* stands as explicit proof of modernism's climate. "The initial and determining act of judgment in [Joyce's] work is the justification of the commonplace," Richard Ellmann argues in his biography of the author (*James Joyce*, 65), an assessment that has been acknowledged without much dispute. Indeed, to say that *Ulysses* fixates on the ordinary—particularly as a unique phenomenon of modernity—is hardly a radical claim. It has become commonplace to say that *Ulysses* explores the commonplace; the ordinary is always, everywhere, in evidence. This chapter, however, proposes to look at what *Ulysses* leaves out, exploring the ways in which the ordinary by its nature slips away and showing how *Ulysses* responds to this instability. By cataloging the experiences of a single day, *Ulysses* both attempts to represent the reality of a particular moment in Dublin 1904 and necessarily gestures toward what cannot be included in a literary text, acknowledging a difference between an ordinary event and a representation that often changes the event into something extraordinary. Joyce creates the texture and believability of everyday life by pinning it down while simultaneously letting it go.

Joyce's statement that he "tried to keep close to fact" in writing *Ulysses* emphasizes his aim to record experience without the delusions of romantic idealism. In conjunction with similar claims made by other modernist writers, Joyce's statement is particularly striking, a kind of password into the realm of modernist aesthetic practices. As the material of novelistic realism, as a source of historical specificity, and as a necessary buttress against the flight of the imagination, facts play a significant role in the modernist project to represent ordinary experience. For Joyce, keeping close to fact is a way of tracing a day hour by hour and listing objects empirically, as Woolf would do in her later novels. Both writers, however, recognized that facts can neither adequately reconstitute the world nor totally "sum up" experience; indeed, the facts of *Ulysses* are sometimes uncertain. But Joyce and Woolf both believed in a material world worth representing, an authentic "reality" dense with detail; their realist styles were motivated by a desire to render tangible, quotidian things.[1] And while many writers before Joyce and Woolf may have made statements about the necessity of turning toward common life as a subject for art (notably Wordsworth), Joyce's claim is unique to his particular situation as a modernist and as an Irish writer. In rejecting the mythologizing of an Irish past, Joyce steps away from an Irish nationalism characterized, he believed, by a propensity to overlook facts about modern Irish life. The political aims of Joyce's realism pivot on this desire to strip life of symbolic and romantic visions. "Myth" in *Ulysses,* in this respect, hangs upon "facts," functioning, as Joyce saw it, as a kind of mirror rather than an inspiration. Realist "reflection," as we will see, becomes one of Joyce's guiding aesthetic principles.

In the first part of this chapter, I address a critical record concerning Joyce's career, starting with Joyce's earliest artistic announcements praising Henrik Ibsen. Here, Joyce advocates an unmediated realism, a style that he believes accurately reflects commonplace life.[2] Ibsen's work became a touchstone for Joyce, though Joyce ultimately rethinks the possibility that any literary style can be stripped of point of view or ideology. Inspired by Ibsen's poetics of the everyday, Joyce's early writings attempt to record life "as we see it before our eyes," as evinced by the fragments known as "epiphanies" and extended in later writings even as Joyce leaves his theory of epiphany behind. Whereas many critics have drawn upon the epiphany as a way to interpret Joyce's work, my point is to show how Joyce abandoned this aesthetic concept before any of his works were even published. Joyce is drawn to the romantic nature of epiphanic moments if only to deflate them. Epiphanies are linked with a desire to aestheticize experience, one of Stephen Dedalus's dominant tendencies, but this desire is dangerous largely because it extracts the individual from a context of community and civic commitment. Alternatively, the depiction of banal daily routines in *Ulysses*—more the story of Leopold Bloom than of Stephen Dedalus—demonstrates how Joyce's everyday does not evade historical conditions.

In the second part of this chapter, I will focus on a method of recording fact that becomes realism's endgame, enacting the limitations of a purely factual style: the list. Lists in *Ulysses* attempt to register and record the variety of ordinary moments that flood experience, while gleefully acknowledging realism's defeat. That is, the lists in *Ulysses* contribute to Joyce's epic reconstruction of June 16, 1904, while challenging the notion that one day can be accurately recorded. Lists are part of what makes *Ulysses* an overwhelmingly descriptive novel, in which Dublin 1904 is brought to life: the ethos of the novel is totalizing.[3] And yet the list always points beyond itself and remains open. The list introduces a more modest ordinary style than the epiphany; lists defy the possibility of an epiphany, or even a narrative event, ever occurring. The onslaught of lists in *Ulysses*, especially in the chapter "Ithaca," attempts to equalize all of the items listed. The equality of the list works against the desire to read and interpret particular elements of the novel as more or less important. This feature of the list relates to my last point, which is to claim that *Ulysses* emphasizes an arresting fact about the very nature of interpretation: How we interpret what we read functions as an analogue for how we choose to interpret or to overlook elements of our everyday lives. A reader of *Ulysses* can no more catch every textual detail than he or she can be cognizant of every element of everyday life. The desire to impose meaning, to give everyday life a narrative structure, or to give significance to banal moments, is a desire that often gives rise to complex works of art. But *Ulysses* also suggests that this desire cannot always be fulfilled; the everyday is often a foil to the very act of interpretation itself.

June 16, 1904, marks the "momentous eruption of everyday life into literature," writes Henri Lefebvre in the opening of *Everyday Life and the Modern World* (2). Lefebvre suggests that *Ulysses* is the first great modern novel to document the simultaneous emergence of modernity with the conspicuousness of everyday life (24–29). Although this statement, like Ellmann's, seems hard to refute, critics rarely look closely at how the everyday in *Ulysses* actually operates, in the sense of Lefebvre's call to examine the everyday as the most telling and ubiquitous quality of modernity. In *Critique of Everyday Life,* Lefebvre proposes an examination of everyday phenomena as a means to understanding the composition of the world. *Ulysses,* on some level, catalogs the kind of phenomena that Lefebvre identifies:

> The simplest event—a woman buying a pound of sugar, for example—must be analyzed. Knowledge will grasp whatever is hidden within it. To understand this simple event, it is not enough merely to describe it; research will disclose a tangle of reasons and causes, of essences and "spheres": the woman's life, her biography, her job, her family, her class, her budget, her eating habits, how she uses money, her opinions and her ideas, the state of the market, etc. Finally I will have grasped the sum total of capitalist society, the nation and its history. And although what I grasp becomes more and more profound, it is contained from the start in the original little event. So now I can see the humble events of everyday life as having two sides: a little, individual, chance event—and at the same time an infinitely complex social event, richer than the many "essences" it contains within itself. (57)

Lefebvre's vision is undeniably utopian, suggesting that we have the ability to understand all of life as it may be contained in a pound of sugar or, in the case of *Ulysses,* breakfast kidneys. *Ulysses* traces these links from everyday consumption to class, politics, and capitalism, whereas Lefebvre's study of everyday life does not examine the everyday's specific material manifestations. Most important, *Ulysses,* unlike Lefebvre's vision, is attentive to the limitations of the everyday, acknowledging the inability to trace and catalog every aspect of an individual's life. The "sum total of capitalist society, the nation and its history," are certainly suggested in the overwhelming lists of *Ulysses,* but the novel by no means believes it is capable of documenting everything. The "little, individual, chance event" in *Ulysses,* furthermore, does not always offer knowledge of things "more and more profound." Rather, the novel often disavows the revelations of the ordinary moment, likening itself to a life in which events are frequently insignificant and forgotten. The everyday is important, but—quite simply—not *that* important. By attending to the relative value of the everyday, *Ulysses* tempers its significance.

## Ibsen and Epiphany

> More than any one man, it is he who has made us "our world,"
> that is to say, "our modernity."
> —Ezra Pound on Henrik Ibsen

At eighteen, reading his essay "Drama and Life" (1900) aloud to the Literary and Historical Society at University College Dublin, Joyce imagines Henrik Ibsen as the artist he wants to be. Joyce pays tribute to Ibsen's bold modernity and frank depiction of typical lives, qualities that Joyce believes himself also capable of portraying:

> Even the most commonplace, the deadest among the living, may play a part in a great drama. It is a sinful foolishness to sigh back for the good old times, to feed the hunger of us with the cold stones they afford. Life we must accept as we see it before our eyes, men and women as we meet them in the real world, not as we apprehend them in the world of faery. (45)

Compare this pronouncement with the one that opens this chapter, Joyce's statement thirty years later to Arthur Power about "realism" and "romanticism." Joyce points to a fork in his path: Ibsen on one side and the Celtic Twilight on the other. Joyce declares a necessary shift toward everyday experience, implicitly rejecting a style embraced by such writers as George Russell, Oliver St. John Gogarty, Padraic Colum, and James Stephens, and especially by W. B. Yeats—a movement that looked back to the mythology and folklore of Irish culture as a source of Irish exceptionalism and Irish nationalism. In consciously choosing Ibsen as his master, Joyce strives for realism over romanticism and, as Ellmann argues in his biography of Joyce, attempts to make himself into a European, leaving the visions of the fin-de-siècle poets, especially in Ireland, behind him (78). But the allure of the Irish Literary Revival and the related aestheticism of writers like Walter Pater and Oscar Wilde still mark Joyce's style, from his early collection of poetry, *Chamber Music,* to romanticized moments throughout his later work, which linger even as they are satirized and renounced.[4]

Joyce's conflation of realism and romanticism comes in part from his attraction to these different literary modes, both of which are also evident in Ibsen's work. But Joyce overlooks Ibsen's symbols, emphasizing instead how Ibsen strips away literary convention to make art out of "commonplace" experiences. Joyce maintains this idea of Ibsen in his first published work, a *Fortnightly Review* piece on *When We Dead Awaken* that appeared just a few months after his reading of "Drama and Life" to the Dublin literary group. Here, Joyce praises Ibsen for portraying "average lives in their uncompromising truth," a description that certainly foresees Joyce's early work ("Ibsen's New Drama," 63). But *When We Dead Awaken,* Ibsen's last play and arguably his most symbolic, ends in a stormy avalanche atop a mountain after each character has realized something important about what it means to be "free" in life. Ibsen first titled this play "The Resurrection," emphasizing the awakening of artistic passion amid deadening everydayness. Although Ibsen's storm seems designed to represent the personal struggle of the artist, the young James Joyce, reviewing the play, sees solely what is "realistic."

Committed to an exacting representation of everyday life, Joyce suggests that Ibsen puts modern life directly on the stage, as if his plays can authentically capture the way that people live. Joyce's misreading is striking, and instructive. He apparently believed that Ibsen's everyday does not signify beyond the objects and events themselves: "It is hardly possible to criticize *The Wild Duck,* for instance; one can only brood upon it as upon a personal woe," Joyce writes. "In every other art personality, mannerism of touch, local sense, are held as adornments, as additional charms. But here the artist forgoes his very self and stands as a mediator in awful truth before the veiled face of God" ("Drama and Life," 42). This description of the artist—invisible and elevated—foresees Stephen Dedalus's idea in *A Portrait of the Artist as a Young Man,* in which the artist becomes divine: "The artist, like the God of the creation, remains within or behind or beyond or above his handiwork, invisible, refined out of existence, indifferent, paring his fingernails" (209). This well-known passage illuminates a tension between Ibsen's realism and the aesthete's idea that one should fashion life into art. If the artist strips away all evidence of his own handiwork, only unmediated life remains—the kind of mimesis that Joyce admires in Ibsen. But if the artist still exists "within or behind or beyond or above" the work of art, then the ideal is Wildean; one's life becomes one's art.[5] The aesthete who pares his fingernails is a type Joyce parodied, for the statement is qualified by Lynch, who drolly replies, "Trying to refine them [the fingernails] also out of existence" (*Portrait,* 209). While the notion of "art as life," as Joyce saw it in Ibsen, seems like a supreme fiction rather than an actual possibility, Samuel Beckett described Joyce's most experimental writing as just this sort of unmediated exercise. Writing about *Work in Progress,* the early draft of *Finnegans Wake,* Samuel Beckett explains: "His writing is not *about* something; *it is that something itself*" (*Our Exagmination,* 14). For Beckett, there is a style that can *be* the something it represents. What would this style look like if this something were the everyday?

Joyce's work is inspired by this question, the most important literary question behind *Ulysses.* In the novel's opening chapter, Stephen cautions Buck Mulligan (who imitates Oscar Wilde) by claiming that a flawed mirror is the perfect symbol of Irish art, "The cracked lookingglass of a servant" (*U* 6). This metaphor emphasizes both the inability to "reflect" life exactly and the special role of the Irish artist in composing this "cracked" reflection, thereby showing the ravages wrought by imperial rule. When Joyce holds a mirror to the life of Dublin, what emerges takes on political implications—a portrait of Irish paralysis under Roman Catholicism and British governance. In a 1906 letter to the British publisher Grant Richards defending the bleak and indecent elements in *Dubliners,* Joyce explains how he uses his mirror: "It is not my fault that the odour of ashpits and old weeds and offal hangs round my stories. I seriously believe that you will retard the course of civilization in Ireland by preventing the Irish people from having one good look at themselves in my nicely polished looking-glass" (*JL* 1:63–64). With this notion of unmediated mimesis—here, the mirror is not cracked—Joyce promotes himself as someone like Ibsen and yet also complicates the possibility of exact reflection by suggesting that his stories have an ideological aim. Joyce's realism is not aesthetic mimicry, nor stripped of politics; his style of "scrupulous meanness" reflects a deliberate decision to show the deadening effects of life in Dublin. His realist depictions of "the odour of ashpits and old weeds" both strive to strip away the happy myths of Ireland and imply a dramatic need for change.[6] In this sense, the mirrorlike style of *Dubliners* transforms what it represents; the ordinary is caught in the paradox of its representation.

Yet Joyce also suggests that he is simply telling the truth ("It is not my fault"); he assumes that the stylistic polish of his realism will motivate change and not any subversive ideology inherent in his literary project. Whether or not it is possible to write in such a clear-sighted way, it is fair to say that Joyce's work, as well as Ibsen's, strives to examine prosaic life, bourgeois convention, and the dangers of deluded romanticism.[7] Soon after Joyce wrote his two pieces on Ibsen, he started recording overheard conversations and disconnected descriptions, trying to record life as he directly observed it. He called these fragmentary pieces "epiphanies," of which there are forty that survive, all published posthumously. Many of these epiphanies, like the text of a play, are complete with stage directions, the names of the characters as speech headings, and very often an indication of the tone of a speech in parenthesis. To a reader, there is no obvious reason why these moments are revelatory, or "epiphanic;" they seem to be ordinary moments, recorded with accuracy. Even as we recognize that some of these early epiphanies will appear in Joyce's later fiction (with a clearer sense of context and importance), here, they are inscrutable. Two of these epiphanies allude to Ibsen himself; one is a conversation about Ibsen's age and the other is an actual description of the dramatist:

> [Dublin: at Sheehy's, Belvedere Place]
>
> Joyce—I knew you meant him. But you're wrong about his age.

> Maggie Sheehy—(*leans forward to speak seriously*) Why, how old is he?
>
> Joyce—Seventy-two.
>
> Maggie Sheehy—Is he?
>
> (*Poems and Shorter Writings*, 171)

> Yes, they are the two sisters. She who is churning with stout arms (their butter is famous) looks dark and unhappy: the other is happy because she had her way. Her name is R. . . . Rina. I know the verb "to be" in their language.
>
> —Are you Rina?—
>
> I knew she was.
>
> But here he is himself in a coat with tails and an old-fashioned high hat. He ignores them: he walks along with tiny steps, jutting out the tails of his coat. . . . My goodness! how small he is! He must be very old and vain. . . . Maybe he isn't what I . . . It's funny that those two big women fell out over this little man. . . . But then he's the greatest man in the world. . . .
>
> (*Poems and Shorter Writings*, 196)

The first epiphany makes its way into *Stephen Hero* as part of a "Who's Who" game that Stephen plays one evening at a parlor house meeting. The second, dreamlike epiphany alludes to the fact that Joyce was beginning to learn Dano-Norwegian himself (largely so he could write Ibsen a letter). Rina, moreover, is the name of the elder Miss Tesman in *Hedda Gabler.* But what is stylistically interesting about the epiphanies is the tension between their symbolic and realistic representations. Are these moments meaningful, or are they insignificant? There is very little *to say* about them. Does this make them an ideal example of an ordinary style? Because the epiphanies are so spare, they leave a reader with a feeling of unease, a desire for more context and definition, especially because by now we are conditioned to look for significance in something called an "epiphany," a word that of course alludes to the feast day commemorating Christ's manifestation to the magi. But the epiphanies in Joyce's early notebooks do not seem like extraordinary moments. In this sense, Joyce's epiphanies are different from Stephen's theory of epiphany, which is an idea about the revelatory power of the everyday that Joyce's work ultimately rejects.

In *Stephen Hero,* a work that Joyce kept unpublished in his lifetime, Stephen conceives of his theory of epiphany one night when overhearing a conversation much like one Joyce would have recorded in his collection of epiphanies:

> He was passing through Eccles' St one evening, one misty evening, with all these thoughts dancing the dance of unrest in his brain when a trivial incident set him

> composing some ardent verses which he entitled a "Villanelle of the Temptress." A young lady was standing on the steps of one of those brown brick houses which seem the very incarnation of Irish paralysis. A young gentleman was leaning on the rusty railings of the area. Stephen as he passed on his quest heard the following fragment of colloquy out of which he received an impression keen enough to afflict his sensitiveness very severely.
>
> The Young Lady—(drawling discreetly) . . . O, yes . . . I was . . . at the . . . chap pel . . .
>
> The Young Gentleman—(inaudibly) . . . I . . . (again inaudibly) . . . I . . .
>
> The Young Lady (softly) . . . O . . . but you're . . . ve . ry . . . wick . . . ed . . .
>
> This triviality made him think of collecting many such moments together in a book of epiphanies. By an epiphany he meant a sudden spiritual manifestation, whether in the vulgarity of speech or of gesture or in a memorable phase of the mind itself. He believed that it was for the man of letters to record these epiphanies with extreme care, seeing that they themselves are the most delicate and evanescent of moments. He told Cranly that the clock of the Ballast Office was capable of an epiphany. (*SH* 210–11)

Two types of epiphany are possible, according to Stephen: instances of "vulgarity of speech" or "memorable phases" of the artist's mind. Two different styles of epiphany thus emerge—prose poems and dramatic notations—as Robert Scholes and A. Walton Litz discuss in their notes to *Dubliners* (254). This passage from *Stephen Hero* is often referred to as an explanation of Joyce's own methods—especially as Stephen's practice of recording epiphanies so neatly mimics Joyce's—but it is important to distinguish between the author and his protagonist, to separate Stephen's aesthetic theory from Joyce's. Nowhere in *Dubliners* or *A Portrait of the Artist as a Young Man* do we find Stephen's explanation of "a sudden spiritual manifestation, whether in the vulgarity of speech or of gesture or in a memorable phase of the mind itself." Although many critics have been quick to note that this definition of epiphany does not appear in any work Joyce published, the implications of this elision still have not been fully grasped.[8] Joyce left this theory behind, turning away from his notion of heightened experience in favor of more mundane moments that resist epiphanic transformation.

Stephen's theory of epiphany is at odds with Joyce's presentation of everyday life in *Ulysses*, a work that shows how life cannot be organized artfully into epiphanic events; rather, experience is flooded with moments that are difficult to privilege, harder to "read into." The materialism of lists, as we will see, provides a way of leveling out experience, parsing it into many items with no connecting narrative to signal which items are more significant than others. Disavowing epiphany—and its accompanying idea that life can be made into art—*Ulysses* turns to a different aesthetic, one that resists transformative moments. This turn is not only aesthetic, but political. First, every epiphanic moment emerges out of a context with which it must then reengage for the effect of the epiphany to register. It is this *context,* ultimately, that interests Joyce: the conditions or state of affairs that already exist, with which an individual must be involved to effect change. Stephen in *Ulysses* is more attentive to this context; he is three years older and back from his flight to Paris—reintegrated, metaphorically, into the Irish context from which he flew. Now, Stephen teaches history lessons to young schoolboys. Likewise, daily routine in *Ulysses* does not overlook or escape historical conditions—as it does in Stein's depiction of life during the Second World War—but in fact directly engages with the material circumstances of a generation lost to the war (the very boys Stephen teaches), in a novel set in 1904 but written, of course, between 1914 and 1921. *Ulysses* advocates ordinary activities that are fundamentally social in nature and embedded in the politics of empire—not unlike the activities of London that Clarissa Dalloway identifies with on her walk—but indeed very different from Stein's depiction of individual habit as a kind of political evasion.

Second, Joyce's amplified, Rabelaisian realism might be viewed as an affront to the proper English reader—a slap in the face of imperialist propriety, as readers like Woolf and H. G. Wells felt it to be. Woolf's critique of *Ulysses,* a novel that the Hogarth Press declined to publish, centered on what she viewed as the vulgarity of Joyce's material (a subject I address in the next chapter). In a letter to Joyce, Wells condescendingly suggests that Joyce's crude facts emerged in part because of his Irishness, because he needed to rebel:

> You began Catholic, that is to say you began with a system of values in stark opposition to reality. Your mental existence is obsessed by a monstrous system of contradictions. You really believe in chastity, purity and the personal God and that is why you are always breaking out into cries of cunt, shit and hell. As I don't believe in these things except as quite provisional values my mind has never been shocked to outcries by the existence of waterclosets and menstrual bandages—and undeserved misfortunes. And while you were brought up under the delusion of political suppression I was brought up under the delusion of political responsibility. It seems a fine thing for you to defy and break up. To me not in the least. (*JL* 1:275)

The tone of this letter ("As I don't believe in these things . . .") suggests that Wells sees himself as more advanced; perhaps Joyce will someday write in Wells's style if he can emerge from what oppresses him. But of course scatology is one method of realism, not a mark of immature literary development. Joyce's "crudeness" finds later manifestations in such works as *Midnight's Children* and *Gravity's Rainbow,* in which scatology may still be shocking but also seems necessary to a particular style that equalizes previously debased elements.

Joyce's lavish materialism in *Ulysses* makes a case that heightened moments are much rarer than the stuff from which they emerge. This central feature of *Ulysses* is latent but less pressing in Joyce's early work, which also represents commonplace events and questions Stephen's romanticizing tendencies. Though the concept of epiphany is introduced in *Stephen Hero,* it is also already renounced in favor of more materialist moments. After Stephen has caught up with Emma Clery on the street, declaring his desire for her, he realizes that the heightened drama of the event is ludicrous, hardly romantic. Describing this interaction later to his friend Lynch, Stephen is distressed to feel only "the commonplace side of the adventure" (*SH* 203). The moment looks forward to a diary entry at the end of *Portrait* describing Stephen's exuberant talk with E. C. in which he describes himself as "a fellow throwing a handful of peas up into the air" (246). No matter how much Stephen wants these moments to be perfect gems of experience, they are not. The deflation of a possible epiphany—the kind of deflated moment so typical in *Ulysses*—reveals the "commonplace" side of interactions, exposing (though also sympathizing with) deluded and romantic sensibilities about art, friendship, and love. Many of the epiphanies that make their way into *Portrait* highlight ordinary language, or idle chatter, and pay careful attention to the materiality of certain scenes. When ordinary, materialist elements are lost, then the epiphany becomes ludicrous. Only in preserving an everydayness does the epiphany retain meaning.

One example of how the everyday gets lost when it is transformed occurs in the second chapter of *Portrait,* when Stephen attempts to write a poem to E. C., suggestive of the "Villanelle of the Temptress" from *Stephen Hero.* But this time, the romanticism of the villanelle is most certainly mocked. Stephen is inspired by three epiphanies, which occur at different moments in his life, all introduced with the phrase "He was sitting," and marked by an intense observation of physical objects and the language of casual conversation. These moments are similar to Joyce's early epiphanies, seemingly locked into insignificance as mere instances of naturalist description. The first epiphany describes his aunt's kitchen as she examines a picture of a starlet in the evening paper; the second epiphany describes Stephen watching the fire in the breakfast room at which tea is being made. The third of these epiphanies occurs aboard the last tram, as Stephen and E. C. leave a party. Stephen fails to kiss her, and the next day he retreats to his desk to compose a poem, titled "To E—C—": "He knew it was right to begin so for he had seen similar titles in the collected poems of Lord Byron" (*Portrait,* 64). Stephen's deep desire to write like a romantic poet fails to catalyze a great poem:

> During this process all those elements which he deemed common and insignificant fell out of the scene. There remained no trace of the tram itself nor of the trammen nor of the horses: nor did he and she appear vividly. The verses told only of the night and the balmy breeze and the maiden luster of the moon. (65)

Stephen vaguely realizes that the urgency and weight of his feeling can only be rendered if he utilizes facts and commonplace things—a poetics of the everyday. Without yet knowing it, Stephen has these resources at hand. He even remembers a similar moment when he tried to write a poem about Parnell, and ended up composing a list instead:

> His brain had then refused to grapple with the theme and, desisting, he had covered the page with the names and addresses of certain of his classmates:
>
> Roderick Kickham
> John Lawton
> Anthony MacSwiney
> Simon Moonan
>
> (64)

Stephen's list of names clearly identifies something more "real" than the romantic luster of his failed poem to E. C. At the least, the list points to his friends' nationality and their particular economic status (marked by where they live), which would signal their relationship to the nationalist fight that Parnell led. The list becomes a more accurate description of Stephen's theme, an ordinary style that emerges out of a failed romanticism.

Joyce ironizes Stephen Dedalus in *Ulysses* when he becomes detached from everyday realities and shows proclivities for turning lists into symbols; Stephen still has not entirely given up his overwrought poetical ways. Stephen reads deeply into commonplace things, as he thinks in "Proteus," composing a list of what he sees: "Signatures of all things I am hereto read, seaspawn and seawrack, the nearing tide, that rusty boot. Snotgreen, bluesilver, rust: coloured signs" (*U* 37). Stephen's desire to experience the Aristotelian theory of sensory perception wrenches symbolism from the refuse and colors on Sandymount Strand. He tries both to control how he senses his environment and to order the environment itself, testing the "ineluctable modality of the visible," the eye's inability to modify what it sees (*U* 37). Stephen's instincts—his desire to see "signs"—shape his distinctly metaphoric use of language, dense throughout "Proteus." Sitting on a rock in the sand, Stephen observes: "These heavy sands are language tide and wind have silted here" (*U* 44). Stephen thinks *about* language and finds it heavy, full of discoveries. But if language is like sand, then every element is equal, as are the tiny granules composing a beach. While this opening of "Proteus" has been read as Stephen's meditation on art and his ability to draw inspiration from the mundane (snot, a rusty boot), the moment also marks Joyce's critique of Stephen's attempt to transfigure the ordinary into legible, neatly defined signs, and it reveals nature's resistance to Stephen's privileging of distinctly heightened experiences. Stephen cannot control, order, or transform every sensory perception, but rather he is a "servant" to the stimuli that come his way. *Ulysses,* in this context, attempts to record events but does not aspire to transform them as Stephen does. Ultimately, lists in *Ulysses* become the optimal form for trying to contain material facts against literary transformations, for tempering the fundamental paradox of representing ordinary life. However, *Ulysses* also acknowledges that there is no language that is not, on some level, interpretative and therefore transformative. Though the young James Joyce saw in Ibsen's drama the possibility of a transparent representation of ordinary experience, *Ulysses* relishes the impossibility of such a style.

## The Lists of *Ulysses*

> For utterly impossible as are all these events they are probably as like those which may have taken place as any others which never took person at all are ever likely to be.
>
> —*Finnegans Wake*

More than most novels, *Ulysses* encourages a reader to devise strategies to draw out meaning from its surplus and difficulty. A few of these strategies have now become almost impossible to ignore, like reading for the mythic correspondences or marking the stylistic technique of each chapter. *Ulysses* foregrounds the act of interpretation: its interpretations are often known before one starts reading, and the novel seems particularly responsive to new readings given the extraordinary amount of material from which to draw and make meaning. The ability to choose patterns from the encyclopedic range of the novel marks perhaps the most striking way that *Ulysses* celebrates everyday life: just as the lists of *Ulysses* cannot totally capture or sum up everyday experience, so too does *Ulysses* defy a reader's desire to interpret with authority and completeness. Although the work encourages us to choose patterns and symbols from all that it offers, ultimately there is too much information in *Ulysses* for a single interpretation to dominate. Because *Ulysses* demands so much from a reader, it also can be fatiguing. *Ulysses* risks losing a reader's attention. The work is actually constructed so that it reflects upon a reader's own experience of perceiving the everyday: *Ulysses* makes us aware of what we notice, and makes sure that even the most conscientious reader will leave something out.

In *Ulysses*, a reader is confronted—on a much larger scale than in Joyce's earlier work—with the problem of representing ordinary experience, if only because the styles of *Ulysses* are marked by their discontinuities from one chapter to the next. The novel almost seems to be searching for a style best suited to its ordinary subject matter. Representing ordinary experience *as* ordinary becomes an especially marked aim in the lists of *Ulysses*, in that the language of lists is usually quite banal, hardly "literary." A list is associated with a functional mode of recording, as with a list of things to get done or a list of things not to forget. Furthermore, the list is distinctly the language of the nonevent, of "filler" in Franco Moretti's sense, and not of plot development. The Russian structuralist Juri Lotman includes the calendar and the telephone directory as examples of "texts without plots," arguing that some violation of the list form must occur in a narrative (237). Considering that Joyce draws upon and mimics exactly these kinds of plotless texts, we might understand *Ulysses* as an attempt to create narrative out of the nonevent. Lotman, much like Hugh Kenner, considers the list a "closed" system, through which language marks what lies within and what lies outside the boundaries of knowledge.[9] However, Joyce draws upon the list not as a system of limitation—like a calendar or telephone directory—but rather as a method for embodying the everyday's fundamental openness. A list in *Ulysses* often points to what exists beyond what gets included in it; in this sense, the novel violates the convention of list-making itself.

Joyce's lists attempt to record the exact history of one day in Dublin, from what Bloom eats to the geographic layout of the city. Lists populate the prose of every chapter in *Ulysses*, resonating metaphorically but always establishing a contextual "reality" of time and place. In this respect, lists go hand in hand with Bloom's approach to experience. The first sentence of the chapter "Calypso" describes Bloom by way of a list: "Leopold Bloom ate with relish the inner organs of beasts and fowls. He liked thick giblet soup, nutty gizzards, a stuffed roast heart, liver slices fried with crustcrumbs, fried hencods's roes. Most of all he liked grilled mutton kidneys which gave to his palate a fine tang of faintly scented urine" (*U* 55). Documenting what Bloom likes to eat, this list also points to Bloom's earthiness, a contrast to Stephen's idealism. A list like this one sets out to include rather than to narrate events, and point to many examples of a single point, as many different "inner organs" as Bloom likes to eat. This list also calls attention to the deep delight Bloom takes in consuming savory foods—it suggests a kind of excess of consumption that marks the novel itself.

Like an epic catalog, lists strive for an authoritative account of what has happened, an objectivity important to collective self-definition and national identity central in the Greek epic that Joyce evokes. For instance, Homer's great list of ships—not from the *Odyssey* but from the *Iliad*—implicitly states, This is what happened; this is who was here. *Ulysses* likewise aspires to historical accuracy on the minutest level. In this sense, lists emphasize Bloom's embeddedness in the fabric of history. Bloom is less tempted than Stephen by romanticizing, by the pull of epiphany, by the desire to escape Dublin. In the chapter "Cyclops," Bloom tells the rabid Irish nationalist "citizen" that Ireland is his nation; "I was born here," he says (*U* 331). And indeed, Bloom's citizenship is established by his generosity toward his fellow Dubliners, a long list of people to whom he gives his time, his condolences, and his money. He is not naturally drawn to the self-importance of the epiphany, but rather to the democracy of a list.

This difference in literary style marks the political differences between Bloom and Stephen. Bloom's definition of citizenship is "to have brought a positive gain to others," as we learn in "Ithaca" (676). In contrast, Stephen chafes against obligations to his family; he dreams of his escape to Paris, from where he has just returned. When Stephen and Bloom finally talk late at night in the cabman's shelter, the conversation is about work and nation. Bloom defines patriotism as "all creeds and classes" working for "a comfortable tidysized income." Stephen responds, "Count me out," and concludes, "We can't change the country. Let us change the subject" (*U* 644–45). While Stephen disagrees with Bloom on the nature of civic commitment and social change, Bloom disagrees with Stephen's views about what he calls "the eternal affirmation of the spirit of man in literature" (*U* 666). This phrase of course closely resembles the "sudden spiritual manifestation" of epiphany, and conjoins Stephen's politics with his aesthetics. The epiphanic moment is thus associated with Stephen's desire to free himself from the context of his surroundings, to raise himself above life by making his life into art. And thus the decontextualizing pull of the epiphany becomes politically irresponsible.

*Ulysses* is a novel more interested in the history of a particular time and place than in individual, revelatory experience. As Kenner has argued, what attracted Joyce to the Greek story of Odysseus's wanderings was not the myth, but the facts: Joyce wanted to know about the actual historical man Odysseus, who was not just an epic hero but an ordinary commercial traveler.[10] Joyce's reliance on the facts of Dublin life makes *Ulysses* a paradigmatic novel for Ian Watt's theory of the rise of the novel. The predominance of idiosyncratic facts, especially those of private life, constitutes one of the key elements of the novel in comparison to the myths and civic ideals of classical literature, according to Watt (176–207). It is no surprise that Joyce removed the Homeric titles from *Ulysses* before it was published, retracting one of the novel's most authoritative heuristics. Proust would do something similar for *In Search of Lost Time,* dropping the architectural titles (Porch, Apse, Window) that were to give his voluminous novel symbolic structure (*Correspondance* 18:359). The epic myth behind *Ulysses,* as many critics have argued (diverging from T. S. Eliot's reading of the novel) is ultimately overpowered by the particularities of Joyce's story.[11] Joyce's reliance on *Thom's Official Directory* emphasizes this preoccupation with the particular: he stuffed the novel with details of Dublin life whose portent lies largely in their sheer quantity, verifying the novel's historical nature rather than its overt symbolism. *Thom's* supplies *Ulysses* with facts about what constituted Bloom's day, including the time of sunrise and sunset, ships in the Dublin port, weather, births and deaths, sporting events, and more than two hundred street addresses, allowing critics Clive Hart and Leo Knuth to construct maps of each episode in *A Topographical Guide to James Joyce's Ulysses* (1981). Joyce was obsessed with such facts; he wrote letters to his Aunt Josephine in Dublin to check that what he remembered was right, including the possibility that Bloom and Stephen could enter Bloom's home without a key and that "an ordinary person [could] climb over the area railings of no. 7 Eccles street" (*JL* 1:175). If Dublin were to be destroyed, Frank Budgen reported Joyce saying, it might readily be reconstructed from the evidence contained in *Ulysses* (*Making of Ulysses,* 69).

But what has become apparent is that not all of these facts are exact. Hart and Knuth suggest that *Thom's* itself is riddled with mistakes (misspellings, duplication of addresses, wrong shop names) and that Joyce purposely transposed the mistakes and created several errors of the same kind (*Topographical Guide,* 14). Certain events in the novel, as more recent critics have noted, are characterized by an interpretative open-endedness. The multiple appearances of the Man in the Macintosh or Molly's Gibraltarian background are teasingly indeterminate, a phenomenon that Philip Herring traces in *Joyce's Uncertainty Principle* (1987) and which Derek Attridge similarly identifies as a marker of the text's postmodernism.[12] Inaccuracies and indeterminacies like these contribute to a representation of ordinary experience marked by slip-ups and confusions, on a textual level as well as on the level of character. As Jules David Law has suggested, Joyce's everyday includes the unintentional in the sense laid out by Freud in *The Psychopathology of Everyday Life* ("Simulation," 202). Everyday mishaps—errors of language, slips of the tongue and pen, bungled actions—become representative of an individual's desires and neuroses. Consider Martha's love letter to "Henry Flower," in which she writes "world" instead of "word," suggesting a fantasy world of words preferable to the world of Dublin. A slip of the pen reveals a personal desire; the facts of *Ulysses* similarly include mistakes, representative of the everyday as something that an individual cannot always consciously control.

Nor is it possible for an individual to account for every aspect of his or her day; the ordinary is by nature easily forgotten. In the "Ithaca" episode in *Ulysses,* on a scale closer to Defoe than Homer, Bloom's "budget" sums up his experience, accounting for what Bloom has done by way of how much he has spent. "Debit" begins with his morning breakfast, "1 Pork kidney, 1 Copy *Freeman's Journal,*" and ends with the expenses at the cabman's shelter, "coffee and bun" and "Loan" to Stephen Dedalus (*U* 11). The list recapitulates, in a different form, what a reader has traced in previous chapters: from Paddy Dignam's funeral (at which Bloom paid five shillings "In Memoriam") to the penny tramfare that returned Bloom from Sandymount. But missing from Bloom's budget is the expenditure of eleven shillings at Bella Cohen's that a reader may remember from "Circe," marking this event as uncertain (real or hallucination?) and also suggesting that Bloom's list of expenses is not totally accurate, or cannot include all elements of experience.[13] The epic catalog is subverted, and the trustworthiness of the "historical" text is again called into question.

Many of the lists—in "Ithaca" and elsewhere—suggest an ability to go on and on, not unified by an organizing aim and energetically spiraling out of control. In this way, the lists deflect the possibility of epiphany, as they include thing after thing without a clear mark of what is most important. In "Circe," for example, the list of things that Bloom's "bodyguard" distributes increases like "loaves and fishes" (the third item in his list); its final items are "cheap reprints of the World's Twelve Worst Books," obliquely suggesting that not everything written has a special value or that some writing might even be disregarded (*U* 485). Certain lists point to a world beyond the text—to events that the reader cannot access or even know for certain have happened. Consider the list of subjects that Bloom and Stephen discuss on their walk home: "Music, literature, Ireland, Dublin, Paris, friendship, woman, prostitution, diet . . . the Roman catholic church, ecclesiastical celibacy, the Irish nation, jesuit education, careers, the study of medicine . . ." (*U* 666), or the list of items on Bloom's kitchen dresser: ". . . a chipped eggcup containing pepper, a drum of table salt, four conglomerated black olives in oleaginous paper, an empty pot of Plumtree's potted meat, an oval wicker basket bedded with fibre and containing one Jersey pear . . ." (*U* 675). Although both of these lists have an imprint of accuracy and completeness, as if the text can tell us everything about what Bloom and Stephen say to one another, or what Bloom sees on his dresser, what becomes clear is that many other items might be added to each list without changing the overall effect. The latter list could include other edible items or objects from the kitchen (the kinds of things dominating the list) without changing its suggestiveness. The list—with its round "bedded" fruits and slippery substances—evokes Molly's body, which must be on Bloom's mind, but many other items could serve this function. Furthermore, each list circles around what is not mentioned there: absent from the first list is a sense of whether Stephen and Bloom actually get along; absent from the second list is whether things are distinctly different in the kitchen after Molly's tryst with Blazes, signaled by the empty Plumtree's potted meat and the basket Blazes brought. Avoided is an explicit account of Bloom's thinking. The lists of "Ithaca" aim to disclose but also to dramatically hold back information, more often than not omitting what a reader may really want to know. Like the eleven shillings missing in Bloom's budget, this list suggests that some things will always inevitably be left out.

The catechistic prose of "Ithaca" also reveals how even the most exacting language of lists cannot render a clear account of action (or hallucination), but in fact makes events seem far removed from the language describing them. For instance, the text asks what happens when Bloom makes tea for himself and Stephen: "What concomitant phenomenon took place in the vessel of liquid by the agency of fire?" (*U* 673). This language seems generated to amuse a reader by emphasizing the sharp disjunction between language and actual experience, by defamiliarizing the ordinary in Shklovsky's sense. A reader must put together the fact of boiling water from the circuitous language describing it. As Karen Lawrence points out, this language does not characterize the simplicity of the domestic event, as does the homely language of "Calypso," when Bloom makes tea for Molly (*Odyssey of Style,* 186–87). If we read *Ulysses* primarily for its language and style—a method that distinguishes poststructuralist and more recent readings of the novel—then the language of "Ithaca" most dramatically illustrates the gap between a reality and the representation of it.[14] It is not possible to "show forth" the ordinary world (as Stephen espouses with his theory of epiphany) without considering the effect of language upon the presentation of the event itself.

The sheer plurality of styles in *Ulysses* also emphasizes this gap, as if no style will suffice for its realism, for ultimately there is no style that will leave the ordinary untransformed. It is, as Barthes would say, an incredibly "writerly" work, one that foregrounds the act of composition rather than enables a reader's passive ease, one that is as interested in style and grammar as it is interested in the everyday. *Ulysses* of course stylizes some of the ordinary or popular patterns of speech—the tired, flaccid clichés of "Eumaeus" or the saccharine prose of women's magazines in "Nausicäa." These varied styles mark the lack of a standard or objectively "right" approach in representing the ordinary; not even an Ibsen-eque realism can transpose the commonplace into written text. One description in "Ithaca" arguably spoofs Ibsen's style. Stephen imagines an advertisement for stationery that is staged as a dramatic scene between a man and a woman:

> Solitary hotel in mountain pass. Autumn. Twilight. Fire lit. In dark corner young man seated. Young woman enters. Restless. Solitary. She sits. She goes to window. She stands. She sits. Twilight. She thinks. On solitary hotel paper she writes. She thinks. She writes. She sighs. Wheels and hoofs. She hurries out. He comes from his dark corner. He seizes solitary paper. He holds it toward fire. Twilight. He reads. Solitary. (*U* 684)

The scene is baffling, and comic. A reader has no idea why the woman is writing or why the tension between the couple is so severe. Again, something important here has been left out. Gifford notes that the description has a Hauptmannesque flavor (*Ulysses Annotated,* 575), but the stark chill and tension between the couple could also echo many of Ibsen's dramas, and certainly strikes a chord with Joyce's *Exiles,* a play modeled distinctly on Ibsen.[15] Although the passage may suggest that Joyce eventually grew less enamored of Ibsen's work (enough to parody it), it also suggests that Ibsen's style became one of many styles; perhaps Joyce did not appreciate it less but realized that no pure realism could capture "average lives in their uncompromising truth," as he believed early on.

Franco Moretti argues that the language of *Ulysses* denies an authoritative style. Each literary style is "equivalent" in the sense that "all [are] equally arbitrary, all equally incapable of imposing themselves," thus each style is "irrelevant" as an interpretation of reality or as a formalization of literary language (*Signs,* 206). Moretti acknowledges the impossibility of a language that is commensurate with—or that can directly reflect—the ordinary events of the novel. And yet, the styles of *Ulysses* do privilege a kind of realism that may be more "mirrorlike" than the others, given that at least five of the early chapters are characterized by a similar stream of consciousness. This sustained style does in fact "impose" itself as an interpretation of reality. But Moretti's point nonetheless holds weight: the shifting styles in the latter part of *Ulysses* emphasize the impossibility of a single kind of reflective language, suggesting a fundamental failure of language to represent ordinary reality. Of course, this failure is also a success: the acknowledgment of the distance between word and event is partly what gives the novel its immense energy and its charm. Often at the expense of realism, the novel's self-awareness foregrounds the fact that we are *reading* a novel and undercuts the seriousness of a Flaubertian struggle for transparency or exactitude, for *le mot juste.* The list ultimately becomes the style closest to the everyday—a style that is not quite the "something itself," in Beckett's phrase, but which introduces a tempered, more contingent kind of literary transformation in its refusal to decontextualize events and objects from their surroundings.

Joyce's lists, particularly in "Ithaca," critique the transformation from ordinary to "literary" language and correspondingly from ordinary to poetic experience—the kind of phenomena that Stephen Dedalus cultivates. That is, the novel calls attention to the failure of language to retain a mirrorlike quality, and it equates Stephen's mode of interpretation with desire to transform the world. Joyce shows how language transforms reality by making the lists poetic, as evidenced in the lyrical lines throughout "Ithaca" that are incorporated into the chapter's lists. "The heaventree of stars hung with humid nightblue fruit" describes the "spectacle" that confronts Bloom and Stephen when they step outside to the garden (*U* 698). Alliterative and cadenced, the language responds to the surprising brilliance of stars in the night sky. The description of what Bloom admires about the quality of water, similarly, starts as a list and becomes a poem, ending with the phrase: "the noxiousness of its effluvia in lacustrine marshes, pestilential fens, faded flowerwater, stagnant pools in the waning moon" (*U* 672). This is not Stephen's language, but a dramatic and wry variation of it, another voice altogether. The poetic eruptions are evidence of the novel's literary showmanship, suggesting that the text itself holds a seeming power over its own textuality. Joyce's realism brings to light the process of *how the ordinary becomes literary,* and this accounts for the novel's reflexive turns. As in other chapters, an unidentifiable narrator—what critics have called the "Arranger," or the "novel-writing machine," or the novel's "consciousness"—seems ahead of a character's own observations, providing commentary on the events unfolding and the ways in which these events are represented.[16]

Some of the objects in *Ulysses*'s lists resonate with literary significance because they keep reappearing, seemingly by a will of their own, or by the hand of the Arranger: a potato in Bloom's pocket, soap bars for Molly, "Sweets of Sin," "Plumtree's potted meat," and the "throwaway" constitute some of the novel's more famous objects. Because many items turn up in several chapters, they become leitmotifs, encouraging a reader to make meaning from their reappearances. *Ulysses* also presents the reader with hysterically funny lists, especially in the "Cyclops" episode, such as the list of Irish heroes engraved on the citizen's girdle (*U* 296). In such cases, the list departs from the novel's realism to point to the arbitrariness of list-making, including disparate items that in no way fit. They signal an inability to totally embed the ordinary in a naturalized context, and the inevitable significance of anything that has been transcribed. When Bloom pieces together the various incidents that relate to the name of the race-winning horse, "Throwaway," of which he is reminded when he sees Boylan's betting tickets on the kitchen dresser, he finally realizes why his morning meeting with Bantam Lyons was so odd. Little did Bloom know that in handing Bantam a newspaper, telling him, "I was just going to throw it away" (*U* 85), he was giving Bantam a betting tip and triggering the rest of the events narrated in his long list. The ordinary moment earlier in the day now becomes markedly significant; the ordinary returns and makes itself important. Yet this transformation holds true for only some of the objects in *Ulysses;* the other items on the kitchen dresser (plates, saucers, a chipped eggcup, Epp's cocoa, jam jars, onions, etc.) do not get reconsidered. For every object that emerges as a leitmotif, there are dozens of others overlooked among the glut. And in this sense, the list's transformations are much more modest than what is achieved through epiphany or myth.

Coupled with this mixture of elements is the fact that the grammar of a list is not like the grammar of a sentence. With little other than commas or semicolons adjoining its elements, a list allows a reader to make individual connections between its parts. A list is a stricter version of the generally paratactic style of much of *Ulysses,* a style that critics like Barthes and Julia Kristeva have pointed to as less hierarchical than the sentence.[17] In this way, Joyce's lists do have a realistic effect, capturing the strange, comic mix of things and ideas that constitute a moment. On the other hand, the lists may suggest that we all organize what we encounter in some rudimentary fashion—that is, we make a list before we make a sentence or before we fully interpret an experience. One of the major issues of *Ulysses* is the nature of how we interpret the everyday: What do we notice? What do we prioritize? What do we leave out? And what is the role of the literary in this negotiation between the individual and the everyday? These questions are central to the novel's reputation, since the question of how we interpret the everyday contributes to how *Ulysses* itself continues to be open to so many critical interpretations.

In a moment from "Aeolus," the text comments on the limitations of its own plotting, with a sly sense that "events" in real life are usually much less important than novels make them out to be. When a messenger boy lights J. J. O'Molloy's cigarette in the newspaper offices of the *Freeman's Journal,* we read about the "trivial" as if it were the grand deus ex machina upon which the rest of the novel depends:

> Pause. J. J. O'Molloy took out his cigarettecase.
> False lull. Something quite ordinary.
> Messenger took out his matchbox thoughtfully and lit his cigar.

> I have often thought since on looking back over that strange time that it was that small act, trivial in itself, that striking of that match, that determined the whole after course of both our lives. (*U* 140)

The passage mocks the work of a newspaper when journalists concoct an "event" out of insignificant phenomena. Reporting an event in a newspaper necessarily adds significance to the event itself, a development amplified by modern media. Blanchot notes that the transcription from real life to newspaper event "modifies everything" ("Everyday Speech," 18). This moment from "Aeolus" points not only to the burgeoning industry of journalism but acknowledges that recording an ordinary event in a novel also markedly changes the nature of the event. The moment pokes fun at the conventions of the novel; the narrative "event" becomes the butt of the joke. In *Ulysses Annotated,* Gifford cites this passage as a parody of Dickensian coincidence, though Joyce could be making fun of many novelists who fabricate overly important plot structures out of trivial acts, including Thomas Hardy, whose "tricks and subterfuges of melodrama" Joyce disliked.[18] The lighting of a match is the kind of "event" that could end up playing a part in a complicated narrative design, but Joyce departs from this novelistic ruse, assuming that lighting a cigarette may function as just that: lighting a cigarette.

Joyce's realism was inspired by what he saw in Ibsen, a mirrorlike reflection of the world. In *Ulysses,* Joyce flashes several mirrors, each one mimetic but showing a uniquely different reflection. One thing that unifies the episodes in *Ulysses* is a sense of life as stranger than novels make it out to be, of the everyday as more varied and random than any literary account of it. Bloom thinks in "Ithaca" when piecing together the Throwaway incident that his "Reminiscences of coincidences" have become "truth stranger than fiction" (*U* 675), a sentiment carried over into *Finnegans Wake,* where the "utterly impossible" events of the novel are still not quite as impossible as what might happen in real life. Accidents are more likely in life than they are in literature. If literature were to replay all of life's accidents, it would not seem believable, a phenomenon that Aristotle understood with his distinction between the probable and the possible as defined in the *Poetics.* In comedy, Aristotle argues, the probable must be considered; events must be likely to occur, and matters of chance must have some meaning. But in tragedy, when the situations are drawn from real life or historical events,

> what convinces is the possible; now whereas we are not yet sure as to the possibility of that which has not happened, that which has happened is manifestly possible, else it would not have come to pass. (636)

In real life, Aristotle suggests, everything is possible, whereas in imaginary futures, or in works that are imagined, it is difficult to know what is possible. *Ulysses* suggests that life is not easily made into neat fictions even though humans may wish to organize experience through structure and meaning. We look back with a sense of what's most important, creating a "retrospective arrangement" of everyday life (*U* 91). To fashion fictions out of our lives—to give them beginnings and endings, in Frank Kermode's words—is to make sense out of events that do not necessarily have a pattern.[19] If Joyce was an aesthete, or a proponent of the mythical method that Eliot thought would usurp the novel, then he also laughed at and disapproved of these proclivities, presenting the everyday as something particular, something open to whatever comes its way. Ultimately, lists in *Ulysses* become the ideal form for constructing this openness, and for resisting the transformations of ordinary experience. For Joyce and for modernism more broadly, the desire to make ordinary experience strange and new is not the ultimate aim, for language will always change what it represents. Distinguished by its attempt to approach the ordinary as closely as possible, *Ulysses* comprehends the ordinary by keeping it open, by letting it go.

# Chapter Two

## Virginia Woolf and the "Cotton Wool of Daily Life"

[Poetry] has never been used for the common purpose of life. Prose has taken all the dirty work on to her own shoulders; has answered letters, paid bills, written articles, made speeches, served the needs of businessmen, shopkeepers, lawyers, soldiers, peasants.
—Virginia Woolf, "The Narrow Bridge of Art"

Virginia Woolf's prose has frequently been called "poetic," a description that alludes to the rhythm and sound of her sentences, the lyric plotlessness of her novels, and the self-conscious interiority of her characters. Woolf's friend E. M. Forster once claimed that Woolf's "problem" was that she should have been a poet, not a novelist.[1] But the term "poetic" invites question, largely because it suggests that Woolf does not tackle the pedestrian world of ordinary life and that her novels disdain "prosaic" subjects. Although Woolf sought to strip away novelistic conventions to render the inner workings of the mind, she knew that the modern novel could not flee from the external world of everyday *things*, from "the common objects of daily prose, the bicycle and the omnibus," as she writes in "A Letter to a Young Poet" (214). Her characters do not dwell solely in their heads. They dwell, for instance, in London streets and public parks, where vagrants sing for money and airplanes advertise overhead.

Woolf's finest writing calls attention to ordinary experiences in a world full of ordinary things. Celebrators and critics of modernism often focus on Woolf's interest in the "mind" or the "moment of being" but overlook the "ordinary." A grounding claim of this chapter is that Woolf's modernism is not only concerned with recording the subjective mind or heightened experience, but deeply invested, stylistically and ideologically, in representing the ordinary.[2] Moreover, Woolf conceives of ordinary life, even at its most private, as constituted by sociopolitical factors as much as by the personal necessities of living. Inner life can itself be ordinary in the sense that a person's private thoughts can be similar to another's, partly because people may be influenced by the same environments. Woolf's novels present the ordinary in these terms, though her essays often conflate the inner life with exceptionality, a discrepancy that suggests Woolf's essays overemphasize dichotomies (poetry and prose, inner and outer, exceptional and ordinary) that her novels do not play out.

In "Modern Fiction," Woolf states: "For the moderns 'that,' the point of interest, lies very likely in the dark places of psychology" (152). Many critics have taken this statement (and similar ones) as a point of departure. Elizabeth Abel examines the way Woolf's works "echo and rewrite the developmental fictions of psychoanalysis" (*Woolf and Fictions,* xvi). Most of the introductions to Woolf's major works also pick up on what Abel describes as Woolf's interest in internal states, "the points of origin marked by mother and father," or other "private powerful sources" (3). People reading Woolf for the first time will learn that "the external event is significant primarily for the way it triggers and releases the inner life" (Showalter, introduction to *Mrs. Dalloway,* xx) and that "there is a roominess about so many of Virginia Woolf's characters, a sense of mystery and of the inexplicable; they are rarely enclosed in precise outlines" (Schulkind, introduction to *Moments of Being,* 14). The most recent biography of Woolf, *Virginia Woolf: An Inner Life* (2005) by Julia Briggs, takes as its premise the claim that "Woolf's fiction is centrally concerned with the inner life, and finding ways of re-creating that life in narrative" (ix). Moreover, both Michael Cunningham's Pulitzer Prize–winning *The Hours* and the subsequent Academy Award–winning film based on it, by Stephen Daldry and David Hare, present Woolf as a solitary, deranged artist who listens to voices in her head. A general sense, in both popular and scholarly estimations of Woolf, is that her work explores a fluid state of consciousness, always heightened, never settling on an "outline." My argument is not that these claims about Woolf's writing are baseless. Rather, they fundamentally miss something crucial about her commitment to ordinary experience, about experiences that are neither heightened nor wholly inward.

When Woolf, in "Modern Fiction," asks us to "examine for a moment an ordinary mind on an ordinary day," she demands two things that are seemingly incompatible. She wants her subject to be both "ordinary" and of the "mind," though by her own definitions, the subjective mind seems a shifting, wildly complex thing, receiving "a myriad impressions—trivial, fantastic, evanescent, or engraved with the sharpness of steel" (150). To render the ordinary is to describe things with which every reader is familiar, but Woolf assumes here that the individual mind is a strange, unique entity. How might "modern fiction" represent both psychological interiority and realism rooted in things shared? Woolf bridges this divide, I shall argue, by replicating the way in which individuals do the things that they always do—repeated acts and habits—because these actions are the fabric of what she calls "character." To look inward, as Woolf's characters do, is not to abandon ordinariness or the external world, because inwardness of course is shaped by a myriad of external factors.

First, I will explore how Woolf identifies the ordinary in several of her key nonfiction writings. She associates the ordinary with prose rather than poetry—a distinction that emphasizes her uncertainty about how to treat the "dirty work" typically associated with prose. I then turn at length to *Mrs. Dalloway,* a novel committed to the ordinary as a source of knowledge about another person. The ordinary in *Mrs. Dalloway* lies at the heart of Woolf's representation of character, functioning as a powerful force of life, prevailing over traumatic events. Woolf's representation of the ordinary becomes an enduring fixation, dominating her experimentation in subsequent novels. The main quality of the ordinary is that it eludes representation, or that no representation of it (no matter how experimental) can be totally satisfactory. Woolf searches for a style that will best suit the ordinary, and in this respect her project is much like Joyce's. Her ambivalent use of "facts" in fiction is such a style, as she herself implies in her long essay "Phases of Fiction" (1929). A survey of novelists who represent the ordinary especially well, "Phases of Fiction" also establishes a tradition from which Woolf positions herself. Partly because Woolf was such a voracious and imaginative reader herself, "Phases of Fiction" reveals Woolf's strong attachment to novelists who describe the world *as it is,* who satisfy our need to believe in a fictional world, a world that we recognize. Her determined disassociation from the Edwardians, whose work is entrenched in materialist facts, should be considered in context of her admiration for many older novelists whose use of facts she emulates as a means of achieving the ordinary. Woolf is interested in every manifestation of ordinary life, including its affective dimension: she admires novels in which the reader is entrenched in a particular world, an atmosphere that is taken for granted, a reality into which the reader sinks.

## Poetry versus Prose

In "A Letter to a Young Poet," a long piece written in response to the young English poets of the 1930s (her nephew Julian Bell, John Lehmann, Stephen Spender, Cecil Day Lewis, and Auden), Woolf criticizes poets who are preoccupied with subjective experience, who describe only "a self that sits alone in the room at night with the blinds drawn" (218). The poetry that emerges from such a strategy suffers from abstraction and impenetrability. Even a discerning reader such as Woolf is baffled by it. But Woolf also questions poetry that is too crass in its attempt to include "the actual, the colloquial" (215). She quotes verse from Lehmann, Spender, and Day-Lewis (although she does not cite their names), and notes the abrupt shift from romantic images to common vernacular.[3] The tension she poses between the private language of the mind and colloquial language of public dialogue, also put forth in essays like "The Narrow Bridge of Art" (1927) and "The Leaning Tower" (1940), underlines Woolf's central concern with how the novel should represent the ordinary without making it either overly poetic or jarringly informal.

Woolf's attitude in "A Letter to a Young Poet" echoes her famous response to Joyce's *Ulysses,* a novel that she ultimately felt was "adolescent" in its representation of ordinary experience and that she criticized as "conscious and calculated indecency."[4] Finding fault with similar moments in the work of younger poets, Woolf emphasizes lines like "ease the bowels" and "buggers are after," and then explains:

> The poet is trying to include Mrs. Gape. He is honestly of the opinion that she can be brought into poetry and will do very well there. Poetry, he feels, will be improved by the actual, the colloquial. But though I honour him for the attempt, I doubt that it is wholly successful. I feel a jar. I feel a shock. I feel as if I had stubbed my toe on the corner of the wardrobe. (215)

Ironically, the poet's motives, as Woolf describes them, actually resemble her own. When John Lehmann criticized the "Letter," Woolf maintained that "the young poet is rather crudely jerked between realism and beauty. . . . He doesnt [*sic*] reach the unconscious automated state—hence the spasmodic, jerky, self conscious effect of his realistic language. But I may be transferring to him some of the ill effects of my own struggles the other way round—writes poetry in prose" (*WL* 5:83). Woolf perceives that the genres of poetry and prose were becoming less distinct and that her work, too, struggles with the same balance between "realism," which she associates with prose, and "beauty," which she associates with poetry. Furthermore, although the name "Mrs. Gape" suggests a woman who draws a reader's attention, or astonishes, she may not be so different from Woolf's own charwoman "Mrs. Brown." Both, in her mind, are ill served by poetry and, for that matter, by the realist style of Edwardian novelists. Woolf argues compellingly in "Mr. Bennett and Mrs. Brown" (1924) that such women should not be overlooked. A modern writer must throw away the superfluous, tiresome tools of Edwardian description and represent ordinary character clearly and completely. Of course, Woolf's feminist aims also underscore her concern with character: Mrs. Brown represents the type of woman (older, unsupported, burdened by her duties) who is often overlooked both in literature and in life. Woolf suspects that the 1930s poets—privileged, male, and mostly homosexual—may not have the capabilities to represent a "Mrs. Gape."[5] But fundamentally, she quarrels with the younger generation of poets not so much because of their motives—with which she is explicitly sympathetic—but because of their method. Only the novel, the prose of the world, in Hegel's notable formulation, is suitable to an age when the inwardness of the "beautiful soul" has been overridden by the plurality of a social world.[6] The form of the novel, "so clumsy, verbose, and undramatic, so rich, elastic, and alive," Woolf writes in "Mr. Bennett and Mrs. Brown," is well designed to express modern character (102).

An essay such as "A Letter to a Young Poet" reveals the slippery boundaries between poetry and prose, and Woolf's somewhat unconvincing attempt to separate their provinces, as if poetry should be saved for the lofty world of interior thought and only the novel should treat an ordinary public world. As Pericles Lewis has argued, the blurring of modernist genres can be explained in part by modernity's relationship to religion: the privatization of religious values described by Charles Taylor and Max Weber meant that many modern novelists sought to represent religious experience as distinct from the materialism of the realist novel that preceded them ("Churchgoing," 675,689). The modernist novel picks up elements of poetry—associated with a private world—and poetry, as Woolf notes, picks up elements of prose. The poetry that Woolf admires and mentions in her essay to the 1930s poets (Eliot and later Yeats) unmistakably draws upon what she calls "the actual, the colloquial." Thus, Woolf's objection to the younger poets ultimately hinges on her opinion of the poetry' s *quality,* not the issue of whether realist elements could be represented in poetry, since she actually respects much of the poetry that was becoming more prose-like at the time.

In her critical essays on the novel, Woolf insists on the danger—for the artist—in retreating to the purely subjective, to the entirely interior, to what she viewed as overly poetic. The unstable associations she makes among subjectivity, interiority, and poetry are influenced by the artistic experiments of her time. She recognizes one of the most pressing issues posed by literary modernism and the artistic developments that followed: To what extent should writers depict the facts of an external world, "to disenchant and disintoxicate," as W. H. Auden wrote ("Writing," 27), and to what extent should they represent psychological depth or inner vision? Which is the more authentic reality? Woolf's engagement late in her career with the poets of the 1930s highlights her persistently mixed feelings about literature's responsibility to a "real" or external world outside the world that modernist experimentation, according to many, was trying to represent. The word "real," of course, is bandied about by Woolf to mean almost anything, as she strives to redefine it. Woolf sympathizes with the younger generation's desire to supplant the imagination with a more politically minded realism, especially in response to the inexplicable violence of the First World War, and England's political and economic difficulties during the summer of 1931, when the letter was composed.[7] But her own artistic struggle is slightly different. Her work is not split between representations of "inner" versus "outer" or "personal" versus "political."[8] Rather, her representation of ordinary experience reconciles two sides of a dichotomy that is often understood as dominating literary modernism.

Woolf articulates this aim at the start of her unfinished memoir, "A Sketch of the Past" (1940), where she distinguishes between "moments of being" and "moments of non-being." She describes her childhood as one long period of ecstasy, a "moment of being" marked by the sound of waves crashing outside her nursery room window at St. Ives. While lying in bed is a nonevent, Woolf's affective sense of this childhood experience is not. But Woolf acknowledges that her childhood certainly consisted of more than these mornings lying in bed: "If I could remember one whole day I should be able to describe, superficially at least, what life was like as a child. Unfortunately, one only remembers what is exceptional. And there seems to be no reason why one thing is exceptional and another not" (69–70). Parts of the day that are not lived consciously, and thus not remembered, constitute what she calls "non-being," of which her adult life seems to be full. As an example, Woolf gives the events of the day before: "ordering dinner; writing orders to Mabel; washing; cooking dinner; bookbinding" (70). While Woolf seems somewhat wearied by all of these events (if we can call them events), she emphasizes their role in revealing character—in this instance, these events reveal something about who *she* is, as she describes herself in her memoir.

"A Sketch of the Past" shares Wordsworth's idea in *The Prelude* that childhood serves as a "base" for the rest of life. Woolf's famous "moments of being" echo Wordsworth's "spots of time," in which the everyday is renovated by the memory of defining, revelatory experiences. But Wordsworth also explains that "memory and thought" are not necessarily contingent upon conventionally "big" moments. Memory will frequently cling to the mundane:

> Who, looking inward, have observed the ties
> That bind the perishable hours of life
> Each to the other, and the curious props
> By which the world of memory and thought
> Exists and is sustained. More lofty themes,
> Such as at least do wear a prouder face,
> Solicit our regard; but when I think
> Of these, I feel the imaginative power
> Languish within me. . . . (282)

Following Wordsworth, Woolf is especially interested in the prose of life, not in the "lofty themes," since prosaic events constitute the bulk of one's experiences and are thus crucial to literary representations that aim at realism. What differentiates Woolf from Wordsworth, however, lies in the spiritual meaning that Wordsworth attributes to these "curious props" of life, from the rowboat episode in book 1 of *The Prelude* to the tempestuous walk at Christmastime in book 12, which point to a divine presence in the world, or at least to a power beyond human understanding.

In comparison, Woolf cannot attribute a definite meaning to the patterns she sees in life, a problem that concerns not only her personal philosophy but how she structures the novel. She suggests the impossibility of arranging life into distinct events, with certain moments (however un-lofty) marked as the most important, an impossibility put forth in an often quoted passage from "Modern Fiction": "Life is not a series of gig lamps symmetrically arranged; life is a luminous halo, a semitransparent envelope surrounding us from the beginning of consciousness to the end" (150). The non-being in which individuals are enmeshed does not offer moments that can be pinned down or propped up as icons of experience or as signs of divine order. If life does have a pattern, it comes from humans rather than from a higher source. Behind the "cotton wool," Woolf writes in her memoir, we see art's connection to humanity:

> It is a constant idea of mine; that behind the cotton wool is hidden a pattern; that we—I mean all human beings—are connected with this; that the whole world is a work of art; that we are parts of the work of art. *Hamlet* or a Beethoven quartet is the truth about this vast mess that we call the world. But there is no Shakespeare, there is no Beethoven; certainly and emphatically there is no God; we are the words; we are the music; we are the thing itself. And I see this when I have a shock. ("Sketch," 72)

Order—a pattern to life—is made visible by an instance of "shock." The revelatory moment allows one to see behind the diffuse non-being of the world, what Lefebvre calls the everyday's *astructural* quality (*Critique*, 2:163). But of course, shock is brief, and life is long. To represent ordinary life in the novel is a challenge to the novel's form (one that marks the works of Joyce and Proust as well) in terms of both the order and teleology that a novel requires. A person might experience a moment of shock that offers a revelatory insight, but the problem is how to integrate this moment back into the fold of everyday life, the place where real change can actually manifest itself. The Bloomsbury group in fact serves as a model for fostering political change not through rupture and shock, but through domestic spaces and bourgeois institutions—for making political work a kind of ordinary habit.[9] But how are the politics of the ordinary reflected on an aesthetic level? The novel's challenge in describing how everyday life operates is both structural and related to the believability of character, Woolf's chief novelistic concern.

The significance of non-being in Woolf's work has received considerably less attention than the shock or ecstasy that Woolf also describes, but non-being is crucial to her aesthetic project. In "A Sketch of the Past," she explains: "Often when I have been writing one of my so-called novels I have been baffled by this same problem; that is, how to describe what I call in my private shorthand—'non-being'" (70). The ordinary, forgettable events of the day, Woolf suggests, must exist in her novels. In *Mrs. Dalloway*, Woolf of course creates "one whole day," not of her childhood, as she wishes she could do when writing her memoirs, but of Clarissa Dalloway's adult life: Clarissa buys flowers, mends a dress, meets an old friend, takes a nap, throws a party. The party stands out in many respects—marked by the presence of the prime minister as well as the most significant people from Clarissa's past—but this temporary reprieve is a defining feature of how unordinary events get integrated back into the continual flow of ordinariness. As Lefebvre has argued, anomalies often serve as a confirmation of the ordinary. Certain types of pleasure, if they happen repeatedly (as Clarissa's parties do) give the ordinary its emphasis, its cycle of suspension and reinstatement (*Critique*, 1:201–27). The overall ordinariness of the day's events enables the focus of the novel to be Clarissa's character and how it is constituted.

Woolf's distinction between moments of being and non-being, like her distinction between poetry and prose, demonstrates her awareness that the modern novel cannot represent only heightened moments of self-consciousness, but must be made up of more mundane moments that make up one's life. Woolf's ambivalence about how the novel should respond to the subjective, to the interior, reveals a red thread running through modernism: despite the desire to get at psychological depth, many modernist writers sought to retain and amplify the ordinary as both an internal and external phenomenon. This idea—for Woolf—has its origins in the early modern period, in the work of Michel de Montaigne, who in "On Repentance" argues that the true test of character is not public life but "to be orderly at home, in our common actions" (239). In her 1924 review of a new translation of Montaigne's essays, Woolf describes how he imparts his distinctive personality (indeed, his "soul") by enumerating his everyday habits ("Montaigne," 64–66). On a large scale, we might acknowledge many modernist novels as grappling with this representation of an ordinary human being living ordinarily. If modernism rejected or subverted conventional literary devices (plot, closure), many modernist works still preserve and even privilege the coherence of character. Representing ordinary experience becomes the means by which characters are best revealed, an idea at the heart of Woolf's essays on the novel.

Woolf even suggests that a writer must be more attuned to ordinary experience than other artists if she is to establish the believability of a character, of a life lived. In a 1911 letter to her sister Vanessa Bell, she writes: "As a painter, I believe you are much less conscious of the drone of daily life than I am, as a writer. You *are* a painter. I think a good deal about you, for purposes of my own, and this seems to me clear. This explains your simplicity" (*WL* 1:475). Revealing the characteristic rivalry between these sisters, Woolf feels that her work as a writer is harder, that the issue of representing daily life in language is a problem that her sister does not face. Composing the stuff that establishes character, a writer must be attentive to daily life's dull "drone," a rhythm or flow of events that lies outside the considerations of Vanessa Bell's representational art. As Christopher Reed has suggested, Bell's paintings (even her more abstract works) were very naturally bound up with domestic life, in the sense that she was involved in painting home interiors (walls, chairs, tables, doors, etc.) especially as part of the Omega Workshop's experiments. One of the reasons that Bloomsbury art is often elided from mainstream modernism, Reed argues, is *because* of its interest in domestic life, since modernism, based on Le Corbusier's model, is predicated on a critical standard of antidomesticity (*Bloomsbury Rooms,* 147, 2–5). Woolf's work shares with her sister's a preoccupation with how daily life is constructed. It puts the domestic back into the modern, balances shock with ordinariness, and values non-being as essential to who one is.

"We are going in the direction of prose," Woolf claims in "The Narrow Bridge of Art" (1927), an essay in which she looks to poetry for "beauty, purity, transcendence," but ultimately rejects it in favor of a new kind of novel, one largely characterized by the ordinary work of prose, with just "something of the exaltation of poetry" (24). But as much as Woolf pushes for a new form for the novel, the actual fiction she produces is rooted in what will render the ordinary, which is sometimes stylistically less radical than her essays on the modern novel would have us believe. Despite her distaste for Edwardian "materialism," so passionately stated in "Mr. Bennett and Mrs. Brown" and "Modern Fiction," Woolf does not actually reject the representation of what she calls in this essay "the fabric of things" (112). She transforms, but does not reject, the literary realism of the past. Her most successful works render ordinary experience and do depend upon facts and fabric.

## *Mrs. Dalloway*

> All the same, that one day should follow another; Wednesday, Thursday, Friday, Saturday; that one should wake up in the morning; see the sky; walk in the park . . . it was enough.
>
> —Woolf, *Mrs. Dalloway*

If *Mrs. Dalloway* explores how people respond to change—the shift from war to peace, the pressures within the class system, and the realizations wrought by a family's growing older—then we might understand Woolf's focus on ordinary events as showing how her characters normalize these changes. In a novel where nothing happens twice, but much that happens presumably has happened before (Clarissa's walk through London, Lady Bruton's luncheon, Elizabeth's omnibus ride), Woolf suggests that no two events are exactly the same, even if they seem everyday. In a Bergsonian sense, no action is the same because each action is affected by time. "If everything is in time, everything changes inwardly, and the same concrete reality never recurs," Bergson writes. "Repetition is therefore possible only in the abstract: what is repeated is some aspect that our senses, and especially our intellect, have singled out from reality, just because our action, upon which all the effort of our intellect is directed, can move only among repetitions" (*Creative Evolution*, 46). Change pervades every moment of our existence, essentially making repetition of any event impossible. *Mrs. Dalloway* explores this experience of the ordinary as something always somewhat strange insofar as it always exists in a new moment of time. Yet as Woolf explains in "A Sketch of the Past," repetition of everyday actions is what we use to orient and control our lives, relying on the sameness of what has gone before. Though we might not be aware of it, Woolf writes, we are protected by change, comfortably covered in the "cotton wool of daily life" (72).

In his study of Proust, Samuel Beckett describes the way in which temporality dominates our day-to-day existence, the way that time, as Bergson also accounts for it, is an adversary to the human desire for regularity: "There is no escape from the hours and the days. Neither from tomorrow nor from yesterday. There is no escape from yesterday because yesterday has deformed us, or been deformed by us" (*Proust,* 13). Woolf's novel foresees Beckett's theory: daily life in *Mrs. Dalloway* functions as something that her characters crave as a natural reaction against the deformations of time. As Peter Walsh notes, walking around Regents Park: "Those five years—1918 to 1923—had been, he suspected, somehow very important. People looked different. Newspapers seemed different" (*MD* 78). London pedestrians go about their daily business as before but nonetheless seem fundamentally different after years of war. Changes, as they affect a day in the life of Clarissa Dalloway, however, are not illustrated by sudden acts of self-awareness but by the desire—felt by so many characters—to preserve the ordinary flow of events, the moment passing.

*Mrs. Dalloway said she would buy the flowers herself.* Woolf's novel opens with an ordinary task, suited by a simple sentence—the rhythm of natural speech, set apart as a single paragraph. Yet move quickly down the page and the task is tinged with a sense that "something awful was about to happen; looking at the flowers, at the trees" (*MD* 3). Clarissa's death anxieties, foreshadowing and echoing Septimus Smith's, complicate the early morning freshness of her day. The first page of *Mrs. Dalloway* oscillates between an ordinary task and a heightened event, running an errand and plunging toward death. Similarly, Clarissa is both an ordinary woman and a woman who feels extraordinary emotions: "she always had the feeling that it was very, very dangerous to live even one day. Not that she thought herself clever, or much out of the ordinary" (*MD* 9). This back-and-forth style characterizes the novel ("She would not say of any one in the world now that they were this or were that"); Clarissa's simple actions, her walk through London and her party preparations, as well as the movements of other characters throughout this June day, make up the substance of the novel's action. They dominate and absorb moments of anxiety or self-realization.

Experience in this novel can be heightened, as Woolf's moving account of Septimus Smith illustrates. But even Septimus is best revealed when he is doing ordinary things, when he briefly reverts back to his behavior before the war. Unselfconscious routines reveal who these people are—to the other characters in the novel and to us, as readers. When Clarissa thinks about Peter Walsh, at the novel's opening, she cannot remember what he is doing *now,* but remembers things about him that are constant. Much of what is seemingly important gets forgotten, leaving a person composed in memory by what seems trivial: "He would be back from India one of these days, June or July, she forgot which, for his letters were awfully dull; it was his sayings one remembered; his eyes, his pocket-knife, his smile, his grumpiness and, when millions of things had utterly vanished—how strange it was!—a few sayings like this about cabbages" (*MD* 3). Clarissa knows Peter based on little things—his eyes, his sayings, his habit of fiddling with a pocketknife.

Of course, Clarissa does remember these things about Peter, and thus endows them with significance; she paradoxically removes them from their ordinariness. And so Peter's pocketknife resonates with importance—a symbol of his sexual energy, the fear Clarissa felt about marrying him, and his sadly tamed danger and masculinity. There are many moments, like this one, in which simple habits not only reveal character but also can be read symbolically. For instance, Clarissa sits on her sofa sewing her green dress when Peter, just returned from India, surprises her. While Peter wonders how she could be doing what she's always been doing (has she changed at *all?*), Clarissa's sewing is more than just her routine. The episode distinctly echoes Penelope's weaving and waiting for Odysseus to return; it acquires mythic importance. Allusions to Odysseus's journey draw attention to Woolf's response to Joyce's *Ulysses,* which she read in 1918 and then reread in 1922. As with the glut of materialist details in *Ulysses,* however, by no means are all of the ordinary actions in *Mrs. Dalloway* so heavily loaded. In fact, most of them are not. Habits, by nature, do not signify something symbolic; they are not exceptional moments. To wholly transform habit into something beyond a representation of character would undermine the realist project that *Mrs. Dalloway* undertakes. Woolf wants to depict the way habit functions, the way habit composes a life.

In Beckett's study of Proust, Beckett is compelled and repelled by habit: it reminds a person of physical obligations, and ties him to his animal self. But habit is also the lifeblood of a play like *Waiting for Godot,* as it is for the characters in Woolf's novel. In his deadpan manner, Beckett states that habit is the substance of "life":

> Habit is a compromise effected between the individual and his environment, or between the individual and his own organic eccentricities, the guarantee of a dull inviolability, the lightning-conductor of his existence. Habit is the ballast that chains the dog to his vomit. Breathing is habit. Life is habit. (*Proust,* 18–19)

Habit in Proust's novel serves as Marcel's attempt to control time, to regulate change. As Beckett puts it, Proust is obsessed with how "the laws of memory are subject to the more general laws of habit" (18), and this dynamic profoundly influenced Woolf's work as well.[10] But Woolf's ideas about habit differ from Beckett's, and are closer to Proust's, in that she sees habit as something that reveals rather than degrades character. (The habits of Beckett's characters are almost always *bad* habits.) The routine needs of the body, while sometimes bothersome, are part of who a person is. For instance, Woolf describes Peter eating his solitary dinner at a restaurant—reinforcing the simple reality that people must eat, including this Englishman, who orders Bartlett pears for dessert (*MD* 176). The question of whether these Bartlett pears suggest anything significant is raised by the fact that a family touring London watches Peter closely. Point-of-view shifts: the family waits for some telling detail from him; they want him to be a representative Englishman. But the ironic tone of Woolf's description of how the family views Peter emphasizes that Peter's dinner is a necessity, not a significant event: "it was his way of looking at the menu, of pointing his forefinger to a particular wine, of hitching himself up to the table, of addressing himself seriously, not gluttonously to dinner, that won him their respect (*MD* 175). Peter's dinner is a far cry from Krapp's obsession with bananas. Other events in Woolf's novel are presented as events that will conceivably happen again—like actions for which Proust depends upon the *imparfait.* Clarissa has bought flowers before, and she will most likely buy flowers again, from the same Miss Pym. In fact, as Victoria Rosner points out (in a felicitous allusion to Beckett), Clarissa's flower-buying habit is "the pleasure of a dog on a leash," since she goes out only to shop and returns by exactly the same route home (*Modernism,* 149). Repetition of such actions allows characters to negotiate the changes between the present and the past, so that events from long ago become part of the immediate moment, as J. Hillis Miller has noted in his celebrated essay on repetition in *Mrs. Dalloway.*[11]

Woolf takes the ordinary as her central subject—an ordinary that is not always symbolic of something else. "Ordinary" (like "character") is a catchword for Woolf. In many of her essays, she draws attention to writers who represent it well. The fiction of Turgenev, Austen, and her friend Forster (among others) locates and fixes on ordinary experiences and ordinary things, often through an attention to facts. Woolf's comment on these writers mixes praise with a desire to translate their aesthetic into something more like her own. In her essay on Jane Austen, for instance, she praises Austen's ability to take the "trivial" and make it profoundly revealing of character. In Austen's novels (as in Woolf's), "there is no tragedy and no heroism," just commonplace moments of living ("Jane Austen," 138). These moments embody the repetitions of any day—for instance, a man and woman talking on the stairs before dinner—but these moments can also spark a character's self-revelation:

> But, from triviality, from commonplace, their words become suddenly full of meaning, and the moment for both one of the most memorable in their lives. It

> fills itself; it shines; it glows; it hands before us, deep, trembling, serene for a second; next, the housemaid passes, and this drop, in which all the happiness of life has collected, gently subsides again to become part of the ebb and flow of ordinary existence. (142)

Woolf's praise for Austen is striking because it so aptly describes her own fiction—especially the "housemaid" passing, for nearly all of Woolf's novels include servants, characters who embody and control domestic routines, whereas Austen's novels rarely mention servants at all. While it would be easy to read this passage as a description of a modernist epiphany, it is equally important to highlight the ordinariness of what Woolf describes, and implicitly her indebtedness to Austen's materialism. Woolf locates a moment, not solely in an Austen novel but characteristic of her own—perhaps the charged, unspoken intimacy between the Ramsays at the end of "The Window" or Isa's quickly stifled attraction to Haines in the opening scene of *Between the Acts.* The "housemaid passing" interrupts the glow and shine of human connection, much like "Mrs. Gape" is a jarring "shock" to poetic reverie. But these moments "drop" back into the flow of ordinary life. As she makes clear in "A Letter to a Young Poet," Woolf actually wants to represent these interruptions, these deflations, the way that the everyday is a mixture and ongoing flow of events. Her interpretation of Austen reveals as much about Woolf's ethos and era as it does about Austen's. The ordinary is a point of fascination for Woolf, alluring because it is so hard to pin down; its natural "ebb and flow" denies a stable moment of recognition.

The paradox of the ordinary becomes part of Woolf's text itself, addressed and played out by the major characters and many minor ones. That is, Woolf's technique of multiple points of view emphasizes the nature of perception and overlooking: some characters perceive events and objects as significant whereas others overlook these very familiar things. Woolf peoples the streets of London with a variety of pedestrians, some of whom see the city with bright-eyed attention. Maisie Johnson, "in London for the first time," sees "the stone basins, the prim flowers, the old men and women, invalids most of them in Bath chairs—all seemed, after Edinburgh, so queer" (*MD* 28). She is a girl much like Joyce's Eveline—used to old ways, repetitions, familiar objects—but Maisie now stands terrified in a big city, "twisting the knob of the iron railing," much as Eveline does, paralyzed at the Dublin port (*MD* 29). All of the day-to-day events of the city seem strange. Maisie (who is never mentioned again) demonstrates how the ordinary can be entirely decontextualized when put into such fresh focus, as Woolf does in describing it. But the "stone basins" and "prim flowers" are not strange to everyone. This difference of perception reflects upon the paradox of narrative representation whereby the act of describing inevitably deepens the importance of what's being described. Although Woolf includes *many* things (a technique amplified in Joyce), everything described is nevertheless given significance, to some degree, by the act of literary representation.

As Woolf worked on this scene in Regent's Park, she found that the only way to go forward was "by clinging as tight to fact as I can" (*WD* 2:272). Facts, here, are the names, affiliations, and occupations of pedestrians—described with brevity, but nonetheless comparable to the materialist style of Woolf's Edwardian predecessors. For instance, a reader finds a similar collection of facts when turning to the opening pages of Arnold Bennett's *Riceyman Steps* (1923) in which a man walks through the industrial streets of London's Clerkenwell in the autumn of 1919. His physical appearance (stout, with a slight limp), manner of dress (hatless, neatly suited), and occupation (bookseller) are emphasized in the novel's first paragraphs, along with many other details that Woolf presumably would have criticized for being "outside," lacking depth, as she writes in "Mr. Bennett and Mrs. Brown" (105). Bennett's style, according to Woolf, overlooks the essential character of the individual, perhaps evident in his description of the charwoman Elsie, who is seen almost solely from the "outside," as a man might see her.[12] And yet, even as Bennett overlooks something crucial about the constitution of character, his materialist style serves a specific purpose, stabilizing the reader in an ordinary physical world. Woolf's work, in comparison, similarly relies on the "outside," but in a way that foregrounds the elusiveness of the ordinary and the paradox of its representation. Maisie has many counterparts (the list of people who fill the opening scene of the novel) who are not so pointedly aware of their surroundings: Scrope Purvis, who sees Clarissa on the curb; Edgar J. Watkiss, who carries lead piping; Sarah Bletchley, who holds her baby; Mr. Bowly, who has rooms at the Albany; Mrs. Coates, who looks up at the airplane; and Mrs. Dempster, who saves crusts for squirrels (*MD* 4–29). These minor characters of various social classes populate Regents Park and the streets surrounding it as they would any other day of the week. Woolf briefly attends to each, but like Maisie, they are never mentioned again—with the exception of Mr. Bowly, who shows up at Clarissa's party, like a Joycean leitmotif. Clarissa must inevitably pass these people. They are noted as if they are regular, recurring aspects of London. Woolf thus depicts the ordinariness of walking through London and also acknowledges (explicitly through Maisie) that representing the ordinary has the power to transform it.

Like this pageant of pedestrians on the London streets, resuming their lives after the war, Woolf's deliberate pairing of Septimus and Clarissa threads together the experience of shell shock with the experience of ordinary existence continuing.

As she explained in her introduction to the Modern Library edition of the novel, Septimus was intended to be Clarissa's "double" (*Essays IV,* 549). The relationship between these two characters, rather than posing a dichotomy of experience, emphasizes Clarissa's own sense of vulnerability after the war, and specifically after her illness, as well as Septimus's struggle to connect to a world that Clarissa, by virtue of "being part of it," embodies (*MD* 5). Clarissa's renewed vitality and love of what she calls "the ebb and flow of things" (*MD* 9) hinges on her theory of human connectedness, of finding meaning from the people and events around her rather than from within herself. Whereas alone, taking her prescribed afternoon rest, Clarissa acknowledges what she "lack[s]" ("something central which permeated"), she feels wholly alive when walking through the streets of London (*MD* 34). Every pedestrian she passes reinforces her own sense of promise: "what she loved was this, here, now, in front of her; the fat lady in the cab" (*MD* 9). Clarissa's daughter Elizabeth inherits this attraction to the everyday flow of events: the "procession" of people, as she calls it sitting atop an omnibus, constitutes the stuff of life. While different from Clarissa in many ways, Elizabeth also hopes that what humans forget, what does not get remembered in the flow of each day might be apprehended by some larger force. Elizabeth thinks:

> Forgetfulness in people might wound, their ingratitude corrode, but this voice, pouring endlessly, year in year out, would take whatever it might be; this vow; this van; this life; this procession, would wrap them all about and carry them on, as in the rough stream of a glacier the ice holds a splinter of bone, a blue petal, some oak trees, and rolls them on. (*MD* 151–52)

Somehow "life" must be preserved—not in amber, but in ice, frozen in time, and moving into a vast ocean where all melts and joins. But who can remember every fragment of life, every process of the day, the flow of all the hours? The idea that these fragments—the little things, the ordinary tasks—are what constitute "life" is the central assertion of the novel, voiced most persistently by Clarissa. She believes that the movement and flow of each day, in its ordinariness, is more important than grand action, even if she cannot recall these things specifically: "being part of it" (*MD* 5), "that divine vitality" (*MD* 7). The deictic language of Clarissa's embrace ("this, here, now" [*MD* 9]) emphasizes her longing after something that, by its very nature, escapes defining. Yet Clarissa's satisfaction with the ordinariness of events and their transitory quality is her hallmark characteristic. As the epigraph that opens this section suggests, each day of the week follows in accordance with what has come before, but for Clarissa, this is "enough."

The word "procession" also summons and reimagines a distinct event in the context of post–World War I England: the procession to bury the unknown warrior in November 1920, an event that drew thousands of mourners to Westminster Abbey and stirred the imagination of the country.[13] While the procession offered a form of mourning for the casualties of the First World War—an outcome difficult for England to comprehend in its magnitude—Woolf's "procession" commemorates life embodied by small, organic things. The images ("a splinter of bone, a blue petal, some oak trees") suggest tangible and natural materials, though their piecemeal nature also evokes the fragility of living. This procession echoes the way in which Clarissa (and the Regents Park pedestrians) seeks out a protective "cotton wool," to "wrap them all about and carry them on." Vulnerable, Clarissa nonetheless desires participation in an urban, exterior world filled with an array of people.

Alternatively, Septimus has turned inward after his mental breakdown, denying the external world. Septimus cannot handle the stuff of life that he calls "real things," for "real things were too exciting" (*MD* 155). Septimus vacillates back and forth between recognizing these "things" and seeing them metamorphose into a vision of war; he has lost the identity that routines and habits establish. Now, everything is heightened experience: "He lay very high, on the back of the world. The earth thrilled beneath him. Red flowers grew through his flesh; their stiff leaves rustled by his head" (*MD* 74–75). Septimus's poetic interior visions—modeled largely after Woolf's own—render a mind deranged by inexplicable pain and devastating loss.[14] For instance, sitting on a park bench with his wife, Rezia, Septimus transforms a man in a gray business suit walking through the park into a uniformed soldier arisen from the dead (*MD* 76). Septimus cannot see the man as Clarissa sees the fat lady in the cab—as an ordinary stranger going about his daily business—but envisions a macabre scene of war instead.

Yet hope remains that Septimus might recover. In one scene, he seems to remember how he felt before the war or before his breakdown, and we learn something about his previous personality. This scene, late afternoon as Rezia sews hats and Septimus lies on the sofa, centers on Septimus's relationship to the ordinary. For a brief moment, as Septimus addresses the materiality of things around him, he seems able to function without fear. Surrounded by domestic objects that threaten to metamorphose into something else, he has difficulty opening his eyes, but "gathering courage, he looked at the sideboard; the plate of bananas; the engraving of Queen Victoria and the Prince Consort; at the mantelpiece, with the jar of roses. None of these things moved. All were still; all were real" (*MD* 155–56). Septimus's comfort with the ordinary objects of a living room seems a temporary stay against confusion. He chooses the ribbons for the hat that Rezia is making; "so real, it was so substantial, Mrs. Peters' hat" (*MD* 158). And instantly Rezia thinks: "He had become himself then, he had laughed then" (*MD* 158). Similar to Clarissa's sewing, Rezia's hat-making is an ordinary routine, one that Septimus, for an instant, participates in. Sewing suggests an assembling of things, a creation of something whole from individual parts, similar to Clarissa's final party. To "assemble" is what Clarissa must do when, in the middle of her party, she hears of Septimus's suicide, his final disassembling, a turning way from what he in the hat-making scene briefly embraced.

Some of Woolf's critics argue that Septimus's experience is a mark of the novel's modernist style in that modernist fiction is particularly well suited to depict heightened experience, especially trauma. If *Mrs. Dalloway* is a representative text, then the novel's repetitions, nonchronological form, and stream-of-consciousness style preserve rather than "reorder" the trauma they embody.[15] Recent discoveries in the field of trauma psychology have enriched our understanding of the relationship between literature and trauma, from which this body of criticism on *Mrs. Dalloway* builds. But the assumption that the representation of trauma in *Mrs. Dalloway* is what makes it modernist does not account for the essential role of the ordinary. First, representations of trauma are not unique to modernism, as Septimus himself comprehends when rereading the literature that he went to war to "save":

> How Shakespeare loathed humanity. . . . This was now revealed to Septimus; the message hidden in the beauty of words. The secret signal which one generation passes, under disguise, to the next is loathing, hatred, despair. Dante the same. Aeschylus (translated) the same. (*MD* 97)

Septimus, having seen the horrors of humanity during the war, now sees the horrors of humanity depicted in the literature that—ironically—persuaded him to fight for England in the first place. He sees himself reflected back. A reader need only look to Lear on the heath or Ugolino in hell to experience the way in which madness, terror, or trauma is enacted. In *Wars I Have Seen* (1945), Stein notes the parallel between Shakespeare's tragedies and her experience in occupied France during World War II. "We spend our Friday afternoons with friends reading Shakespeare," Stein writes. "We have read Julius Caesar, and Macbeth and now Richard the Third and what is so terrifying is that it is all just like what is happening now" (105). Terrifying events were represented through syntactical disruptions, repetition, and nonchronological form long before the arrival of literary modernism.

Second, to argue that traumatic experience demands a different kind of narration—or that trauma itself is unnarratable—is contrary to Woolf's distinction between non-being and a highly memorable event. As she explains in "A Sketch of the Past," Woolf finds non-being much harder to narrate. To offer another example, here from a 1924 diary entry, Woolf notes how she cannot exactly describe what marks each day in a house to which she has just moved: "Indeed most of life escapes, now I come to think of it: the texture of the ordinary day" (*WD* 2:298). Woolf proceeds to describe a traumatic scare—her niece Angelica Bell was hit by a motor car—and the details she remembers are vivid: a telephone call, the long wait in the hospital, the evasive nurse, the anguished look on her sister's face. The traumatic is etched in her memory so as to be printed on the page, unlike the time Woolf spends at home. Woolf contrasts the sharpness of trauma with the dullness of habitual experiences, which are often much harder but necessary to remember and record.

Most important, in the case of Woolf's novel, the narrative drive of *Mrs. Dalloway*—that is, the way it ends—represents an affirmation of the ordinary, not the traumatic. When Clarissa hears of Septimus's suicide, in the middle of her party, she feels at first deeply startled, largely because she recognizes her own proclivity to "plunge" toward death. Her physical reaction to Septimus's death ("her dress flamed, her body burnt" [*MD* 201]), suggests that she could herself be engulfed or consumed by suicide; his death prompts her to imagine her own. If Clarissa had killed herself—as Woolf had considered, according to her introduction to the Modern Library edition of the novel—then Clarissa's day would have been far from ordinary. But the fact that Woolf changed her original plan suggests that Clarissa's everyday living prevails over death. Clarissa recovers a sense of happiness that Septimus's death threatens to obliterate. Leaving her party for a moment and retreating to a back room, she arrives at a sense of joy. While she admires and even envies Septimus's courage, she wants to go on living: "A thing there was that mattered; a thing, wreathed about with chatter, defaced, obscured in her own life, let drop every day in corruption, lies, chatter. This he had preserved" (*MD* 202). Septimus's suicide "preserves," paradoxically, the same flow of events that Elizabeth watches from atop the omnibus, "this vow; this van; this life," like the ice of a glacier preserving a splinter of bone. Septimus's death somehow keeps intact a human desire for purity or unadulterated experience that, for Clarissa, the "chatter" and "corruption" of life sometimes obscure. Unable to see life after the war as simple or pure, Septimus cannot maintain his connection to ordinary things, and yet his suicide propels Clarissa to reconnect with "life": "this life, to be lived to the end, to be walked with serenely" (*MD* 203). While Clarissa's happiness—her conclusion that "she felt glad that he had done it; thrown it away while they went on living" (*MD* 204)—might seem perverse, it is essentially an assertion of life ("this, here, now,") over inwardness, trauma, or death. Woolf asserts the force of Clarissa's everyday living.

By doubling Clarissa and Septimus, Woolf emphasizes that Clarissa's desire for the continuation of ordinary days is a conscious choice very different from Septimus's choice to plunge from a window. The possibility that ordinary behavior is largely conscious behavior is different from a conception of human behavior articulated by Freud, whose works had a very powerful hold over Woolf and her milieu.[16] Woolf's depiction of ordinary behaviors underscores the skepticism that she felt about Freud's theory of the unconscious pathology behind everyday life. When Woolf finally turned seriously to Freud's late essays in 1939 at the outbreak of war, what disturbed her most were the ways in which his ideas about the unconscious seemed to reduce individual freedom (Lee, *Virginia,* 722). At a time when it was imperative for Woolf and others to believe in individual freedom and action amid a mob mentality, Freud's understanding of the aggressive and destructive impulses of humanity and of group psychology were terrifying to her. Although *Mrs. Dalloway* does not explicitly engage with ordinary experience as a mode of opposing war and destruction, what it does advocate is the ordinary as an individual choice against extreme forms of violence.

The power of the everyday to trump trauma is a possibility that Woolf's other works put forth as well. Woolf's use of the word "procession" to signify the flow of ordinary events—events that paradoxically resist representation—also occurs in *Jacob's Room* (1922), a novel that aspires to represent the elusive character of Jacob Flanders. As his loaded last name suggests, Jacob will soon become a victim of the same war that drove Septimus to suicide. The "procession" of events that make up Jacob's life are nothing but "shadows," in Woolf's opinion, as if Jacob's character disseminates into the unknown, along with the First World War's warriors. In a rare instance of authorial intrusion (which her subsequent novels generally avoid), an omniscient Woolfian narrator presents a theory that is worth quoting at length, as it exemplifies the connections Woolf makes between an ordinary moment and individual character:

> It seems then that men and women are equally at fault. It seems that a profound, impartial, and absolutely just opinion of our fellow-creatures is utterly unknown. Either we are men, or we are women. Either we are cold, or we are sentimental. Either we are young, or growing old. In any case life is but a procession of shadows, and God knows why it is that we embrace them so eagerly, and see them depart with such anguish, being shadows. And why, if this and much more is true, why are we yet surprised in the window corner by a sudden vision that the young man in the chair is of all things in the world the most real, the most solid, the best known to us—why indeed? For the moment after we know nothing about him.
>
> Such is the manner of our seeing. Such the conditions of our love.
> (*Jacob's Room,* 60)

This passage illuminates many Woolfian themes: the difficulty of knowing another person, the transience of meaningful moments, the shiftiness of perspective, and the desire to pin down character. Woolf here also attempts to collapse the inner versus outer dichotomy that motivates her engagement with the 1930s poets; she does not want to say that individuals are solely defined by subjectivity. Moreover, Woolf's young man foresees Mrs. Brown, the "old lady in the corner opposite," whom Woolf hopes the modern novelist, departing from more traditional representations of character, will not ignore. The interior image—of a person by a window, suddenly recognizable—also makes its way into *To the Lighthouse,* whose first chapter (very much *about* Mrs. Ramsay's inscrutability) is titled "The Window." Lily Briscoe's abstract representation of Mrs. Ramsay attempts to solidify, to stabilize, an emotion she cannot precisely describe, similarly associated with death's contribution to a "procession of shadows." More significant, the above passage identifies the moment when an ephemeral procession becomes something "the more real, the most solid." Essentially, "shadows" become "real" when they are allied with an ordinary moment, a young man sitting in a chair. Though the tone of the passage is markedly melancholy, the situation cannot be called traumatic. Rather, the movement from "shadow" to "real" enacts the aim of Woolf's fiction: characters come alive when they are depicted through moments of non-being. Woolf suggests that these kinds of moments most define the "manner" and "conditions" of living—a sentiment that characterizes the turn away from heightened events in favor of the ordinary in *Mrs. Dalloway.* Protected in cotton wool or preserved in a procession, ordinary moments embody the substance of Woolf's characters and constitute the prosaic fabric of her fiction.

## Facts and Things

> It is precisely the random moment which is comparatively independent of the controversial and unstable orders over which men fight and despair; it passes unaffected by them, as daily life. The more it is exploited, the more the elementary things which our lives have in common come to light.
>
> —Eric Auerbach, *Mimesis*

Although Clarissa's celebration of life depends upon her theory that everyone is connected, class distinctions identify the everyday as an experience fashioned by a particular ideology. The first page of *Mrs. Dalloway* reveals that Clarissa's everyday consists of servants, country houses, and a familiarity with those in positions of power. Class necessarily determines just what sort of ordinary tasks mark one's life. The everyday experiences of women who work out of necessity are very different from those of women who take walks when they wish and throw parties. The ordinary—as a genre of events and things—differs based upon how much control a person has over her environment. Characters such as Lucy, or Mrs. McNab from *To the Lighthouse,* do the cleaning and cooking, whereas Clarissa Dalloway and the Ramsays do not. To what extent, then, is Clarissa's "one day" a privilege of the upper class? How does the everyday in Woolf's novel account for characters who lack agency, who cannot decide to buy the flowers themselves?

Although every individual's life necessarily entails certain routines of self-maintenance, the ordinary also has an economic, cultural, and gendered specificity that defies simple totalizing, a point that many theorists who valorize the everyday's revolutionary potential often overlook. "The most certain chances of liberation are born in what is most familiar," writes Raoul Vaneigem, celebrating everyday life as a powerful agent in opposing a capitalist system (*Revolution,* 3). The notion of everyday life as potentially defiant or rebellious assumes that individuals always have control over the everyday or that most people are dissatisfied with their own ordinary habits. Rezia Warren Smith, for instance, is instinctively repulsed by Sir William Bradshaw's "proportion" and "conversion," and wants to protect Septimus from the doctor's authoritative orders. Bradshaw may seem like a bad version of William James, who advocates the salutary effects of habit. But Bradshaw's methods are enforced, whereas James asserts that habits are choices. Unlike Clarissa, who chooses to engage in "being part of it," Septimus has Bradshaw's proportion and conversion imposed upon him, an imposition that Rezia also feels. Before Septimus's suicide, as the couple waits for the doctors to arrive, Rezia finishes sewing her hat and wraps up Septimus's papers, as if protecting the two of them from what the doctors might impose. But Rezia, of course, can do nothing in the face of Bradshaw's swashbuckling. Her everyday is overlooked, lacking any real power.

As Eric Auerbach argues at the end of *Mimesis* (1946), the everyday is constituted by moments that are in fact indiscernible to a dominant order. Literature's ability to unearth these privately concealed moments illuminates something "elementary" and "common" among all individuals, he writes, though the everyday manifests itself differently for each person. Whether or not this revelation of shared humanity ("being part of it") has any real political power (as Auerbach believes it does) is a question that Woolf's later novels continue to explore. My contention is that Woolf clings to what she calls "facts" (and what Septimus calls "real things") both as a mode of literary realism and as an ideological value against the force of trauma. Framing *Mrs. Dalloway*'s commitment to the ordinary within the context of these later novels, however, reveals the ways that Woolf experiments with how to incorporate the facts of material existence, and yet realizes that she cannot ultimately represent every point of view, every ordinary life.

Woolf's representation of everyday moments no doubt favors the perspectives of the upper class. In *The Waves* (1931), Woolf wanted to represent the "life of anybody" but realized that she could only replicate the upper-class voices with which she was familiar. In her drafts, she included the voices of the working classes, but omitted them in the published text for fear of being condescending.[17] Even Woolf's description of servants, often quite sympathetic, is nonetheless limited to how servants are related to the people for whom they work. Similarly, Woolf's stinging portrait of Miss Kilman, for instance, singles out Miss Kilman's bitterness toward the upper class as the most defining feature of her identity. But Woolf's novels—which always mark the disparities between the upper and lower classes and especially between men and women—seem to acknowledge rather than to overlook the radical differences in how the everyday is experienced. "Often nothing tangible remains of a woman's day," Woolf writes in "Women and Fiction" (the essay that served as a basis for *A Room of One's Own*), understanding that the everyday may hold a special valence for women, whose lives go unrecorded (146). Woolf's Mrs. Brown, of course, traveling from Richmond to Waterloo, is a vital example of a woman whose life journey has never constituted a literary epic. Although Woolf's depictions of characters akin to Mrs. Brown (like Miss Kilman or Ellie Henderson), in the end, may not satisfy a reader's need for class complexity, Woolf's novelistic aim is to suggest that a representation of the everyday cannot be reduced to one authentic experience.

Woolf's presentation of the everyday emerges as both diverse and ultimately collective, what Rita Felski describes in "The Invention of Everyday Life" (2000) as "the essential, taken-for-granted continuum of mundane activities that frames our forays into more esoteric or exotic worlds" (78). Maurice Blanchot describes the everyday along similar lines. "The everyday is what we are first of all, and most often: at work, at leisure, awake, asleep, in the street, in private existence," he writes. "The everyday, then, is ourselves, ordinarily" ("Everyday Speech," 12). No matter how famous an individual or how remarkable a day may be, there is an ordinariness about everyone, and every day, that cannot be escaped. That is, Woolf's ordinary accounts for its affective state, and in this sense she represents it as shared. The intersecting points of view in *Mrs. Dalloway* contribute to the "procession" of everyday life that all the characters, regardless of class, experience. Felski further explains:

> Everyone, from the most famous to the most humble, eats, sleeps, yawns, defecates; no one escapes the reach of the quotidian. Everyday life, in other words, does not only describe the lives of ordinary people, but recognizes that every life contains an element of the ordinary. We are all ultimately anchored in the mundane. ("Invention," 79)

Felski's feminist theory of everyday life acknowledges that the experience of modernity comprises various different sites, the domestic as well as the perambulatory pedestrian. Modernity, to be exact, is not predicated on a post-Baudelaire alienation from the home, though of course the everyday attains a new visibility in the nineteenth century, as people are massed together in big cities, and the uniform and repetitive aspects of human lives become more prominent ("Invention," 79). London, for Woolf, is a place where the quotidian is made conspicuous by people passing on the street. By moving in and out of the perspectives of Regents Park pedestrians, Woolf depicts the everyday as both unique to each individual and responsive to a shared environment. The sky-writing airplane, the prime minister's motorcar, and the chimes of Big Ben, for instance, thread through each pedestrian's personal narrative. As Auerbach argues, modernity's emphasis on the "random moment in the lives of different people" sharpens the profound relationship between the individual and a larger sense of shared humanity (488). In exploring the ordinary, we see "nothing less than the wealth of reality and depth of life in every moment to which we surrender ourselves without prejudice" (488). Writing in exile, Auerbach challenges the face of fascism, finding his final example of "mimesis" in Virginia Woolf's *To the Lighthouse,* where he sees Woolf's representation of the overlooked as an enduring sign of what is shared across countries at war.

The two women in the "Time Passes" section of *To the Lighthouse* best demonstrate the balance between the individuality and universality of the everyday. "Time Passes" interrupts the narrative of the Ramsay family's summer holiday and enacts the disruptions of World War I. The famous brackets in "Time Passes" have the effect of purposely subordinating the traumatic events that irrevocably change the Ramsay family. The brackets also give "the sense of reading the two things at the same time," as Woolf explained in her diary, again recognizing (like the doubling of Septimus and Clarissa) that experience is never either/or, never just one thing (*WD* 3:106). "Time Passes"—even more than *Mrs. Dalloway*—dramatically deflects the traumatic and centralizes what is ordinary. Mrs. Ramsay's death, Prue's marriage and death in childbirth, and Andrew's death in battle are all bracketed here, placed within the context of Mrs. McNab and Mrs. Bast cleaning the Ramsay house: dusting bedrooms, wiping windows, sweeping floors, and pausing in the study to sip tea together. These tasks are the only actions with the power to normalize the passing of time during the upheavals of war.[18] The ordinary, located in the housework of two lower-class women, serves as an arresting reminder of what remains in war's wake—the basic and essential routines of human endurance. The women thus embody the struggle of Europe, but also, on a literal level, call attention to the fact that their work differs from the leisure described in the novel's first section.

The only denizens of the Ramsay house in "Time Passes," these servants also emphasize the overlooked or unremembered nature of ordinary experience. Here and elsewhere, Woolf shifts point of view to focus on the forgotten, the banal. The objects of the Ramsay house and the labor of Mrs. McNab and Mrs. Bast deflect away from the terrible events of war; intense pain and loss are not addressed head on, but through the efforts of cleaning and continuing. Woolf describes the sheer effort and physical exertion demanded of Mrs. McNab in cleaning the Ramsay house:

> The books and things were mouldy, for, what with the war and help being hard to get, the house had not been cleaned as she would have wished. It was beyond one person's strength to get it straight now. She was too old. Her legs pained her. (*TTL* 147)

To "get it straight" requires an enormous effort; Mrs. McNab's physical pain appears emblematic of the pain of a world at war. Her attempt to reestablish a sense of continuity and security in the Ramsay home generates a new relationship to the ordinary, particularly ordinary *things.* Domestic objects become more powerful than they once were; they seem to endure longer than humans do. Stability is found in "a jug and basin . . . the sharp edges and firm bulk of a chest of drawers" (*TTL* 137). Objects retain beauty in their solidity, withstanding human questioning: "'Will you fade? Will you perish?' . . . they should answer: we remain" (*TTL* 137). Like the sideboard and bananas that connect Septimus to an external world—or the famous mark in Woolf's "The Mark on the Wall"—the objects in "Time Passes" represent firm elements of habitual, ordinary life, which a world war cannot stamp out.

Alex Zwerdling argues that the "discontinuous structure is largely determined by [Woolf's] wish to highlight historical and ideological shifts" (193), a view that generally dominates critical thinking about "Time Passes." But although the brackets in this section clearly do highlight rather than deflect the shocking events described within them, I am suggesting that "Time Passes" gives as much (if not more) attention to what is described *outside* of the brackets: the mundane housework of two women. Readers may feel jarred by the brackets, but they emphasize (through their grammatical function) that what's inside is subordinate to what's outside. Although violence is depicted in"Time Passes," it is not Woolf's primary focus; it is purposefully indirect. In fact, Woolf specifically cut out many of her earlier references to World War I in this section. War violence, especially male destructiveness, is more explicit in the drafts for "Time Passes" and in a separate version published a year earlier than the finished novel in *Commerce,* a Paris periodical.[19] In the final published version, Woolf chooses to deemphasize, even eliminate, overt references to war. War is acknowledged here first and foremost as a cause of domestic neglect, so that it seems possible to recover through housework ordinary life before the war. In this way, "Time Passes" privileges the routines of cleaning over the shock of war, even as cleaning takes on a dramatically new meaning in conjunction with the losses that shake the Ramsay family and the world outside of their house. The ordinary becomes a means by which the unprecedented magnitude of the war can be managed. Mouldy books are minor in comparison to the destroyed libraries of Europe, but they are objects that can be mourned over, cleaned, and repaired. The powerful, bracketed moments in "Time Passes," emphasizing the devastations of war, put pressure on the ordinary: the ordinary is the place where shock is absorbed, a place where life asserts itself, continuing.

In *Mrs. Dalloway,* a similar contextualization occurs toward the end of the novel, when Clarissa's servants prepare for her party. When the first guests arrive, we see the scene through Lucy's eyes. She frets over the prime minister while Mrs. Walker frets over the soup and salmon. Woolf emphasizes the work in the kitchen when Clarissa's party is in full swing. Other servants—Jenny, Mrs. Parkinson, old Ellen Barnet, and Mr. Wilkins—are all named, like Regents Park pedestrians, drawing attention to the indispensable facts of Clarissa's party, not solely to the heightened sense of human connectedness that Clarissa later feels. Furthermore, the material things of the party are as important as the prime minister's arrival:

> . . . the plates, saucepans, cullenders, frying-pans, chicken in aspic, ice-cream freezers, pared crusts of bread, lemons, soup tureens, and pudding basins which, however hard they washed up in the scullery, seemed to be all on top of [Mrs. Walker], on the kitchen table, on chairs, while the fire blared and roared, the electric lights glared, and still supper had to be laid. (*MD* 181)

The ordinary machinery of the party is neither left out nor subordinated; it is an equal part of the novel's final event. Like the literary still life of "Time Passes," this accumulation of cooking objects calls attention to the labor behind leisure.

In Woolf's last three novels, however, she becomes troubled by this method of including facts and things. If we look at what animates Woolf's continued stylistic experiments, it becomes clear that representing ordinary experience by means of a materialist style emerges as a major uncertainty in her later work. Woolf both spurns and embraces the inclusion of the prosaic; she is afraid that it often complicates or covers up what is "real" about a character. Unlike Joyce, her emphasis on materialist detail is always in reference to building character or building narrative: one of her problems with *Ulysses* was that Joyce's explosive materialism seemed indulgent to her, without a purpose.[20] In her long essay "Phases of Fiction" (1929), for instance, Woolf seems to be of two minds regarding the use of facts in fiction, classifying a collection of writers as "the truth-tellers"—including Defoe, Swift, Trollope, Borrow, W. E. Norris and Maupassant—because they gratify our sense of "belief." Woolf admires the chief truth-teller, Defoe, because "emphasis is laid upon the very facts that most reassure us of stability in real life, upon money, furniture, food, until we seem wedged among solid objects in a solid universe" (95). Robinson Crusoe's catalogs and timetables—analogous to Joycean lists—and the repetitious nature of Defoe's narrative are qualities that Woolf ostensibly celebrates. And yet her own ambivalence about facts softens her praise; "truth-tellers" are liable to fall into the same trap as the Edwardians:

> Truth-telling is liable to degenerate into perfunctory fact-recording, the repetition of the statement that it was on Wednesday that the Vicar held his mother's meeting which was often attended by Mrs. Brown and Miss Dobson in their pony carriage, a statement which, as the reader is quick to perceive, has nothing of truth in it but the respectable outside. ("Phases," 103)

Woolf acknowledges that listing things can never comprehensively represent experience; a writer must convey the inside as well as the outside. Again, "Mrs. Brown" reminds us that the inner life of women, in particular, often gets overlooked by novelistic facts. The use of facts in fiction for Woolf seems both necessary and essentially insufficient.

Though a dramatic departure from her previous novels, *The Waves* (1931) marks Woolf's ongoing struggle with facts. Woolf represents the ordinary as entirely stripped from the external world that facts establish, testing the limits of a material-less world. The Woolf novel most frequently described as "poetic," *The Waves* privileges a lyrical "I": six voices speaking in the emphatic present tense, interrupted by intervals that describe the sun's course over the earth and sea. Rarely can the reader locate specific places, visualize appearances, or contextualize characters in a world outside of sensory experience. Facts exist but are blunted by sensation. When writing *The Waves,* Woolf was involved in her discussions with John Lehmann about the distinction between poetry and prose. She wrote to him:

> I wanted to eliminate all detail; all fact; and analysis; and my self; and yet not be frigid and rhetorical; and not monotonous (which I am) and to keep the swiftness of prose and yet strike one or two sparks, and not write poetical, but purebred prose, and keep the elements of character; and yet that there should be many characters, and only one; and also an infinity, a background behind. (*WL* 4:381)

The "purebred prose" of *The Waves* radically differs from conventional prose styles. The voices in *The Waves* do not replicate the way that people actually talk; rarely are the sensations of the body spoken aloud in real life. But the experiences described in this work are universal: birth, childhood, adolescence, adulthood, old age, death. Six voices represent the voices of *everyone,* or anyone. The language of *The Waves* is "prose," it seems, because it describes ordinary experiences, not extraordinary events. Present-tense utterances are equalized among the others (except perhaps for Bernard's final soliloquy, spoken in the past tense), so that the novel does not demarcate individual moments of being but represents an arc of being not identifiable by any specific time. The ordinary is universal or shared experience, of which actual facts seem to play little part.

In light of its abandonment of an external reality, *The Waves* might even be considered a failure in Woolf's own terms, as Mark Hussey has argued (*Singing,* 82–95). The style of the novel shares with other modernist styles an inability to preserve—as ordinary—the kinds of experiences that dominate how people live most of their lives. With *The Years* (1937), Woolf tries out a very different style in which she records exact dates, particular locations, technological developments, family genealogy, and historical moments. *The Years* systematically traces life in the Pargiter family from 1880 to what Woolf calls the "Present Day." Woolf explains in an early version that the work "is not a novel of vision, but a novel of fact" (*Pargiters,* 9). In this early version, she alternates between nonfiction essays and chapters of fiction, essentially commenting on her story as it develops, and emphasizing institutional and social facts that controlled women's sexual lives—such as not being able to go outside alone, or being compelled to restrict exercise. Similar to the copious footnotes in *Three Guineas,* the facts included in the essays are meant to give credence to the creative work of the text. Other facts, for instance, are the detailed finances of the Pargiter household that make clear why the Pargiter daughters never ask to go to college or art school. In the end, Woolf abandoned the essay/chapter divisions of the novel, and fused the two sections together, retaining facts through the novel's dense materialism. Perhaps more than any of Woolf's other novels, *The Years* details the way English life *looked,* particularly domestic interiors. As in *Ulysses,* where Joyce "tried to keep close to fact," a reader can trace various solid objects—the spotted walrus with a brush on its back or the chair with gilt claws—as they reappear from one era to the next. Woolf expressed disappointment with the final result of her conception, although this novel was her only one to become a bestseller immediately after publication (Briggs, *Inner Life,* 301). Woolf's use of facts in fiction, it could be argued, attracted a readership familiar with a more naturalistic mode of recording ordinary life.

Her last novel, *Between the Acts* (1941), maintains an altered commitment to facts. Set quite specifically on a mid-June afternoon in 1939, just six weeks before the start of the war, the novel describes the domestic functions of English country life, and explores how these functions are tied to a historical English past. In this novel, facts are newspaper stories (of a London rape, of present and imminent war) as well as history texts (an "Outline of History," Mrs. Swithin's favorite book). Woolf wants to connect what gets written down—recorded history—with the unselfconscious rituals and routines that grow out of this past. In this way the novel registers Woolf's 1939 reading of Freud's later works, specifically his conception of the relationship between violence and civilization, and of group psychology. Woolf suggests, however, that everyday actions sometimes have the power to resist or subvert the history that preceded them, albeit in very small ways. Miss La Trobe, the "outsider" who directs the pageant of English history, attempts to show her audience how their origins have shaped them, thus suggesting that they might act differently through the pageant's implicit questioning of how their civilization has "progressed." The whole novel hangs heavy with indications of war—a future toward which Miss La Trobe's history seems to be headed, and which the relationship between Isa and Giles portends. But Woolf's characters are only minor agents of change, assuming what Michel de Certeau describes as small "tactics" of everyday life that resist social and economic systems. These tactics slow down or shift relations, such as Isa's resistance to Giles, but as De Certeau acknowledges, they rarely change the overall organization of power.[21] Miss La Trobe believes her pageant to be a "failure," as the individuals of the audience return home to dinner once the final scene has ended. Facts of the past in *Between the Acts*—what Miss La Trobe's pageant stages—weigh upon the English present in a way that makes it quite difficult for the Swithins and Olivers to act differently from their ancestors. The facts of history dramatically dictate English ordinariness.

Woolf's method of including facts and things ties her work to the writers whom she regularly disparages and to other realist writers (including Austen and Defoe) whom she admires. Her modern realism is not in stark contrast to the realist novels that preceded hers. A novel such as *Between the Acts* depends on facts, foregrounding their intransigence and power, just as *Mrs. Dalloway* foregrounds the elusiveness of the ordinary that facts embody. Woolf's experimentation with facts throughout her later fiction continues to renovate earlier literary styles, in the sense that her work self-consciously engages with the ideological reasons for drawing upon facts; she accepts facts as a means of conveying something "real" in the novel while simultaneously questioning the stability of this representation. In "Phases of Fiction," Woolf explains:

> The novel is the only form of art which seeks to make us believe that it is giving a full and truthful record of the life of a real person. And in order to give that full

> record of life, not the climax and the crisis but the growth and development of feelings, which is the novelist's aim, he copies the order of the day, observes the sequence of ordinary things even if such fidelity entails chapters of description and hours of research. (141)

Here, Woolf describes the novels of the past as well as the novels of the future—the novels she will write. But Woolf acknowledges that in some writers, a concern with factual truth-telling produces empty fiction: "The surface is all; there is nothing beyond" (98). A "fidelity" to facts, in Woolf's fiction, must go beyond the "surface," recording overlooked routines, the minute stuff that constitutes character. Woolf's battle with facts as they are related to what is "truthful" fueled her own works of fiction, and thus she cannot help but see this struggle in so many other novelists whose realism she inherits.

Woolf's representation of the ordinary emerges as the most defining feature of her writing, but her ambivalence about describing facts and things draws attention to her shifting, often inconsistent views about how this representation should work. In his *Rambler* essay "On Fiction," Samuel Johnson argues that a good story emerges from a writer's "general converse and accurate observation of the living world," a line of thinking that Woolf also embraces along with Johnson's notion of the "common reader" ("Rambler," 1243). A writer should not employ the "machinery" of fiction but attempt to replicate life. Of course, for Johnson, fiction has unambiguous moral aims ("Vice should always disgust"). But Johnson assumes, like Woolf, that all lives are worth describing, not just the lives of the privileged or the lives of the famous men that Leslie Stephen recorded in his dictionary. "I have often thought that there has rarely passed a life of which a judicious and faithful narrative would not be useful," Johnson writes in his *Rambler* essay on "Biography," "for the incidents which give excellence to biography are of a volatile and evanescent kind, such as soon escape the memory, and are rarely transmitted by tradition" (1247–48). Woolf's non-being is precisely the material that escapes memory and upon which literary traditions cannot be built. Although her novels experiment stylistically with how to represent these "evanescent" incidents, it is possible, as I have suggested, to understand her entire oeuvre as committed to the representation of the ordinary.

It is worth calling attention to the idea that this dominating feature of Woolf's fiction has deep biographical roots as well, which this chapter has only partially explored. The "cotton wool of daily life" that Woolf describes in "A Sketch of the Past" fills up her diaries and letters, often described with great relish, often described with fatigue. Ordinariness had an allure for Woolf at times, as it represented health and stability in her own life in contrast to the terrifying bouts of illness that threatened to take over her ability to write and function. Woolf drew upon her illness as material for her writing, so that the stability of routine also took on connotations of artistic dullness, or prose over poetry, as she describes in "On Being Ill." Moreover, the sheer magnitude of Woolf's daily writing (on average, Woolf wrote six letters a day and kept a diary for forty-four years) has allowed critics to understand the texture of how Woolf lived, with minute and detailed information about how her days were constituted. In a 1925 diary entry, Woolf realizes that the dailiness of work and marriage often adds up to an unseen and private happiness:

> The immense success of our life, is I think, that our treasure is hid away; or rather in such common things that nothing can touch it. That is, if one enjoys a bus ride to Richmond, sitting on the green smoking, taking the letters out of the box, airing the marmots, combing Grizzle, making an ice, opening a letter, sitting down after dinner, side by side, & saying "Are you in your stall, brother?"—well, what can trouble this happiness? And every day is necessarily full of it. (*WD* 3:30)

For Woolf, the ordinary is the cause of personal triumph, embedded in "common things" and therefore untouchable. Her diaries and letters suggest that ordinary life is a positive value, and one that she would like to substantiate in her novels. In her early plans for *The Waves,* she describes the novel as "life itself going on" (*WD* 3:229). *The Years,* she writes, is "to end with the press of daily normal life continuing" (*WD* 4:152). To understand how Woolf works out her personal theory into her novels—that is, how her novels take what is "hid away" and bring it to light—has been the aim of this chapter. Whether what Woolf calls "happiness" can come from "common things" for everyone, everywhere, is a question that she leaves for her readers to answer.

# Chapter Three

## Gertrude Stein, William James, and Habit in the Shadow of War

She worked every day. She dictated her works to Alice Toklas, who wrote them down. She lived like anyone more or less. She went out to market, bought food. She had that awful dog. She had to take it out for a walk all the time.
—Paul Bowles on Gertrude Stein, "Desultory Correspondence"

And anyway except in daily life nobody is anybody.
—Gertrude Stein, *Everybody's Autobiography*

Gertrude Stein, one of modernism's earliest experimenters and the celebrated "mother of the avant-garde," called attention throughout her life to the ordinary functions of her not-so-ordinary life. Stein's emphasis on habit, in both her autobiographical works and in her fiction and poetry, seems to contrast startlingly with her bohemian years in Paris—her friendships with the great painters of the twentieth century, her rotating salon of artists and intellectuals at 27 rue de Fleurus, her longtime lesbian partnership with Alice B. Toklas, and the innovative and often baffling style of her texts. Gifted with an ability to recognize promising young artists when they were still relatively unknown (Picasso, Hemingway, Braque, to name a few), Stein was by all accounts "modern" before modernism fully arrived. In "Composition as Explanation" (1926), Stein claims that had

World War I not catapulted Europe into the modern age it would have taken her contemporaries thirty years to appreciate the masterpieces that she could recognize early on. The war, according to Stein, effectively forced the acceptance of a new modernist aesthetic.

But what Stein wrote about her pioneering approach to art stands out against her love of habit, something we often associate with conventional, even old-fashioned, living. To Paul Bowles, who was twenty years old when he visited Stein in 1931, her habits seemed markedly run-of-the-mill. One might say that Stein (like Wallace Stevens) deflated the myth of the eccentric writer; she was rooted in domestic habits, and, more to the point, she made these habits the subject matter of her work. Unlike the familiar paradox between the life of the writer and a writer's work—what T. S. Eliot calls "the man who suffers and the mind that creates" ("Tradition," 41)—the relationship between Stein's life and work, marked by habit, consistently became the material for her writings. Stein's household felicities—her late mornings, her love of large meals, her relationships to her servants, her attachment to Basket the poodle (and to subsequent poodles she named Basket)—constituted a life of specific routines that, when the two world wars ravaged Europe, she was exceptionally reluctant to give up. "Wars change the way of life, habits, markets and so eventually cooking," Toklas writes in the cookbook she published after Stein's death (*Alice B.*, 3). While the wars undeniably changed these women's life together and had an enormous influence on Stein's work, wars also had the effect of establishing even more indispensable habits for them. This renewed emphasis on habit becomes the subject matter for Stein's World War II writings. Habits both mask the disruption that war creates, dissolving the consequences of the world into the space of the home, and paradoxically work as a way in which war itself can be best represented.

Stein locates habit—rather than, say, innovation—as the singular most animating force in the English literary tradition. Similarly, William James—Stein's most important early mentor, with whom she studied in the 1890s when she was a student at Radcliffe—celebrates habit as a result of the freedom to choose, and the subsequent indication of a fully formed character.[1] James's belief in habit is striking in and of itself, underscored by the work of Henri Bergson, who also upheld the utility and necessity of habit in *Matter and Memory* (1896). But James's belief in habit stands out against a dominating ethos against habit, articulated by influential intellects like Ralph Waldo Emerson, James's pragmatist progenitor, and Walter Pater, one of literary modernism's key precursors. Stein, in one sense, inherits James's positivism (he sees habit as a means toward self-improvement) and yet she does not understand habit primarily in terms of productive action.

Rather, habit serves a kind of pleasure—the pleasure of repetition. Stein viewed habits as neither life denying, in Pater's sense, nor prosaic: "Repeating is a wonderful thing in living being," Stein writes in *The Making of Americans* (1934), a text in which she praises the "monotony" of middle-class life and lays out the sweeping proportions of her attraction to repetition, both linguistic and thematic (265). The subject of dailiness in Stein's prewar work becomes even more central to her World War II writings. Similar to Woolf's depiction of ordinary life in relation to World War I, Stein's world is one in which habit accumulates value and takes precedence over war's action. One might assume that habits would be disrupted during a time of crisis, or substituted by an active reaction to war's violence, as in Samuel Beckett's case. Beckett's post–World War II work is, in this sense, an acute counterpoint to Stein's. Stein's response to World War II was to keep her life as consistent and as pleasurable as possible. In looking at her World War II writings, however, my intention is not to denounce Stein's real life choices—which have been well documented and are unquestionably problematic—but to look closely at how habit functions in her writings, and to examine the consequences of what she learned from William James.[2] I will also consider Stein's somewhat elliptical emphasis on what she calls "daily island life," and how her historical conception of literature frames her lifelong reliance on repetition, culminating in a strange and exaggerated reliance on "daily island life" during a time of war.

## Habit: "The enormous fly-wheel of society"

> Sow an action & you reap a habit; Sow a habit & you reap a character;
> sow a character and you reap a destiny.
> —William James

The influence of Jamesian pragmatism upon modern poetry, including Stein's, has been well recognized, but James's beliefs about habit, and how these particular beliefs may have influenced Stein, have received only passing attention.[3] Habit is the linchpin for the philosophical way of thinking that James called "radical empiricism" and, later, pragmatism. Moreover, Stein's obsession with habit in her late writings illuminates the uses and limitations of James's model. Originally given as a lecture to Harvard undergraduates, James's essay "Habit" was published in 1887 and was included in his 1890 *Principles of Psychology*. In his essay, James explains the importance of habit as an active and practical application of theoretical ideas to the everyday—and subsequently a means by which individuals can make themselves better. As Louis Menand has argued, the wide appeal of James's pragmatism lay in its essential claim that people can change their behavior according to life experience, rather than be subject to some ideal plan imposed upon them.[4] According to James, habits are ways in which individuals make choices based on their own practical experience, not on some higher ideology or abstract design.

Agents of their own behavior, people create habits by selecting from "a world of pure experience," a term that James uses to designate the "primal stuff" of which "everything in the world is composed" and upon which individuals choose to act (*WWJ* 170). Pure experience is a fluid state of relations, a "stream of consciousness" (he coined the term), and we make choices to enter into pure experience by selecting from, and thus organizing, its chaotic flow. As James's language suggests, his theory of habit emerges from a particular nineteenth-century understanding of the physiology of the mind, analogous to Henri Bergson's theory of intuitive action, of how the body's memory of all past actions informs the mind's decision to act in a particular habitual fashion. Bergson and James shared ideas about the importance of biological evolution in structuring memory, and in developing efficient habits. For both James and Bergson, habit allows individuals to filter external stimuli, to choose how to respond to these stimuli, to limit the chaos of experience, and to cultivate constructive behaviors. In this respect, James's notion of habit differs significantly from the Transcendentalism of Ralph Waldo Emerson, his elder peer (and godfather), who famously claims in "Self-Reliance": "Power ceases in the instant of repose; it resides in the moment of transition from a past to a new state, in the shooting of the gulf, in the darting to an aim" (271). Whereas Emerson considers "repose" an immobilizing kind of habit, James defines habit by its action, its ability to invigorate the self.[5]

Trained in medicine, James understands habit first as a process of the body, with ethical and moral consequences. "Habit," James writes, "is nothing but a new pathway of discharge formed in the brain, by which certain incoming currents ever after tend to escape" (*WWJ* 9). Repeating certain actions creates these "pathways" so that habitual actions lack impediment. Habit, therefore, fosters skill, speed, and decisiveness, all of which Jamesian philosophy promotes. Bergson's famous inverted memory cone in *Matter and Memory*, whose conical point touches a plane of "the world" at the moment when action happens, illustrates how every habit is an evolved distillation of all past actions. According to Bergson, we do not bring all of life's experiences to bear on each event but rather use only what is relevant to the particular situation. For instance, we would be unable to open a door if we remembered every door-opening of the past; there must be a separation between memory and action, and habit is the meeting point between them. Perhaps most important, for James, cultivating habit allows the intellectual spirit to grow. Habit frees up the mind for thought. "The more of our daily life we can hand over to the effortless custody of automatism," James writes, "the more our higher powers of mind will be set free for their own proper work" (*WWJ* 17). The mind functions better when the body has been efficiently maintained. Habit neither stifles the mind nor reminds us only of our physical, material selves ("the ballast that chains the dog to his vomit," according to Beckett). Rather, habit opens a door to intellectual freedom and ease.

But James also acknowledges what others might perceive as a negative feature of habit: repetition, not progression. A contradiction inheres in James's understanding of habit: although habits may lead to self-improvement, habits can also keep one in the same place, repeating the same actions. Oddly (in that it seems against the notion of self-improvement), James admires this very quality of stasis; he becomes nearly poetic (in a passage that one is tempted to read as ironic) in his appreciation of habit:

> Habit is thus the enormous fly-wheel of society; its most precious conservative agent. It alone is what keeps us all within the bounds of ordinance, and saves the children of fortune from the envious uprisings of the poor. . . . It keeps the fisherman and the deck-hand at sea through the winter; it holds the miner in his darkness, and nails the countryman to his log cabin and his lonely farm through all the months of snow; it protects us from invasion by the natives of the desert and the frozen zone. It dooms us all to fight out the battle of life upon the lines of our nurture or our early choice, and to make the best of a pursuit that disagrees, because there is no other for which we are fitted, and it is too late to begin again. It keeps different social strata from mixing. . . . It is well for the world that in most of us, by the age of thirty, the character has set like plaster, and will never soften again. (*WWJ* 16)

James associates habits with character-building behavior. Habits are not the stuff of adolescence, but belong to maturity, with permanence of personality that apparently sets like plaster by the age of thirty. James's admiration for constancy may arise out of his personal fear of incertitude (he was notorious for changing his mind)[6] or out of his anxieties about a fast-changing world in which a sense of home has been lost. Like other urban Americans in the late 1800s, James experienced the modernization catalyzed by the Civil War. This passage might be read as James's craving for social structures that offer each individual a "home" rather than leaving each person to wander endlessly, unhabituated to modern life. In this sense, it is logical that James's way of thinking about habit (as well as Bergson's) continued to hold sway during an era of increasing "acceleration," as the decades between 1890 and 1920 have been described, a time marked by vast changes in urban life.[7]

But James's industrial metaphor—a "flywheel" actually regulates the motion of machinery—draws attention to habit's association with industrial work and the loss of control that working-class individuals had over their everyday lives. It is hard to imagine habit for the fisherman, miner, or deck-hand functioning in the same way that it did for William James. Whereas James may have been able to choose his habits and therefore allow his "powers of mind [to] be set free for their own proper work," the working classes clearly did not have this luxury. In turn-of-the-century America, agrarian labor was being regulated or replaced by urban industry; in a sense, the imposing power structures that Antonio Gramsci calls "hegemony" might be a more accurate way of describing what James, here, calls habit (*Gramsci Reader,* 195). James's metaphor of habit as a "flywheel" is unabashedly elitist: habit keeps "different social strata from mixing" and enforces a separation of class and labor. Given this passage, it seems remarkable that James actually celebrates rather than condemns habit. That is, habit is useful for those who have choice but problematically placement-keeping for those who do not. Despite what he himself reveals about habit's perverse power to keep people in place, James promotes the order that habit provides. For James, who understood the world of "pure experience" as overwhelming, habit served as a "conservative agent," a stabilizing necessity.

The idea that representing habit functions as a way to represent literary "character" might be understood as a slight variation from this Jamesian notion of habit as a fixing "plaster." For instance, in *Narration*—a compilation of four 1935 lectures—Stein presents her ideas on the process by which people form their identities. "Anybody is as their land and air is," she writes. "It is that which makes them and the arts they make and the work they do and the way they eat and the way they drink and the way they learn and everything" (46). While Stein did not view habit as rigidly as James did (or at least not as rigidly as his essay on habit suggests), she did rely on habits as a way to reveal the motivations and energies of her characters. For instance, Jeff Campbell, the young African-American doctor in Stein's story "Melanctha," represents a certain kind of pragmatic habituation and steadiness at odds with, in the end, Melanctha's sensual lability.[8] "Melanctha" bears the conspicuous imprint of a Jamesian sense of habit, defending "regular living" over "excitements" (*Three Lives,* 84). In seeing habit as character forming, Stein and James noticeably depart from another dominant nineteenth-century influence, Walter Pater, who asserts the weakness of habit in his conclusion to *The Renaissance* (1873). The very thing that attracts James to habit (it builds character) repulses Pater. Pater disparages habits, which form a "thick wall of personality" around the individual self, dulling the senses into sameness (60).

In response to a Victorian celebration of work and habit (in particular, to Ruskin), Pater emphasizes the primacy of the senses, not automatic action. Whereas James defines habit in terms of personal choice, Pater views habit as unconscious action. Both value individual agency, but one sees habit as personal will and the other as a lack of receptiveness to the world. Forming unconscious habits, for Pater, functions as an evasion of "experience," of perceiving life fully and completely. A life spent "in art and song" engages the senses most persistently, an idea not unlike Shklovsky's belief in art's ability to defamiliarize the ordinary through a heightening of sense perception. One's life can be ostensibly quite ordinary (as was Pater's), but the affective experience of it should be charged with a luminous intensity. In this sense, Pater argues against the first valuation of the ordinary—inattentiveness—but not against the ordinary as a genre or a style. Furthermore, for both Pater and Shklovsky, art does not necessarily cause a rupture with the ordinary world, but a sanctification of it.[9] Paterian aestheticism, as Wolfgang Iser has described it, consists of an "endless series of unconnected moments" without a wider context that would allow for the moment's consequences (*Pater,* 139). Every Paterian moment is unique and risks irrelevance from the next. In perhaps his most famous passage—his conclusion to *The Renaissance*—Pater declares:

> To burn always with this hard, gemlike flame, to maintain this ecstasy, is success in life. In a sense it might even be said that our failure is to form habits: for, after all, habit is relative to a stereotyped world, and meantime it is only the roughness of the eye that makes any two persons, things, situations, seem alike. (60)

"Success" does not consist of training oneself in efficient habits, but in experiencing everything as if for the first time. Life is but an "interval," and to rely on habits is "on this short day of frost and sun to sleep before evening" (61). Instead of repeating actions over and over again (essentially, an act of delusion, since no moment can ever be repeated exactly), we are urged to get "as many pulsations as possible into the given time" (61).

Pater represents the kind of habitless man of whom James is most critical. While they both believe that the world is essentially a state of flux, Pater wants to embrace flux, and James warns that we must not, as coherent individuals, dissolve into it. Toward the end of "Habit," James observes:

> There is no more miserable human being than one in whom nothing is habitual but indecision, and for whom the lighting of every cigar, the drinking of every cup,

> the time of rising and going to bed every day, and the beginning of every bit of work, are subjects of express volitional deliberation. (*WWJ* 17)

Bergson would agree. In *Matter and Memory,* the man of action is defined by his ability to bring to bear only relevant past experiences and act on them in the present moment, whereas "to live only in the present, to respond to stimulus by the immediate reaction which prolongs it, is the mark of the lower animals" (153). James's essay on habit might in fact be read as a roundabout critique of late-nineteenth-century aestheticism, a movement closely related to a modernism of heightened sensory experience. James also hints at the kind of life led by his cosmopolitan brother Henry; the "habit of excessive novel-reading and theatre-going," he writes, encourages a life of sensual indulgence, which in turn produces "true monsters" rather than men of action (*WWJ* 19). James's condemnation is clearly inflated, but he does recognize something with which many would agree (even excessive novel readers): it is not possible to burn, to maintain ecstasy, every minute of one's life. The body would give out, the self obliterated. Despite Pater's credo, our lives cannot consist solely of gemlike moments, and this is something that even those literary modernists most influenced by Pater recognize. Although Pater may stand behind modernist notions like Yeats's unity of being and Joyce's epiphany, these heightened moments are rooted in, even protected by, the things we do every day. What Woolf calls "the cotton wool of daily life" surrounds and guards against too many "moments of being." To maintain Pater's ecstasy is to live a life of naked shock, never clothed against a world that is sometimes harsh and dangerously unpredictable. Habits, like Woolf's soft cotton wool, represent an attempt to stabilize and protect against uncertainty. And most important, for Stein, habits provide domestic comfort, a source of great pleasure in her work.

Stein not only rethinks Paterian ecstasy, suggesting that there is deep satisfaction to be found in habit, but her work also serves as a counterpoint to Freud's understanding of repetition as neurosis. Although Freud, like James, believes that the sense organs instinctually protect the individual from too much external stimuli ("*Protection against* stimuli is an almost more important function for the living organism than *reception of* stimuli" [*Beyond,* 30]), Freud suggests that repetition often works against this kind of self-protection, against an individual's tendency to reduce or remove internal tension. The "beyond" of Freud's *Beyond the Pleasure Principle* (1920) refers to a kind of repeating that does not function on the basic level of protecting the self but in fact reenacts a traumatic event. In this sense, Freud's understanding of repetition does not affirm individual agency as Jamesian habit and the Paterian moment both do. (This denial of choice was one reason that Woolf, like Stein, was resistant to Freudian theory.) But in another sense, Freud and Pater both repudiate habit, and offer a dominant paradigm of the origins of modernism. Philip Fischer, for instance, cites William James as an example of the nineteenth-century moralistic belief in habit's efficiency against which Pater and Freud both rebelled.[10] This dichotomy (nineteenth-century habit versus modernism's break from it) constitutes the most prevailing framework for understanding habit in relationship to literary modernism. Yet the example of Stein offers a powerful challenge to this notion of habit as something that literary modernism left behind. For Stein, repetition is the source of daily pleasure, not a staging of past trauma and certainly not a mark of failure.

Stein in fact celebrates habit as the essential basis of writing in "What Is English Literature," the first of her 1934–35 *Lectures in America.* "What is English Literature" also emerges from Stein's lifelong interest in the relationship between habit and political stability, a subject that dominates her later war writings. She imposes her own theory of habit upon a grand narrative of English literary history, tracing the trajectory from Chaucer to the twentieth century by way of the "daily island life" that characterizes the greatness of the country's literature, to which she, albeit an American, also contributes. According to Stein, England's insularity produced a homogenous, prosperous, and seemingly untroubled way of life. Thus, poets and writers in England have always been obsessed with themselves, with dailiness, and with the "enumeration" of things that make up their daily life. Imperialism, rather than opening up new ways of living that lay beyond England, fortified the importance and hegemony of Englishness:

> The thing that has made the glory of English literature is description simple concentrated description not of what happened nor what is thought or what is dreamed but what exists and so makes the life the island daily island life. It is natural that an island life should be that. What could interest an island as much as the daily the completely daily island life. And in the descriptions the daily, the hourly descriptions of this island life as it exists and it does exist it does really exist English literature has gone on and on from Chaucer until now. (14–15)

In Stein's characteristically general overview of English literary history, writing about "daily island life" becomes almost a historical habit; to fit within the literary tradition requires that a writer succumb to national self-absorption.

The literature of England describes, in particular, *things.* The "poetry of England" Stein writes, "is the poetry of the things with which any of [the English people] are shut in in their daily, completely daily island life" (15). It is worth considering whether Stein's statement here might be applied to twentieth-century literature that deemphasizes plot, that tells "not of what happened nor what is thought or what is dreamed but what exists." *Tender Buttons* (1914), Stein's early and experimental long poem, might be read as a series of object lessons, a study of things in the sensory world, as designated by some of the titles in the first section, "Objects": "A RED STAMP," "A SELTZER BOTTLE," "A LONG DRESS," "A CHAIR." Even in the later two sections, "Food" and "Rooms," the poem pivots on nouns, a fact that Stein acknowledges in her last essay in *Lectures in America,* titled "Poetry and Grammar." Stein explains that after finishing *The Making of Americans,* "I then began very short things and in doing very short things I resolutely realized nouns and decided not to get around them but to meet them, to handle in short to refuse them by using them and in that way my real acquaintance with poetry was begun" (228). According to Stein's distinctions between parts of speech (and between prose and poetry), "Poetry is doing nothing but using losing refusing and pleasing and betraying and caressing nouns" (231). She energetically welcomes into poetry the "things" that Woolf associates with prose. Stein's exuberant use of prepositions (her favorite part of speech) in *Tender Buttons* throws these nouns—these objects—into fresh focus, playfully pushing us to see them anew, to be attentive to things that might otherwise seem utterly banal.

This attention to objects changes the very nature of their ordinariness. The objects attain a kind of vivid immanence, while nonetheless resisting any obvious epiphany or clear statement of "meaning." The transformation of Stein's objects is modest, like what happens to some of the more conspicuous items in Joyce's lists. In this sense, Stein's early work might be said to be more experimental than her World War II writings: the later works reveal an entrenchment in habit, an absorption in it. Between attention and absorption lies a delicate and sometimes imperceptible shift, a movement at work in many modernist texts that guard against the dangers of pulling objects and experiences out of context. As Lisi Schoenbach has argued, Stein's "pragmatic modernism" differs from the avant-garde aim to defamiliarize habitual experience. Schoenbach compares Stein with the surrealist writers whom Stein disliked, arguing that the surrealist aim to "shock" has negative social consequences in the sense of promoting an aesthetics of rupture and opposition that does not necessarily instigate the definitive social change to which their artistic manifestos aspire.[11] But at the heart of this claim about Stein's more subtle aesthetic, "to contextualize rather than defamiliarize," as Schoenbach puts it ("'Peaceful,'" 240), is the possibility that the same criticism could be made of Stein. That is, while reintegrating aesthetic shock back into a social fabric is essential to actually creating change, sometimes it becomes necessary to draw away from habit, to pull oneself out of it. Stein's inability to extricate herself from ordinary experiences during a time of war ultimately marks the limits of her modernism.

In the sense of selecting and observing ordinary objects, Stein's technique in *Tender Buttons* calls to mind William James's 1904 essay "A World of Pure Experience," in which he describes the different kinds of relations that make up how we perceive objects in the world, as expressed through prepositions in the language of philosophy. "Philosophy has always turned on grammatical particles," James writes: "With, near, next, like, from, towards, against, because, for, through, my—these words designate types of conjunctive relation arranged in a roughly ascending order of intimacy and inclusiveness" (*WWJ* 197). James points out that relations among people are as varied as these prepositions signify. Habits are implicitly necessary in a world in which experience is not naturally standard or fixed: "Taken as it does appear, our universe is to a large extent chaotic. No one single type of connection runs through all the experiences that compose it" (*WWJ* 197). His observations could apply to Stein's interest in the same parts of speech. Indeed, one way that critics have understood *Tender Buttons* involves reading Stein's selection and rearrangement of objects as an enactment of the Jamesian notion of perception.[12]

In "What Is English Literature," Stein offers us another pattern for understanding her early work that emphasizes how habits are formed by national affiliation. According to her, twentieth-century writers are interested in "daily island life" in a way somewhat different from that of their predecessors. The writing of "now"—by which she means American writing—"does not go on so well now for several reasons, in the first place they are not so interested in their island life because they are in short they are not so interested. And in the next place it is not as much an island life" (15). The emphasis on daily things takes a turn as England's empire diminishes; although American writing extends the English tradition, according to Stein, it does not emphasize "island life" because America is not an island. Metaphorically, Stein seems to say that American writers cannot describe a habitual way of life because collective habits do not exist in America. American writing depends on what Stein calls "separation" and "lack of connection," terms that she only obliquely explains but that presumably distinguish between England's tradition and America's nonconvention (51, 53). In *Narration*, Stein concludes: "One may say that in America there is no daily life at all" (6). Essentially, the "pluralism" of American life (to use James's term), and the variety of its landscapes resist anything so uniform as "daily living." Tapping into the myth of the self-made American, Stein suggests that individuals in America create their own habits.

According to Stein's logic in "What Is English Literature," the quintessentially American writing of Henry James detaches itself from "daily island life" and marks the future of American writing. She points to James (here and elsewhere) as her most influential literary precursor. As Jonathan Levin has suggested, James's late prose style, with its endlessly delaying and qualifying subjects, may be what Stein means by "separation" and "lack of connection" (*Poetics,* 148–49). That is, Stein distinguishes between the material realism of the English literary tradition and a new kind of linguistic abstraction begun by Henry James (counterpart to the emerging abstraction in modern art). However, abstraction and nonspecificity were what William James famously disliked in his brother's writing, preferring grammatical clarity and plot-driven action.[13] Stein falls somewhere in between the James brothers. She learned something of linguistic abstraction from Henry James but embraced material objects with the clear perception that William James celebrates, what he called "attention" to the influx of sensory stimulus. In *Tender Buttons,* Stein toys with the "relations" between objects; loving the things of daily life, Stein calls attention to that with which we are familiar. Essentially, she describes the stuff of ordinary life, of habit, but she abstracts this stuff by rearranging its relational context. Exemplifying Shklovsky's idea of making "the stone *stony,*" Stein's prose continually works against habitual associations between objects; she challenges our habits of linguistic sense-making. However, in her World War II writings, Stein shows characters trying to establish habits that make sense during a time of war. What we see in *Tender Buttons*—a refusal of the ways in which we habitually associate things together—emerges, in her later writings, as a very different reliance on the power of habit in ordinary lives.

Stein's attraction to habit and repetition grow out of Jamesian philosophy, but her celebration of comfort, pleasure, and ease are uniquely her own. As Ann Douglas has suggested, Stein's love of the popular—the common stuff of ordinary life—should make us question the way she has been read as a highbrow experimenter. In Douglas's account, Stein represents the average American consumer, who loves mass-produced things, and whose work reflects this ethos (*Terrible Honesty,* 121–22). Representing the habits of ordinary people serves as a way of representing pleasure, even during a time of war. It is no surprise that Alice B. Toklas shared this desire for pleasure, for she was the one who maintained many of the couple's domestic habits. In fact, one of her cookbook's chapters, "Food in the Bugey During the Occupation," reveals that the couple managed to keep a plentiful kitchen much as they did before the war (*Alice B.,* 201). Under the clothes of habit, one of Stein's most persistent literary subjects is war—war's relationship to art and war's relationship to everyday life. Born in the wake of the Civil War, which served as a prototype for the twentieth century's wars, as Stein suggests at the beginning of *Wars I Have Seen,* she lived and wrote through World Wars I and II, which marked the modernization of Europe (4). Stein refuses to treat war through heightened experience. Her World War II writings, in particular, avoid relating chaotic or disturbing events, or even a climax. Only the repetition of the everyday, and a hope that at least the everyday might continue, remains during the war. Stein's focus on habit became not just a guiding ethos of life, but a timely refuge. Her World War II writings foreground habit's crucial utility as well as habit's ultimate political inadequacy.

## "Suspended in Time"

> If time exists your writing is ephemeral. You can have a historical time but for you the time does not exist and if you are writing about the present the time element must cease to exist. . . . In [*Wars I Have Seen*] I described something momentous happening under my eyes and I was able to do it without a great sense of time. There should not be a sense of time but an existence suspended in time. That is really where I am at the present moment. I am still largely meditating about this sense of time.
>
> —Gertrude Stein, "Transatlantic Interview"

Taking her cue from English literature that details "daily island life," Stein during World War II focuses on daily life in France. Stein previews this approach to war in her short anecdotal work *Paris France* (1940), written just before *Mrs. Reynolds* and *Wars I Have Seen.*[14] In *Paris France,* Stein suggests that France is the place where modern art and literature flourishes. Though the twentieth century is embodied by America, she writes, it finds its artistic achievement in Paris: "So Paris was the natural background for the twentieth century; America knew it too well, knew the twentieth century too well to create it, for America there was a glamour in the twentieth century that made it not be material for creative activity" (24). In *Paris France,* Stein continues a literary tradition of emphasizing the "material," or materiality of daily life, describing French food, fashion, and culture. Despite the "phoney war" between France and Germany (from September 1939 to May 1940)[15] during which *Paris France* was written, Stein claims: "Really not, french people really do not believe that anything is important except daily living and the ground that gives it to them and defending themselves from the enemy. Government has no importance except insofar as it does that" (8–9). The conversational, blithe tone of this statement (and of the whole work), emphasizes Stein's confidence that French "daily living" will always be protected, despite the increasing chance of another world war. The subject matter of *Paris France,* accordingly, is not government or politics, but the daily life that French politics protects. When World War II fully erupts, Stein's focus is still daily life in France.

*Wars I Have Seen* and *Mrs. Reynolds* both fixate on domestic experience: the rationing of food, wine, and tobacco, the dependence on neighboring farmers, and the closeness of a small community against the threat of impending violence.

Begun as a journal or daybook, *Wars I Have Seen* recounts the quotidian details of life in two French villages, Bilignin and Culoz, where Stein and Alice B. Toklas lived from 1939 to 1944, against the advice of their friends and American officials. Stein and Toklas were protected ostensibly by their friend Bernard Faÿ, a Nazi collaborationist, a professor of American culture at the Collège de France, and the translator of the French edition of *The Autobiography of Alice B. Toklas.*[16] Essentially, they were safe as long as they kept silent and neutral. Stein explained her reasons for not leaving France—a decision that, in retrospect, seems astonishing—in an essay published by the *Atlantic Monthly* in November 1940 titled "The Winner Loses: A Picture of Occupied France" (and added as an appendix to *Wars I Have Seen*). In this essay, Stein describes a visit to the American consul in Lyon just before the Franco-German armistice. At the consulate, she and Alice Toklas were told to flee to either Switzerland or America:

> They all said "Leave," and I said to Alice Toklas, "well I don't know—it would be awfully uncomfortable and I am fussy about my food. Let's not leave." So we came back, and the village was happy and we were happy and that was all right, and I said I would not hear any more news—Alice Toklas could listen to the wireless, but as for me I was going to cut box hedges and forget the war. (181)

In keeping with her love of habit and her resistance to change, Stein chose to stay in France, where she had lived for thirty-five years. Her conversations with local farmers, after returning from the consulate, verifies this choice. The farmers tell her, "We have cows and milk and chickens and flour and we can all live and we know you will help us out in any way and you can and we will do the same for you" (182). Once the armistice is signed, and the French are relieved from German bombardment, Stein celebrates the way that ordinary life might continue under the new Vichy regime. "The Winner Loses" closes on this note: "But anyway our light is lit and the shutters are open, and perhaps everybody will find out, as the French know so well, that the winner loses, and everybody will be, too, like the French, that is, tremendously occupied with the business of daily living, and that will be enough" (191). Stein suggests that the French are more concerned with the repetitions of daily living than with the actual war. The French, technically "losers" to the Germans, are actually "winners" in the sense that their daily lives can now resume. Yet the strangeness of living under the Vichy regime, as Stein documents in *Wars,* belies her initial sense of freedom.

Stein recorded in her journal up until the occupation was at an end—until the Americans arrived—and *Wars* mimics the repetitive passing of time also tabulated in *Mrs. Reynolds.* Despite the war—or rather, as Stein makes clear, *because* of the war—*Wars* emphasizes the practicalities and pleasures of daily life: food, farming, and the weather:

> It is a queer life one leads in a modern war, every day so much can happen and every day is just the same and is mostly food, food, and in spite of all that is happening every day is food, I had a dear friend who used to say Life dear Life, life is strife, life is a dear life in every way and life is strife in every way. (7)

Stein's "friend" would become her own literary invention, Mrs. Reynolds, who repeats this very saying, "Life dear Life, life is strife." Stein essentially takes her own experience living through the war and turns it into fiction. As we will see in *Mrs. Reynolds,* repetition of event and an emphasis on habit become a mode of narration, created out of Stein's actual sense of how time progresses (or does not progress) during the war. Rather than focus on the facts or chronology of war, Stein and Toklas protect themselves from the shock of war's events; their daily habits serve as a mode of self-preservation, in William James's terms, as a "most precious conservative agent." Throughout *Wars,* Stein insists that daily life can and *should* continue: "There is nothing to be curious about except small things, food and the weather" (65), Stein writes. "So in every way the French people defend themselves that is they lead their normal life" (101). Daily living is a "ballast" for Stein and Toklas, to use Beckett's metaphor; it allows the French to live calmly through occupation—however self-deceiving—with a sense of control.

Living becomes leveled by repetition. The absence of chapter breaks in *Wars* and the dense retelling of familiar material denies the reader a coherent sense of change. The only way to know that time has indeed passed is to look for sentences, usually at the start of paragraphs, that announce the actual date: "To-day we were at Aix-les-Bains, end of June 1943" (29), or "I was out walking this afternoon the first week of January '44" (82), or "To-day we were over in Belley the third of August, nineteen forty-four" (146). War skews temporality, causing repetition: "War makes things go backwards as well as forward," Stein explains (2). Stein describes having to buy a wristwatch to go outside, so that she knows when the six o'clock curfew is approaching, but the notion of time existing in the countryside never feels appropriate to her. As the epigraph above suggests, Stein worked to rid *Wars* of "a great sense of time." She neither wanted time imposed upon her life in the country nor upon her narrative.

Maintaining domestic routines works against the "queer" quality of wartime that Stein describes. Stein notes the death of "real" feeling and the sense of strangeness that dominates life in the twentieth century. Foreseeing Paul Fussell's claim that World War I put an end to earnestness, Stein says of the movement away from nineteenth-century realism to twentieth-century methods of representation (a frequent topic for her): "Anybody can understand that there is no point in being realistic about here and now, no use at all not any, and so it is not the nineteenth but the twentieth century, there is no realism now, life is not real it is not earnest, it is strange which is an entirely different matter" (28). Life is "not real," according to Stein, suggesting that life now does not conform to what is conventionally considered realist in literature. We might also understand Stein's statement here as an explanation for the limitations of her diary-like style. Ostensibly unmediated, and certainly more accessible than some of her earlier experimental work, Stein's style in *Wars* nonetheless recognizes the inability to express the "unreal" quality that characterizes war. The overall point of the work, Stein offers toward the end, is to render the "suffocating cloud" (155) under which ordinary life continues, an effect similar to what Stein calls the "shadow" of war in *Mrs. Reynolds.* Moreover, Stein conceives of habit as a mode that reflects cultural transformations: the biggest change from the nineteenth to the twentieth century, according to Stein, is discernable on the level of everyday events. Thus habits paradoxically become the best way in which to represent war.

And yet the conspicuous absence of violence in Stein's text calls into question the positive function of habit. Essentially, the war is being fought in Stein's own backyard. German soldiers (however unwelcome) sleep one night in the house where she and Toklas live, taking with them the next morning a servant's pair of slippers, all of their peaches, and, "to be disagreeable," the keys to the house (139). Although the experience frightens Stein's servants, the violence done to Stein and Toklas's home life is certainly not great. Stein's text never confronts violence on a grand scale; rather, she prefers stories that relate the insidious nature of wartime upon ordinary life. Toward the end of the work, when it is clear that France will be saved from the Germans, Stein describes how women who "kept company" with the Germans were forced to have their heads shaved: "It is called the coiffure of 1944, and naturally it is terrible because the shaving is done publicly," she writes (160). Stein describes this event with a wry, matter-of-fact acceptance, maintaining a relationship to war that seems both defiant (not involving herself) and troubling (refusing to see beyond the war's effect on domestic and local life). To an extent, Stein's experiences during wartime illuminate William James's belief that habits can be a remarkably protective shield against too much violence upon the senses. Habits serve to clarify one's "relations" to the world when war amplifies our sense that, as James writes, "our universe is to a large extent chaotic" (*WWJ* 197). But Stein's reliance on the routines of village life also reveals habit's most extreme limitations: Stein avoids confronting the mass destruction and death intensifying all around her.

Stein never aggressively opposes the war, nor does she celebrate the Jamesian "man of action." Stein loves pleasure and habit, not antagonism and revolution. As John Whittier-Ferguson has suggested, "Stein was by temperament and conviction 'conservative' in the word's broadest sense: she was opposed to change" ("Stein in Time," 120). *Wars I Have Seen* exposes Stein's parochialism; despite Stein's avant-garde writing, her actions during the war were unremarkable, no different from many other people's actions. In *France under the Germans* (1993), Philippe Burrin maintains that many French people lived through the occupation with the sole goal of "getting through it," behavior that was not so different from showing a measure of support for collaboration (viii). Stein's similarity to others who lived through the war, however, should not be shocking. As the politics of many other pioneering modernists will confirm, aesthetic practices do not necessarily correspond to radical or leftist politics. *Wars I Have Seen* depicts life during the occupation as motivated by material needs and everyday desires, not by the Résistance. Threaded throughout her narrative, Stein's fickle support and dislike of the Vichy government seems subservient to her overall desire for the stability and peace found in ordinary domestic life. Stein's politics in fact seem to change over the course of time that *Wars* documents, as she negotiates the political powers that will best ensure peace in France. At first, she enthusiastically supports Philippe Pétain, leader of the Vichy regime, even resolving to translate his speeches into English, but she never completes this project (Bridgman, *Gertrude,* 314–18). The four-page introduction she prepared for the volume in 1942 goes so far as to present Pétain as the savior of France.[17] But by the end of *Wars,* as Zofia Lesinska has noted, it is very clear that Stein no longer supports Pétain; he is now a "crazy man," and then "an old man, a very old man," and finally, "everybody has forgotten all about him" (*War Autobiographies,* 331).

According to Barbara Will, Stein may have taken on the Pétain translation project as a way to protect herself and Toklas, especially given the fact that Stein translated Pétain's speeches quite literally, in contrast to her normal proclivity to translate loosely and creatively ("Lost," 652–57). Will contends that Stein may have known more about the real dangers of living in France during the war (specifically, the deportation of Jews) but that she suppressed what she knew (as well as her creative mode of translation) to protect her life. Will's argument, in this sense, would appeal to those who are baffled by what Stein's World War II writings leave out and by the strange fact that Stein simply submitted to the conditions of war. But if Stein did *not* know more than what she acknowledges in her writings, then it is clear that she essentially responded to France's concessions to the Germans in the way that most of her neighbors responded, a possibility that is also quite likely give Stein's natural aversion to change. Like most French people (the "everybody" Stein frequently cites), Stein initially supported the Vichy regime but turned toward the Résistance movement as it gained strength. Her World War II writings, in this respect, epitomize France's silent majority and challenge postwar distortions of history that fail to remember the mass public support for Vichy between 1940 and 1942. According to the best figures, only 2 percent of the French adult population could be considered members of the Résistance, a figure notably at odds with the myth of *la France résistante* developed at liberation (McMillan, *Twentieth-Century France,* 147–49). Stein's World War II writings demand our attention even more for their value in representing how many people thought or lived through the war than how they represent the circumstances of just one protected modernist writer.

## A "perfectly ordinary couple living an ordinary life"

*Mrs. Reynolds,* a fictional account of Stein's own experience, illuminates this complex and seemingly resigned response to war. The novel tells the story of a couple living under "the shadow of two men": Angel Harper, who represents Adolf Hitler (the bad "angel") and Joseph Lane, who represents Joseph Stalin. While *Wars I Have Seen* is written in a dense albeit relatively straightforward style, *Mrs. Reynolds* returns to Stein's first experimentations with prose—maintaining an insistent present tense, repeating words and phrases, and emphasizing simple rhymes. Yet Stein's treatment of history in *Mrs. Reynolds* radically differs from that of her *Three Lives* (1909) or *Tender Buttons* (1914), both of which are about the "ordinary" but are set in a dehistoricized "continuous present," a phrase Stein coined to describe her first attempts to escape chronological narrative.[18] *Mrs. Reynolds* also rebels against chronology, but represents a specific time in history—the rise and fall of Nazism and Fascism in Europe. Thus her attempt to suspend time is much more complicated than in her early work: the repetitive habits of Mr. and Mrs. Reynolds jar against the encroachment of real historical horror, even as Stein revises what is meant by history.

In her strikingly worded epilogue—the section of the novel that has attracted the most attention—Stein suggests that *Mrs. Reynolds* is a "historical" novel, but not "historical" by familiar definition. She writes:

> This book is an effort to show the way anybody could feel these years. It is a perfectly ordinary couple living an ordinary life and having ordinary conversations and really not suffering personally from everything that is happening but over them, all over them is the shadow of these two men, and then the shadow of one of the two men gets bigger and then blows away and there is no other. There is nothing historical about this book except the state of mind. (331)

To render a state of mind, Stein's "ordinary" lacks all specificity: the couple's conversations never develop; Mr. Reynolds's type of work is never named; and it is unclear where the characters are living. Despite the cultural differences in daily living that Stein stresses in "What Is English Literature," habits essentially function in the same way for everyone whether in the United States or in Europe, living in the age of Hitler and Stalin. Stein's epilogue to *Mrs. Reynolds* obscures a personal or historical context, refusing to acknowledge a link between the Reynoldses' routines and Stein's experience living in two French villages during the German occupation. In this sense, *Mrs. Reynolds* is a historically nonspecific story of "anybody." Constructed by repetition rather than a series of different and related events, the novel essentially redefines "historical" as the repetitions of everyday living rather than dates and geographical locations.

The obscurity and sheer length of *Mrs. Reynolds* present a new challenge to the reader. The novel enacts how tedious the war felt for Stein. Even Richard Bridgman, an early champion of Stein's work, admits that the novel "cannot be advanced as a pleasurable reading experience" (318). Like other modernist styles that attempt to embody the everyday, the style of *Mrs. Reynolds* allows for a reader's affective disinterest. Not only on the level of style, but also on the level of character and event, the novel is enigmatic, shuffling causes and effects and shying away from explanations, as if war, under any circumstances, is inexplicable. Joseph Lane, for instance, is introduced as a "shadow" similar to Angel Harper, but he receives considerably less treatment in the novel, and gradually disappears, though no reason is given for his disappearance. Angel Harper's flashbacks to a disturbed childhood and Mrs. Reynolds's surrealistic dreams are also sometimes perplexing, as when Harper remembers his desire, at age ten, "to cover his face with a black veil, and put transparent paper over one leg and to hang something behind to be a tail and he liked to be alone so he could not fail" (99). Ominously predicting his distorted desire for power and his fear of failure, this flashback might be read metaphorically, though not to complete satisfaction. The simple, exacting rhymes ("veil" / "tail" / "fail") complicate the seeming seriousness of the psychological critique; indeed, a tension between a playful style and serious subject matter characterizes the whole work. Perhaps because of the difficulties imposed upon the reader, and perhaps because of Stein's unusual and unsettling confrontation with World War II in this work, *Mrs. Reynolds* has typically been passed over by critics.[19]

Consisting of twelve parts (undifferentiated except that Angel Harper grows older), the novel is virtually plotless, recording Mr. and Mrs. Reynolds's habits during World War II: rising early in the morning, going to work (for Mr. Reynolds) or visiting neighbors (for Mrs. Reynolds), taking exercise, eating dinner, and going to bed. Aside from their concerns about the supply of food and heat, Mr. and Mrs. Reynolds go on living more or less as they did before. Stein writes: "They wanted to know what the news was, but after all, it would do just as well to know the news tomorrow as today. In every way the news was the news of yesterday, and yesterday was another day and so was tomorrow" (88). Stein's prose captures a monotony that pervades existence on the home front, analogous in some senses to Samuel Beckett's postwar creation of characters obsessed with repetition (Molloy sucking stones, Krapp eating bananas). War aggravates the sense of empty waiting as Mr. and Mrs. Reynolds wonder what will happen next. War, in an affective sense, is boring. But in Stein's text, the repetition of habits enables her characters to live as fully as they can. The couple is not consumed by the existential angst of repetition; rather, they maintain a sense of control in repeating actions that give them pleasure. Mr. and Mrs. Reynolds find satisfaction in fulfilling their everyday needs:

> Well they had eaten a great deal and that made them tired, they were not used to eating so much and they went to bed early and after all they did sleep very well, they thought they would not but they did. Yes said Mrs. Reynolds waking up not early but late, yes life is strife, dear life, dear life. And she sighed a little. (197)

Mrs. Reynolds's easy maxim, "life is strife" (echoing Stein's "dear friend" described in *Wars*), seems to have little bearing on the Reynoldses' actual existence during the war; her "sigh" sounds almost playful, especially since the opening of the work announces: "All the world knows how to cry but not all the world knows how to sigh. Sighing is extra" (10). Though Stein certainly acknowledges the war's shadowy effect upon the Reynoldses' everyday life, their habits function as a guard against this darkness. And despite what the above quotation states, Mr. and Mrs. Reynolds quite frequently eat and sleep "a great deal." The repetition of habit serves to protect these individuals from the world at war, from James's "pure experience." For Mr. and Mrs. Reynolds, living during a time of war, habit keeps the self intact, preserving and protecting their state of being.

The facts of war consist of the chronological counting of Angel Harper's age. That is, the text marks time by counting Harper's birthdays. Part 5 opens:

> Angel Harper was forty-six
> Exactly forty-six.
> Really when Angel Harper was forty-six he was in a fix. And so was anyone. And every one. Believe it or not it is true and it made every one pretty blue. (128)

While Harper's increasing age marks Mrs. Reynolds's growing anxiety about his rise to power, the nursery rhyming of Stein's style works against the acknowledgment of any real threat. Facts establish a material reality, but on the other hand, facts cannot entirely be trusted as a complete register of what is happening in the world. In this way, Stein does not use facts quite in the same way that Joyce and Woolf do, but she does acknowledge the limitations of a factual style. Furthermore, Stein's strange spoofs of Hitler and Stalin (which involves psychologizing Harper's childhood) as well as Mrs. Reynolds's refusal to believe that Harper will live, undercuts the seriousness of the facts about the war; the text tries to suppress anxiety about Harper's rise. Detached from the "news" and removed from the war efforts, this suppressed anxiety colors Mr. and Mrs. Reynolds's lives. Mrs. Reynolds's cousin explains: "I do not know whether what is happening makes any difference to me or not, and not knowing whether what is happening makes any difference to me or not is very tiring" (286). War has an odd, unnamable effect on domestic things, even though the Reynolds never suffer from severe shortages: "Every day is another day when Angel Harper is forty-seven, even cake gets to have another meaning and as to candy and milk and cream and oatmeal, dear me said Mrs. Reynolds looking forward, I do wish I did not have to say so" (141). Sweets and comfort foods, "candy and milk and cream and oatmeal," are objects of culinary attention and satisfaction, however temporary that satisfaction might be. Ordinary habits are not epiphanic moments during wartime, but they do acquire "another meaning." Stein suggests that fulfilling basic needs serves as a singular source of pleasure for these characters.

A comparison between Stein and Beckett, in this context, is too striking to be overlooked. The war plays a fundamental role in Beckett's depiction of habit in his post-1945 work. The experience of witnessing a performance of Beckett's *Waiting for Godot* or *Endgame* can be mind-numbing (much like reading *Mrs. Reynolds*), as Beckett's characters are preoccupied with the banal: the weather, what they will eat, and their dependencies on one another. They resort to the clichés of conversation, as Clov says in *Endgame:* "all life long the same questions, the same answers" (5). But unlike Mr. and Mrs. Reynolds, Beckett's characters are marked by intense mental anxiety and real physical suffering, suggestive of what Beckett himself was personally aware.[20] Against Stein, Beckett's presentation of material and bodily needs is indeed grim. For example, the meager radishes, turnips, and carrots swapped between Estragon and Vladimir echo the real food shortages Beckett experienced during the war; the reliance of blind, immobile Hamm upon Clov comprehends the deep dependencies of soldiers, or hostages who have been forgotten; and the master and servant suffering of *How It Is* resonates against the historical reality of concentration camps. Habit in these works is central to survival, a small comfort against the possibility that no one (or no god) watches over individuals. As Hamm suggests, "Nature has forgotten us" (11). It is not surprising that Beckett's plays—especially *Waiting for Godot*—have had a powerful effect on prisoners, since Beckett's work understands the basic human condition as marked by controlled routines that deny spontaneous choice (Knowlson, *Damned,* 370).

Choice is a central uncertainty in Beckett's work: his characters are caught in a Jamesian "flywheel" that seems to regulate the monotonous revolutions of their lives, whereas Stein's characters are able to actually exercise some measure of control over how they will act during a time of war. While Beckett shares Stein's concern with the habits of ordinary people, his characters cannot be described as "really not suffering personally." Rather, Beckett's characters feel that living is an essential burden, a torturous prolongation of pain, but they bear life out anyway. Suicide is an evasion of essential humanity, and a rejection of perhaps the only choice we have—to live—as the famous last words of *The Unnamable* attest: "You must go on, I can't go on, I'll go on" (476). Habit and repetition are so central to Beckett's work that he repeats his characters through names and personalities: the Molloy, Moran, Malone, Macmann and Mahood of the trilogy, the Pim and Bom of *How It Is,* and the confusing similarities between Estragon and Vladimir. Indeed, the coherence of identity hinges on repetition. The lowest level of human survival—the repetition of bodily functions—reminds us we are alive: "What matters is to eat and excrete," Malone states (*Malone Dies,* 210). Beckett's work examines the animal drive to exist in a world that is clearly unjust, where human relations are defined by painful dependencies. Stein, on the other hand, aims to transcend or "suspend" the human condition through her use of repetition, to posit Mr. and Mrs. Reynolds "outside of history." This couple continues to do what they desire during the war, despite the political circumstances.

Because time's movement forward is equated with Harper's rise to power, Stein's novel strains between the inevitable forwardness of time and the ways in which Mrs. Reynolds can control or rebel against this inevitability. *Mrs. Reynolds* engages with the war very generally by asking a question relevant to any "ordinary" person, as Stein's epigraph reinforces: In what ways is it possible to resist war on the level of the everyday? For Mr. and Mrs. Reynolds, their habits do not change: the resistant "tactics" that De Certeau describes are for them their sustained ways of life. The work suggests that war deeply affects the kinds of things people do every day, while nonetheless emphasizing that Mr. and Mrs. Reynolds do not change their routines and habits. The ordinary might be a means of maintaining the cherished present tense.[21] Ostensibly third-person omniscient, the novel's point of view draws on the language and style of Mrs. Reynolds's dialogue, so that the work seems to privilege not only her experience but her voice (a technique, for instance, similar to Joyce's point of view in *Dubliners*). In this way, *Mrs. Reynolds* echoes Stein's earlier stories in *Three Lives,* "The Good Anna" and "The Gentle Lena," in which unreliable narration reveals a discrepancy between voice (innocent, trustworthy) and content (defeated lives ending in death). Marianne DeKoven suggests that the innocence of what she calls "obtuse narration" in *Three Lives* might be a defense against despair; the stories avoid judging or pitying characters who themselves do not see their lives as pitiful (29–32). In *Mrs. Reynolds,* the discrepancy between voice and content works differently: the childishness of Mrs. Reynolds's point of view creates something close to dramatic irony. Her perception of war (simply put, "war is bad") offsets the complexities of the war's continuation. Whereas no one would argue with a child who perceives of a war as "bad" (it seems a response worth protecting), Mrs. Reynolds's innocence borders on delusion, since we know that she is not a child.

Irrationally hopeful, Mrs. Reynolds depends upon the prophecies of two saints, St. Odile and St. Godfrey, rather than actual "news" from the front lines. These saints, the narrator tells us, have predicted Angel Harper's death at age fifty-five. The last paragraph of the novel suggests that the war's end, represented by his death, has indeed been foretold:

> Mrs. Reynolds remembered the next morning that she had said that Saint Odile had not been mistaken, and said Mrs. Reynolds she Mrs. Reynolds was not mistaken in believing in Saint Odile because Saint Odile had not been mistaken. Angel Harper was not fifty-five alive. (330)

Though Mrs. Reynolds is "not mistaken," it is never clear throughout the novel whether St. Odile's prophecy can be trusted. Thus, a vague sense of luck hangs over the novel's conclusion: Mrs. Reynolds is lucky enough to have her trust in St. Odile unchecked; perhaps others, more attuned to the "news," consider an Allied victory the result of human agency. The saints' prophecies in *Mrs. Reynolds* might therefore seem a sly (and troubling) evasion of historical explanation, of causes and effects, rather than a vigorous refutation of war's cause-and-effect logic.

The role of prophecy in the novel is just one issue that has caused critics to question the political implications of Stein's novel. Its plotlessness and innovative wordplay led one early reader to believe that it had nothing to do with life during the war and that Stein was even indifferent to the war.[22] Ellen Berry has argued, alternatively, that the saints' prophecies might be read as Stein's rebellion against the teleological telling of history—an argument similar to the way some critics read Stein's use of the present tense as symbolic opposition to Angel Harper's increasing age and war's movement forward. Berry suggests that the "counting" of Harper's age is overturned and reversed by a look back to what the prophets have predicted all along (*Curved Thought*, 123–31). Berry associates Stein's "wandering" mode of representing time (prophecy disrupting linear flow) with female subjectivity. Like many sensitive critics of Stein's work (Marianne DeKoven, Maria Diedrich, Lisa Ruddick), Berry links Stein's writing with what Julia Kristeva calls cyclic or repetitive time (113, 131). And yet this sort of reading, if applied to *Mrs. Reynolds*, underscores a disjunction between aesthetic practices and a political reality outside the fictional terrain that *Mrs. Reynolds* calls to mind. Disrupting Harper's rise to power on the level of verb tense complicates the question of whether Mr. and Mrs. Reynolds have anything to do with the war's end: Are they decent citizens by simply waiting out the war—opposing it on aesthetic grounds—or does the novel suggest that they should have been more actively involved in opposing Angel Harper?

More recent critics have moved away from the gender dichotomies that Berry puts forth, arguing that the work posits an inextricable connection between the aesthetics of "daily life" and the politics of World War II. Phoebe Stein Davis, for instance, argues that the novel does not define the domestic in opposition to the war, "but as a sphere inseparable from it and necessarily altered by it" (582). Davis points out that Mr. and Mrs. Reynolds lose their "home" during the war, even though they never actually move away from it. Stein writes: "All this time Mrs. Reynolds was ready to come home. She and Mr. Reynolds had not been away but she was ready to come home" (130). As this passage suggests, war robs "home" of its accustomed qualities. War might not physically impose upon the Reynoldses' life, but it dramatically destabilizes what was formerly taken for granted. Thus, in a Jamesian sense, habit serves as a means for Mr. and Mrs. Reynolds to assert their "home" under the threat of change. But like James's understanding of habit's power to "keep different social strata from mixing," Stein's celebration of the Reynoldses' habits identifies a dangerous kind of self-absorption. Perhaps Stein's commitment to ordinary life during the war opposes the institution of male warfare and violence, but as *Wars I Have Seen* also confirms, her reaction to the twentieth-century's worst crimes illuminates an extremely problematic escapism, cloaked as pacifism and anchored in habit.

In *Wars I Have Seen* and *Mrs. Reynolds,* Stein's startling description of how habit functions during a time of war exposes both habit's usefulness and its limitations. Stein focuses on the habits of ordinary life as a mode of protection; habits become Woolf's "cotton wool of daily life," a domestic shield against surrounding trauma. But habits, as defense, also enable a dangerous blindness to what, especially in retrospect, demanded action. As William James recognizes, habit might protect against the shock of "pure experience," but well-established habits also separate those who can choose their actions (like Stein) from those whose lives are controlled by compulsory routine. During the Second World War, the massive mechanization of death became a sick enactment of James's "flywheel," and the use of tanks, airplanes, and more sophisticated artillery a product of increased industrial output on the home front. Stein's choice of a title, *Wars I Have Seen,* ironically points to the wars that she *did not see:* a reader understands more about domestic life during the war than about worldwide destruction and casualties on the battlefield. To take political action, to revolt against the status quo, to document the war's violence, to join the Résistance as Beckett did—all would have been actions antithetical to her habits and to her personal and artistic temperament.

Stein's World War II writings implicate her modernism in a paralyzing and troubling preoccupation with the daily. Habit, in both *Mrs. Reynolds* and *Wars I Have Seen,* creates "an existence suspended in time," as she described her method in "Transatlantic Interview," conducted in the last year of her life (103). Although Stein's use of habit works against a movement forward or backward, challenging a sense of linear temporality, her reliance on habit also sheds light on a surprising conservative tendency in her work. Stein's desire to suspend time illuminates an obstinate refusal, on some level, to accept "momentous" change. In a way, we could call Stein's Word War II writings nostalgic, in the sense that they resist, even rebuke, the forward movement of time. Though Stein was an early exemplar of modernism, her depiction of habit aligns itself as readily with a nineteenth-century ethos. Her optimism about life, certainly influenced by William James, and her unwillingness to confront the dark side of war's violence dramatically differ from the ironic or bitter ethos of so many other modernists who wrote about war. From James, Stein inherits an American pragmatic view of the world, in which humans could control their lives through habit. Other twentieth-century thinkers, notably Freud, offer ways of thinking about habit that might illuminate human obsessions or self-betrayals. But Stein never accepted this notion of modern psychology. Her aesthetic seems both ahead of and behind her time.

# Chapter Four

## Wallace Stevens's Commonplace

The fundamental difficulty in any art is the problem of the normal.
—Wallace Stevens, "Adagia"

Wallace Stevens once claimed that his aim was "to try to make poetry out of commonplaces: the day's news" (*SL* 311n). "Commonplace," a word that Stevens began using in the mid-1930s, at first suggested the contemporary events of his time. But "commonplace" also came to signify more local concerns for Stevens: the patterns of work, the changes in the weather, or the best place to buy bread and fruit. The term shifts in meaning for Stevens and registers the various pulls upon his poetry, becoming a touchstone for the kinds of activities that poetry might address. Ultimately, commonplaces might be defined as life's habitual acts, registered in a contemporary political climate and stripped of sentimental elements. The particularity of these acts is less important for Stevens than the state of mind and the style of the commonplace. At times, Stevens uses the words "ordinary" and "normal" to signal the same quality. Toward the end of his career especially, Stevens valued the dependable routines of ordinary life over the rarer moments of inner clarity or imaginative vision, and his poetry deeply reflects this focus. His work dwells on repetition of commonplaces, what he calls "The Pleasures of Merely Circulating" (1936) or what "Notes toward a Supreme Fiction" (1942) augurs as "A thing final in itself and, therefore, good: . . . round and round, the merely going round, / Until merely going round is a final good" (*CP* 149, 405). In most cases, the ordinary is not transformed into something else but endures as a final good. "Final" does not suggest an endpoint or resting place, but a spinning back into experience rather than spinning out of it. Stevens settles into the ordinary as a satisfaction with the material rather than the spiritual, the local rather than the exotic, and the constant rather than the unknown.

Stevens's work is committed to the "sufficiency" of ordinary experience, to use another one of his words, balanced between two poles that he called imagination and reality. But his work has often been understood as primarily concerned with the machinations of the mind, though in a sense different from how Woolf's work has been received along these lines. Stevens's lifelong fascination with the imagination has pointed critics to an essentially "abstract" quality of his poetry. Whether "abstraction" is a negative feature depends upon the critic. Charles Altieri celebrates Stevens's abstraction and emphasizes its connection to the principles of modern abstract art, whereas Marjorie Perloff looks at "Notes toward a Supreme Fiction" and argues that Stevens's abstraction avoids the political realities of the Second World War.[1] Christian Wiman has argued against the strength of Stevens's work altogether, suggesting that if Stevens is influential over the next fifty years, then the break between "poetry and American culture will be complete."[2] If Stevens's poetry is "abstract" or removed from the world, then it is also said to be "philosophical"; perhaps more than the work of any other modernist poet, Stevens's poetry often serves as the foundation upon which theorists make claims within the field of ordinary language theory, phenomenology, or philosophy of mind.[3] Alternatively, Helen Vendler, Alan Filreis, and James Longenbach, though very different in approach, implicitly doubt Stevens's abstraction: Vendler by arguing that his "harsher" poems spring from "passionate feeling," Filreis and Longenbach by positioning Stevens within the sociopolitical currents of his time.[4] I agree with these three critics insofar as my argument calls attention to Stevens's lifelong interest in the commonplace, not the abstract, as the most defining feature of his finest work. Even though Stevens's claim that "it must be abstract" in "Notes toward a Supreme Fiction" would seem to point otherwise, the "notes" and "toward" of the poem's title emphasize provisionality and that this abstraction will never be reached. Experience must always be of *this* world. The "supreme fiction" remains abstract only as it materializes into "An abstraction bloodied, as man by thought," as Stevens writes in "Notes" (*CP* 385). Abstract notions are never static in Stevens: they shift to account for the "flawed words and stubborn sounds" of human imperfection, of a limited vocabulary, of experiences at a far remove from the ideal (*CP* 194).

Stevens's treatment of the commonplace emerges out of the conflict between an abstract world and an "actual world." The latter term comes from a 1952 letter, to which I will return, in which Stevens comments on the role of poetry in the aftermath of the Second World War. The "actual world" in Stevens's poetry does not announce itself through "facts" as it does in modernist novels that establish the ordinary through a dense materialism. And unlike the poetry of some of his peers, Stevens's poetry is not known for its depiction of "particular" things. One might think that the commonplace is composed of particulars, but for Stevens the commonplace is as much an approach to things as it is the things themselves. In this sense the commonplace is shared. In "The Course of a Particular"—one of his last poems—the "cry" of leaves has meaning only unto itself; it cannot be abstracted to other situations, to other people. The particular thus become perilous: "until, at last, the cry concerns no one at all" (*OP* 124). While Stevens has been criticized, during his lifetime and still, for the politics of his "particular" kind of life—especially the sense that he was removed from the realities of the Second World War—this chapter shows how his theory of the commonplace was deeply mindful of the politics of his times, even as his poetry may not seem as politically engaged as the work of some of his contemporaries. Like Stein, Stevens became more deeply invested in the commonplace during the 1930s and 1940s, and his style develops in response to his dependence upon it. But the commonplace at home for Stevens is neither the antithesis of the war abroad nor a safe retreat. The commonplace is a certain kind of attitude that acknowledges the necessary negotiations between private life and the public world, a back-and-forth movement between one's situation and the way that other people live.

My first objective will be to consider how Stevens's late reflections upon his own life, characterized by one place and one job, shape his understanding of the actual world that poetry might represent. Stevens's construction of his own "normal" existence—the upper-middle-class comforts of Hartford, Connecticut—gave weight to and even catalyzed his theory of the commonplace. I also contend with Stevens's ideas about how poetry must respond to the Second World War. It would be impossible otherwise, from his point of view, for as he says in one letter, "our minds are full of it" (*SL* 356). I then look at how Stevens's commitment to the commonplace informs the substance of his long poem on the subject, "An Ordinary Evening in New Haven." The poem, originating in "Notes toward a Supreme Fiction," essentially *thinks about* rather than represents or replicates ordinary experience, as some of his earlier poems actually attempt to do.[5] Many poems in the Stevens canon are meditative, but "Ordinary Evening" is exceptional in this respect: the poem calls itself "the never-ending meditation" (*CP* 465). The ordinary is a discursive style: a roundabout, circular feat of never pinning down the elusive subject. But this is not an experience of frustration for Stevens. To be in quest of the ordinary, in Stanley Cavell's terms, requires an understanding that the ordinary can never be completely grasped though one is always moving toward it.[6] The improvisational style of "Ordinary Evening" enacts this movement, not because it lacks an order or a plan, but because the poem presents and alters ideas, repeating and modifying as a mode of development, as if an experiment. The poem emphasizes an important theme in Stevens's life and work: his desire to move forward and his image of himself as spinning, circling around the same subjects, maintaining a middle ground between two points. This lack of getting anywhere, this inability to convert experience into something transcendent or idealized—this is a positive quality for Stevens, something that he wills. The poem attempts to get somewhere, but also pulls back from arriving there, in a kind of paradox of movement and steadiness. The commonplace, as embodied by "Ordinary Evening," is not a complete or finished phenomenon but always transpiring.

I conclude by considering how Stevens's very concept of language is affected and informed by his understanding of the commonplace. Although many other modernist writers were preoccupied with ordinary experience and how best to represent it, what makes Stevens unique, in this respect, is how he dwells on language as a satisfying, pleasing medium despite what he accepts as language's limitations. His remarkable language—his dazzling play with words—does not distance us any more from the ordinary, since all language is caught in the paradox of representing the ordinary without transforming it, a fact that Stevens understood quite clearly. Stevens does not try to avoid the paradox, instead he flaunts language's extraordinary capabilities. Ordinary experience, itself elusive, is not at odds with what language can and cannot do. Indeed, ordinary experience is very well suited to linguistic expression, generating a kind of poetry that might be called ruminative or reflective—words that T. S. Eliot used disparagingly to describe nineteenth-century poetry but which describe the vital power of Stevens's poetics.

## The Normal Poet

> Tomorrow I am going to New York to do a number of errands and otherwise nothing at all. Perhaps I shall have my hair cut. I know almost no one there any more, so that I am like a ghost in a cemetery reading epitaphs. I am going to visit a bookbinder, a dealer in autographs, Brooks about pajamas, try to find a copy of *Revue de Paris* for December because of an article about Alain that it contains, visit a baker, a fruit dealer, and, as it may be, a

> barber. An ordinary day like that does more for me than
> an extraordinary day: the bread of life is better than any souffle.
> —Letter from Wallace Stevens to José Rodríguez Feo, February 19, 1952

> The trouble is that poetry is so largely a matter of transformation.
> To describe a cup of tea without changing it and without
> concerning oneself with some extreme aspect of it is not at
> all the easy thing that it seems to be.
> —Letter from Wallace Stevens to Barbara Church, July 27, 1949

Stevens's first conspicuous use of the word "commonplace" occurs in letters to Ronald Lane Latimer, the young publisher of two of Stevens's limited editions. Stevens describes a specific group of five poems, *Owl's Clover,* published in 1936 and then revised for his volume *The Man with the Blue Guitar* (1937) but which he subsequently did not include in his 1954 *Collected Poems.* Dissatisfied with how the poems grapple with art's relationship to contemporary issues, or "to what one reads in the papers," Stevens eventually thought the poems were "rather boring" (*SL* 308). Strikingly, Stevens's notion of the commonplace develops in part out of his first-time attempt to write poems that would address the social issues of his day, in this case the economic difficulties of the 1930s, the appeal of communism in American left-wing intellectual circles, and the rise of totalitarian states in Europe. He thought of calling the collection "Aphorisms on Society" to emphasize the social issues that the poems address, but Latimer apparently persuaded Stevens to use the more lyrical title. Following Stevens's own evaluation, *Owl's Clover* has often been read as a poetic failure.[7] But the subject matter did not disappear for Stevens. The title of the collection (the common name for a weed and herb) suggests something that grows on its own and does not go away, a quality shared with "the day's news."

What continues to concern Stevens is how his poems could or should respond to a much larger crisis—the war. He is aware that the commonplace absorbs what he famously calls "the pressure of reality," and wants his poetry to reflect the complicated influence of wartime news upon the lives of people at home (*NA* 22). One of his letters to Latimer itself is a record of that absorption. Stevens asks: "Is poetry that is to have a contemporary significance merely to be a collection of contemporary images, or is it actually to deal with the commonplace of the day?" And on the back side of the letter, Latimer has scrawled what looks to be a list of items he needed to furnish his editorial offices, including "1 BKCASE," "1 LAMP," and "1 DESKLAMP."[8] The question of socially concerned poetry is met with the necessary arrangements of a workspace. While the combination of consequential and mundane problems is perhaps the cliché of any archived letter, Stevens's approach to poetry is a powerful register of both. One way that Stevens engages with a social world after writing *Owl's Clover* is by looking at other people's ordinary experiences—that is, the way in which other people arrange their everyday lives, and how their days are shaped by the political climate. Seeking out the commonplaces of *others* constitutes Stevens's engagement with the social; he rarely again directly addresses the political issues of his moment. Moreover, the real contentment that Stevens found in his routines of work at the Hartford Accident and Indemnity Company distanced him (physically and in spirit) from cultural, artistic, and political centers of activity, or at least this was his long-lasting self-conception. And yet, the commonplace on which he depends is hardly an easy subject for poetry; the commonplace constitutes life's most pervasive feature—but according to Stevens, it is not always a specific thing.

In a 1940 letter to the critic Hi Simons concerning a poem from *Harmonium* (1923), "The Comedian as the Letter C," Stevens explains the "normal" as something his poetry attempts to "achieve." He reacts against the claim that his work exists in an isolated, imaginative realm:

> People say that I live in a world of my own: that sort of thing. Instead of seeking therefore for a "relentless contact," I have been interested in what might be described as an attempt to achieve the normal, the central. So stated, this puts the thing out of all proportion in respect to its relation to the context of life. Of course, I don't agree with the people who say that I live in a world of my own; I think that I am perfectly normal, but I see that there is a center. (*SL* 352)

Stevens develops an idea about the normal in place of regularly, or "relentless[ly]," addressing contemporary events. He even reconsiders his early poetry as part of a new poetic project. In the above letter, the older Stevens of "Esthétique du Mal" rereads his younger work, recasting "The Comedian as the Letter C" in a light that is more conducive to his new emphasis on the "normal" rather than on the riotous verbal extravagance that also unquestionably characterizes the early poem:

> What word split up in clickering syllables
> And storming under multitudinous tones
> Was name for this short-shanks in all that brunt?
> Crispin was washed away by magnitude. (*CP* 28)

The poem, as many have noted, is highly autobiographical: Crispin's great sea voyage and return home might be understood as a quest for poetic subject matter ("what word"?) and a search for worldly fulfillment in places rich with experience, overwhelming in their "magnitude." The poem, as Stevens understands it in his letter to Simons, discovers "the normal, the central" as an answer to the lifelong dilemma of how to live.

But the normal differs for everyone. One of Stevens's adages, in apparent contradiction to his statement about being "perfectly normal," celebrates diversity: "I don't think we should insist that the poet is normal or, for that matter, that anybody is" (*OP* 193). Wry, Stevens connects his theory of the "normal" with a comment upon his own normalcy. Of course, we can never say his markedly bourgeois life was entirely "normal" if only because the normal cannot be associated with an affluence that was in fact unusual during the Great Depression.[9] Stevens's normal, in this sense, accounts for something like the shifting points of view that Woolf draws upon to illuminate how the everyday cannot be reduced to one kind of experience (a genre). Both writers assume an understanding of the everyday as both unique to each individual and responsive to a shared environment. It is an attitude toward experience with which every human being is familiar, even as Stevens's satisfaction with ordinary experience grows out of a very specific kind of life: a commitment to the rhythms of work, to making money as a successful surety lawyer, and enjoying the simple things (books, pajamas, haircuts) that money can buy. "Money is a kind of poetry," Stevens shamelessly maintains, valuing a secular and material world rather than the world of "silent shadows" and "dreams" considered in "Sunday Morning" (*OP* 191; *CP* 67). His theory of the commonplace over the course of his career is both poetic and personal. To attend to the ordinary, in poetry, is to value the ordinary as "the bread of life." In this vein, Stevens circled through the central routines at the Hartford, where he worked for more than fifty years, and his home on Westerly Terrace, where he lived with his wife and daughter. There is a profound consistency to the demands that compose his life. Although Stevens's poetry does not detail how he spends his days, as his letters often do, it allows a reader to understand the commonplace given one's own particular quotidian.

Stevens's commonplace book, *Sur Plusieurs Beaux Sujects,* registers his proclivity for circling around particular ideas, not unlike his approach to the commonplace in "Ordinary Evening."[10] Stevens transcribed various quotations and aphorisms, choosing and adapting language from other texts in a casual, unsystematic fashion, drawing upon book reviews, catalogs, and periodicals rather than "full-sized" philosophers like Plato and Aristotle, as Milton Bates has noted (2). Although ostensibly addressing "beautiful subjects," his commonplace book contains a prophetic, cryptic passage on the normal from a 1933 architectural review.[11]

Here, the normal is defined as a perfect subject for art. The plainness of the normal inheres in every aesthetic thing:

> And, the normal is not the average, neither in art, in letters, nor in commerce. The average can never rise to great perfection but the normal can be perfectly expressed in any activity of man, be it architecture or poetry—painting or agriculture. . . . Modernity and newness are as inseparable from normality as are the ways of an animal in any chosen period of its long and slow changing evolution. The Normal is not static, it is of the Universe, and with the Universe it forever changes. It is so much with us that it needs no search to find it, no theory to teach its presence. (25–27)

Comparable to Whitman's "divine average"—the occupations of working individuals that constitute a democracy—the normal for Stevens is an "activity" rather than a thing, a movement rather than a fully realized moment. In this respect, Stevens's poetry of the commonplace is distinct from Pound's "image" which "presents an intellectual and emotional complex in an instant of time" (*Literary Essays*, 4). Pound's verbal exactitude compresses the language of the poem and charges it. Stevens finds language that generates more language. The ordinary is a continuum, not to be pinned down. Pursuing the normal, Stevens also realizes, ironically, that the normal "needs no search to find it." It is everywhere but never in one place. Hence Stevens wrote to his close friend Henry Church, editor of the Paris review *Mesures:* "For myself, the inaccessible jewel is the normal and all of life, in poetry, is the difficult pursuit of just that" (*SL* 521). His statement again conflates art and life, the "activity of man" and the poetry he produces. Yet writing about the normal is no easy task. In 1935 Stevens wrote to Latimer:

> You will find occasional references in my poems to the normal. With me, how to write of the normal in a normal way is a problem which I have long since given up trying to solve, because I never feel that I am in the area of poetry until I am a little off the normal. The worst part of this aberration is that I am convinced that it is not an aberration. (*SL* 287)

To write a poem about the normal paradoxically requires writing "a little off the normal," observant but somewhat removed from the thing he wants to embody. Stevens essentially admits that representing the normal without altering it amounts to an impossible task. Nearly fifteen years later, writing "Ordinary Evening," Stevens reconciles himself to this "aberration," believing that only poetry committed to the ordinary can be satisfying, even if this kind of poetry will always fall just short of its aim. Indeed, he acknowledged that the poem in the end "may seem diffuse and casual" (*SL* 719).

Poetic limitation, as it defines Stevens's search for the commonplace, differs from the way that many modernist writers—Pound and others—thought about the possibilities of language. "Words strain, / Crack and sometimes break, under the burden, / Under the tension, slip, slide, perish, / Decay with imprecision, will not stay in place, / Will not stay still," Eliot writes in *Four Quartets,* marking language's inability to represent the shock and disorder of modernity, in particular, a moral burden Eliot identifies with wartime England (19). Moreover, the shored fragments of *The Waste Land* established Eliot's radical discontent with language much earlier in response to the First World War. Stevens's commonplace also emerges out of a specific historical moment, but the commonplace is not simply another expression of (or reconciliation with) the modernist frustration with language. For Stevens, whose subject matter was not customarily the trauma or shock of war, language seems like a trustworthy medium. In this respect, Stevens's work offers a conception of language which accords with American pragmatism, especially as it has been influenced in later manifestations by Wittgenstein. The idea that language is like a set of tools that does work in the world is central to Richard Rorty's claim that language is fundamentally contingent: not "final" or "fixed," but constantly challenged and overturned by other vocabularies, or better tools, that make sense of human experience (*Contingency,* 3–22). Conceiving of language as reinvigorated—if often violently so—by the experience of human suffering (as in a poem like "Esthétique du Mal"), Stevens rarely expressed despair at what language could *not* do. Though he said very little about Eliot as compared with his more local peers William Carlos Williams and Marianne Moore, Stevens wrote of *The Waste Land:* "If it is the supreme cry of despair it is Eliot's and not his generation's."[12] In making a claim for how poetry might register cultural change rather than personal crisis, Stevens instead emphasized often what language *must* do. For instance, he ends "Of Modern Poetry" (1942) with the command: "It must / Be the finding of a satisfaction, and may / Be of a man skating, a woman dancing, a woman / Combing. The poem of the act of the mind" (*CP* 240). This "act of the mind" is not an appeal to abstraction or isolation, but paradoxically an appeal to engage with the world outside of the mind, represented here by the uncomplicated and familiar movements of the body.

But "Of Modern Poetry," like *The Waste Land,* responds to a radically changed world amid war, as Stevens's poetry itself was changing. It poses the question: What should poetry be *now?* And answers with a call for a new kind of language and a new understanding of audience:

> It has to be living, to learn the speech of the place.
> It has to face the men of the time and to meet
> The women of the time. It has to think about war
> And it has to find what will suffice. It has
> To construct a new stage. (*CP* 240)

In his commonplace book, Stevens copied a passage from a 1938 article by Stephen Spender that he could be recalling in "Of Modern Poetry," a context that deepens a political reading of the poem:

> The aim of the serious dramatist is to invent a situation in which several characters reveal—in a way which is spontaneous because it is produced by the situation—the fundamental nature of their being and their attitude to life. Now the poet is someone who devotes his life to exactly such a process of self-revelation as drama attempts to produce in characters: his poems are speeches *from the drama of the time in which he is living.* The dramatist defines in his characters the level at which their feelings blend into poetry. (Bates, *Sur Plusieurs,* 57; italics mine)

Spender sought dramatic forms that were relevant to political and social issues of the 1930s. In his own poems that engage with the complexities of communism, fascism, and the Spanish Civil War, he shifts among images of urban modernity and his own intensely personal expressions (a style, as I have shown, that Woolf argued against, believing the young 1930s poets confused poetry with prose). Stevens, provoked by Spender, addresses the political less directly and less personally. Unlike some other modernist poets, he does not lose faith in language and its capabilities or turn excessively to other languages. "Combing" is his response: a word that means both to search and to groom. Stevens's search is for the normal, and he finds that the words of a poem must (and can) "suffice." He wants "modern poetry" to respond to the simple yet striking moments of ordinary life ("a woman / Combing"), as these moments are somehow the most necessary to modern experience and the most likely to be unacknowledged, undervalued, or unrepresented.

Stevens does not celebrate poetic language that is distinctly different *now* from what it was *then.* This response separates Stevens from poets like Auden and Eliot, whose poetics seriously shifted in response to the Second World War, or from George Oppen, whose silence in the 1930s attests to his belief in the irreconcilability of his poetry and his work with the Communist Party. As James

Longenbach has argued in *Wallace Stevens: The Plain Sense of Things,* both Auden and Eliot needed to distance themselves from their previous utopian or apocalyptic fantasies. "Not having succumbed to the lure of an unobtainable utopia [as had Eliot], he had no need to lament its demise," Longenbach writes. "Not having overestimated the powers of poetry [as did Auden], he had no need to exaggerate its limitations" (196). Stevens's career is significantly different from that of these other modernist poets. Although his poetry certainly changed in tenor and scope, his continuity of thought from the late 1930s through the end of life is dominated by his consideration of the commonplace, a concept that itself signifies change and that receives its fullest treatment in his later volumes.

But why exactly are commonplace moments the most necessary to a modern age or to a world at war? Stevens poses this question to himself in his 1948 lecture, "Imagination as Value." Here he struggles with the utility of poetry in a post-romantic era after the numbing horrors of two world wars. He turns to the commonplace as a quality that needs attention when every situation is charged by extremes, by the highs of heaven and the lows of hell. "The great poems of heaven and hell have been written," Stevens claims in this lecture, "and the great poem of the earth remains to be written" (*NA* 142). "Imagination as Value" is the fullest expression of Stevens's response to the brutalities of the twentieth century, which he attributes to human forces, not to forces beyond the earth or beyond our responsibility. The lecture reflects his direct contact with writers who suffered through the war whom he met through Henry Church: Jean Wahl, who had been sent to the concentration camp at Drancy and partly inspired "Esthétique du Mal," and Jean Paulham, who was briefly imprisoned for his literary work (Filreis, *Actual,* 98–115, 130–37). In the lecture, Stevens argues that the imagination is the human faculty capable of finding the commonplace even in the most severe circumstances: the imagination is not a vehicle of escape, but a requirement of life. "The chief problems of any artist, as of any man, are the problems of the normal," Stevens writes. "He needs, in order to solve them, everything that the imagination has to give" (*NA* 156). This conclusion may seem like a paradox: Why is the imagination necessary to the normal? If the normal is a middle ground, as Stevens suggests it is, then recovering this middle ground is unusually demanding in a modern age of ideological endpoints, of conditions that seem overwhelming.

Frank Kermode takes up Stevens's argument in the last chapter of *A Sense of an Ending* (1966), a study deeply suffused with the language of late Stevens. In his treatment of a British agent imprisoned in German-occupied France, Kermode suggests that if the agent is to survive deprivation and the threat of death, he must conjure a fiction of beginnings and endings—an imposed temporality—through the resources of the imagination. Kermode's idea (and it is drawn from Stevens) is that only by seeking the imagination—creating a "fiction" with a beginning, a middle, and an end—can an individual survive atrocity, an idea that initially seems radically at odds with Adorno's famous statement, "To write poetry after Auschwitz is barbaric" (*Prisms,* 34). The imagination, for many, came to its final end in the totalizing vision of Nazi death camps; poetry must now confront facts, not construct dangerous myths, the great modernist temptation. But for Stevens, the imagination still holds "value": the imagination should never serve as a means of expressing some ideal or ideological vision. Rather, as Stevens writes in "Notes," the poet aims to see the world clearly "with an ignorant eye"—that is, as if for the first time (*CP* 380). His "fictions" are not static myths but rather are always changing. For Stevens, the imagination serves as an agent of perseverance, and poetry—as "Of Modern Poetry" maintains—must simultaneously change to "think about war" (*CP* 240).

This viewpoint may seem possible only from someone safely couched at a far remove from a war-torn continent. And yet Stevens's celebration of the imagination was always contingent upon "the day's news" or "the pressure of reality." In "The Noble Rider and the Sound of Words," originally a 1941 lecture at Princeton, Stevens emphasizes history's influence on poetry. He claims: "The pressure of reality is, I think, the determining factor in the artistic character of an era" (*NA* 22). This claim—or at least the phrase "pressure of reality"—is often cited as an example of how Stevens expresses the tension between imagination and reality, a binary that continues to dominate the way that philosophical issues in his work are often framed. But what has not been noted about Stevens's phrase is that it is a truism of the most obvious sort: (of course) historical events affect the art of a particular era. It is never quite possible nor desirable, according to Stevens, for the imagination to transcend reality, but it is vital or "necessary"—to use the key word from Stevens's essay collection—that the imagination contests the brute facts of modern life. In this lecture, Stevens both distances himself from the events abroad and associates his own local Hartford weather with an international climate in which others also live. The "weather of war" emerges at this time as a frequent phrase, conflating Stevens's own observation of the changes in the weather with the chilling conflicts overseas. "It might be that it would be better to wait a little while, until there is a change of weather," Stevens writes to Henry Church in 1940, suggesting that Church put off publishing the journal *Mesures* that published many of Stevens's poems in French translation, "The crisis of Europe may come out of a blue sky, but I don't expect it to do so. I am afraid that what is going on now may be nothing to what will be going on three or four months from now" (*SL* 365). The sky of Europe is the same sky of Hartford, Stevens suggests, and war will affect everyone beneath it.

The weather, a topic that frequently occurs in Stevens's poetry and in his correspondence (nearly every letter notes the weather), epitomizes a commonplace—something observed daily, a cliché. In this sense, the weather aptly represents what is shared among a group of people, banal and yet important, with which everyone is familiar. The weather is neither escapable nor imagined; it is what really exists. Other critics, most notably Harold Bloom, have equated Stevens's attention to the weather with "a religious man" who "turns to the idea of God" (186). But it is more likely that Stevens dwells on the weather as an earthly, nonreligious reality. "The 'ever-jubilant weather'" Stevens writes, referring to the poem "Waving Adieu, Adieu, Adieu," "is not a symbol. We are physical beings in a physical world; the weather is one of the things that we enjoy, one of the unphilosophical realities" (*SL* 348–49). "The Poems of our Climate" (1942), in this context of "the weather," has been rightly read as a response to the war. The poem acknowledges the inevitably flawed world in which people live, rejecting the aestheticized perfection of a still life for the inherent difficulty of the human condition, concluding:

> The imperfect is our paradise.
> Note that, in this bitterness, delight,
> Since the imperfect is so hot in us,
> Lies in flawed words and stubborn sounds. (*CP* 194)

Stevens's repetition of "imperfect" suggests the French verb tense, the *imparfait,* a tense that signals an action with no clear beginning and ending. Proust depends upon the *imparfait* to establish the repetition of habits and the radical openness of a human life. Similarly Stevens suggests that there is no teleological path to a paradise beyond the earth. The earth is paradise enough, even as our language is "flawed" and our ability to make poetic music is challenged by inhospitable climates like the climate of war, which influences everything. "I make no reference in this letter to the war," Stevens ends a 1940 letter, "It goes without saying that our minds are full of it" (*SL* 356).

Of course, the weather of war also suggests a certain lack of agency, both acknowledging war and yet understanding peace as something that might just emerge like sun from behind the clouds. The phrase reflects Stevens's ambivalence about the role that he or his poetry could play in contributing to "the day's news." Stevens was quite aware that poetry has real limitations, and that his quasi "war poems" would not actually bring about discernable change. Crispin realizes: "The words of things entangle and confuse. / The plum survives its poems" (*CP* 41). While Stevens wrestled with whether poetic language could be separate from what it modifies (the "seeming" and "being" of "Description Without Place" is a fine example), many poems qualify poetry's real power in changing events. In "The Planet on the Table," Stevens's persona Ariel thinks with pleasure of his poems but feels "It was not important that they survive" (*CP* 532). The poems that I have singled out, "Of Modern Poetry" and "The Poems of Our Climate," along with poems including "Dutch Graves in Bucks County" and "Repetitions of a Young Captain," engage with war deeply but obliquely, never identifying specific dates, events, or facts. This aspect of Stevens's poetry obviously sets him apart from other poets of the 1930s and 1940s, especially Auden, whose "Spain 1937," "In a Time of War" (1938), and "September 1, 1939" stand as testaments to the kind of powerful political poems that Stevens did not write.

"Poetry makes nothing happen," Auden writes in his "In Memory of W. B. Yeats," a statement that is often interpreted as an acceptance of poetry's minimal effect on actual events, its lack of agency in the world. Though poetry may make nothing *happen*, however, Auden never said it lacked lasting power. Poetic power lies in the lives of a poem's future readers. "The words of a dead man, "Auden writes in preceding lines, "Are modified in the guts of the living" (81). "Modified" may suggest tempered force, but "guts" suggests that the poem still retains something visceral. For Stevens, especially in regard to the Second World War, poetry felt removed from this possibility of relevance and endurance.[13] In a 1952 letter to Barbara Church right before his *Selected Poems* was published, Stevens wrote:

> There is going to be a *Selected Poems* published in London shortly. I returned the proofs yesterday. The book seemed rather slight and small to me—and unbelievably irrelevant to our actual world. It may be that all poetry has seemed like that at all times and always will. The close approach to reality has always been the supreme difficulty of any art: the communication of actuality, as [poetics?], has been not because it loses identity as the event passes. Nothing in the world is deader than yesterday's political (or realistic) poetry. Nevertheless the desire to combine the two things, poetry and reality, is a constant desire. (*SL* 760)

This letter to Barbara Church, who was driving around Italy surveying the ruins of World War II, might be considered within a context of American prosperity against the gloom of postwar Europe.[14] Stevens never believes that his poetry can actually ameliorate social conditions or change the way that people (or politicians) behave. In fact, he believes that poetry with these aims inevitably loses the power of longevity. Poetic thought, Stevens suggests, should acknowledge the "actual world," but only in a way that allows the poems to maintain their enduring power, not become restricted to contemporary political meanings.

The commonplace became for Stevens an idea that distinguished and even validated his life and work. Moreover, finding important values in the commonplace enabled Stevens—whose life was always materially comfortable—to live completely and fully in the routines that he chose. On some level, Stevens is content to imagine a world beyond Hartford, or the American Northeast, without actually traveling outside the country himself (exceptions include a 1903 camping trip to British Columbia and a 1923 stopover in Cuba). Nor would he give up his work at the Hartford once he became a well-established poet. When Archibald MacLeish invited Stevens to be the Charles Eliot Norton Professor at Harvard for the 1955–56 academic year, Stevens declined, partly out of concern that a leave of absence from Hartford Accident and Indemnity Company would force the issue of retirement. Stevens explains in a letter to MacLeish that the foreseen difficulty of "taking up the routine of the office again" after an entire year away also influenced his decision (*SL* 852–53). The routine of ordinary life deeply satisfied Stevens. The intellectual sphere of the academy never seemed solid enough footing for him, never the "rock" of work.

Furthermore, at a time when most poets made a requisite trip to Paris, Stevens never once traveled to Europe. In an early letter to William Carlos Williams, Stevens mocks his own attraction to more local concerns: "My job is not now with poets from Paris. It is to keep the fire-place burning and the music-box churning and the wheels of the baby's chariot turning and that sort of thing" (*SL* 246). Stevens sometimes offers oblique explanations for his domestic isolation, for why he never travels himself. In one of his late (rather resigned) letters to his friend José Rodríguez Feo, the younger Cuban poet and founder of the literary magazine *Orígenes,* Stevens writes:

> I have been working at the office, nothing else: complaining a little about it but content, after all, that I have that solid rock under my feet, and enjoying the routine without minding too much that I have to pay a respectable part of my income to the government in order that someone else representing the government may sit at the Café X at Aix or go to lectures at the Sorbonne. (*Secretaries,* 198)

With a trace of self-mockery, Stevens appreciates his productive (and recognizably dull) life at the office and suggests that the taxes he pays enable the European intellectual or the university scholar to pursue more leisurely philosophical matters. But as the last two stanzas from "Notes" emphasize, the academic quest for knowledge has its own limitations; "the Sorbonne" embodies a hubristic quest for order and control (dangerous "myths") that experiences of the irrational and blissful beautifully undermine:

> They will get it straight one day at the Sorbonne.
> We shall return at twilight from the lecture
> Pleased that the irrational is rational,
>
> Until flicked by feeling, in a gildered street,
> I call you by name, my green, my fluent mundo.
> You will have stopped revolving except in crystal. (*CP* 406–7)

"Flicked by feeling," the poet celebrates "twilight" understandings, not academic abstractions. Stevens's coda to the poem, addressed to the "Soldier," perhaps fulfills Stevens's desire for a humanist ending that addresses the war. He thought of adding a fourth section called "It Must be Human." However, as Vendler suggests, after the stunning image of a "green" and "fluent mundo . . . revolving except in crystal," the coda seems anticlimactic, an elegiac turn away from the forceful first person of the last stanzas (*On Extended,* 205). The coda is an attempt "to combine the two things, poetry and reality," as Stevens describes his aim in the letter to Barbara Church. Arguably, the images from the highly anthologized seventh section of "Esthétique du Mal" ("How red the rose that is the soldier's wound") are more successful and certainly blunter in their efforts to forge a relationship between aesthetic beauty and human suffering, the soldier's blood and the rose of poetry.[15]

Stevens's love of the commonplace, however, is actually contingent upon and fed by a social world constructed through a circle of friends and acquaintances, of which Rodríguez Feo is an important part. As the above letter suggests, Stevens relishes his distance from the Sorbonne, preferring his daily walk from work to his home on Westerley Terrace and the image of himself dedicated to a masculine, bourgeois vocation.[16] But his wide-ranging and longtime correspondence with specific people all over the world surfaces as his personal method of solving "the problem of the normal," of learning how the commonplace functions for other people, in other places.[17] It is helpful to conceive of Stevens's social world as a negotiation between a private realm at home in Hartford and a public or political realm. As Hannah Arendt has argued, the emergence of the "social," which is neither wholly public nor wholly private, is rooted in modernity (*Human,* 28). Arendt looks back to the Aristotelian distinction between public (*polis*) and private (*oikos*), where life was divided "between activities related to a common world and those related to the maintenance of life" *(Human, 28).* Out of this binary, the social emerges from the forces of a market economy and in particular the formation of a nation-state. The social—what Arendt sometimes describes as a civic realm—might be characterized in its worst manifestations by conformity and mass taste. In its best characterization (and this is what concerns Stevens), the social is constituted by activities that are shared, communicated, and experienced together. Stevens relishes the links between his life and other people's. These links are forged not just through the necessities of living or through the choices one makes politically, but also through the fact that Stevens and his correspondents are living in a particular moment in history and going about their lives simultaneously. Stevens ultimately believes that the commonplace is collective.

A piece of mail from someplace faraway, arriving at his home in Hartford, connected his habitual life with a world beyond. Someone else's commonplaces became for Stevens an authentic journey elsewhere. Although his letters sometimes intimated a longing for other lands, the details his friend sent him seemed to "suffice," for he certainly had money enough to travel had he cared to. Furthermore, Stevens was less interested in the exotic details of life elsewhere—even in faraway locales—than in the essentials of everyday life that his friends recorded, fodder often incorporated into his poems. Barbara Church provided Stevens with generous accounts of her travels throughout Europe after her husband's death, sending postcards—sometimes more than ten at a time—illustrating street scenes, paintings, steamers, vistas, and road stops. A few of her postcards inspire lines in "Ordinary Evening":

> it follows that
> Real and unreal are two in one: New Haven
> Before and after one arrives or, say,
>
> Bergamo on a postcard, Rome after dark,
> Sweden described, Salzburg with shaded eyes
> Or Paris in conversation at a café. (*CP* 485–86)

The relationship between anticipation and actuality links New Haven with European cities, as the traveler imagines a city before he arrives, and exists in the city on arrival. The experience of the "real" always transfigures what one has imagined, and likewise, no place or experience can exist without the imagination's strong impress upon it. Nothing exists in pure abstracts.

In one 1948 note, Barbara Church describes traveling through her homeland after World War II, and Stevens picks up on her description of "blue and white Munich" (*SL* 605). In a subsequent letter to Rodríguez Feo, Stevens compares the colors of ruined Munich with the color of mangos on his dining room table, justifying his unlikely comparison as the imagination's power over the world of facts. For Stevens, facts in the wake of war have the possibility of overwhelming humanity with their stark magnitude:

> We have on the table in the dining room several Hayden mangoes. What healthy looking things they are. A friend who has been to Munich wrote to me the other day of the extent of the destruction of "blue and white Munich." It is like changing records on a gramophone to speak of the red and almost artificial green of mango skins and then speak of blue and white Munich. But unless we do these things to reality, the damned thing closes us in, walls us up, and buries us alive. . . . Reality is the footing from which we leap after what we do not have and on which everything depends. It is nice to be able to think of José combating the actual in Cuba, grasping great masses of it and making out of those masses a gayety of the mind. (*Secretaries*, 128–29)

Reality is something to "combat"—something that can swallow a person unless it is faced clearly, made sensible, Stevens suggests, by making it resemble something that is known. Stevens wants to see Munich's destruction but also resists the "blue and white" by comparing it to the "red and almost artificial green" of "healthy" mangos, tropical fruits that flourish despite Europe's devastation. Power lies in making something more familiar through comparison, but in this case resemblance also seems to defy the reality of what Barbara Church describes. Stevens's notion that "reality is the footing from which we leap" seems naïve in the context of postwar Europe, as if it is possible to fly forth from the rubble. But Stevens nonetheless suggests that he comes closer to the "blue and white" of Munich by bringing those colors into the place of his own home. The Bergamo, Rome, Sweden, Salzburg, and Paris of "Ordinary Evening" become the "things seen and unseen, created nothingness, / The heavens, the hells, the worlds, the longed-for lands"—tangible, for Stevens, in that other people have chosen to live there and have normalized what seems, for Stevens, exotic.

Stevens's attention to the quotidian and rejection of the exotic is one of the most frequent themes in his ten-year correspondence with Rodríguez Feo. Their letters offer the best evidence of the older poet's preference for the day-to-day world of practical things. With playful aplomb, Rodríguez Feo first writes to Stevens in November 1944 asking if he might translate some of Stevens's poems into Spanish. José, as he is usually addressed, frequently peppered "Wallachio" with frank questions regarding poets, painters, and critics. He also quickly revived Stevens's interest in George Santayana, with whom both poets were familiar from having studied at Harvard. "I think you share with [Santayana] that rediscovery of the supreme beauty that small, every-day objects have for the poetic eye," Rodríguez Feo writes in only his second or third letter to Stevens (*Secretaries*, 36).

Perhaps his most open and intimate self-expressions (except for his early letters to his future wife), Stevens's letters to Rodríguez Feo are nonetheless also somewhat patronizing in his assumptions about what Cuba must be like. He most enjoys the details that Rodríguez Feo sends concerning Cuban daily life (the food, the animals, domestic conversations between him and his mother) and disdains his efforts to include American and European literature and criticism in *Orígenes,* for "Cuba should be full of Cuban things" (*Secretaries,* 57). Stevens sometimes overstates the practical in his letters to Rodríguez Feo, partly, it seems, because the young Cuban lived in a world that always tempted Stevens: the warm, southern, pleasure-seeking climate that also lured Santayana. To Rodríguez Feo, who was educated in the Northeast but eventually returned to Cuba, settling for the quotidian sometimes seemed like settling for a cold, Puritan, passionless life. Stevens challenges this sentiment in "Academic Discourse in Havana," where he writes: "Grandmother and her basketful of pears / Must be the crux for our compendia. / That's world enough" (*CP* 143). The "crux" of experience should come from the familial and the familiar; fruit carried home by José's grandmother serves as the essential material for life's "compendia."

In a 1949 letter, Rodríguez Feo writes of his experience of the quotidian during a dreary late fall, describing his sad acknowledgment of how humans spend the greater part of their lives:

> And the anguish remains: the realization that after all one *cannot* live at the peak or "cumulus" of intensity. That life must be dull, monotonous, if then, later, we are to enjoy moments of excitement or discover a mysterious relation between the quotidian and the marvelous. But if you are not prepared, and I thought I was, to accept life as something shot with dull moments, and the notion, Christian?, that for a moment of joy there are ten of boredom, much more horrible than suffering, or perhaps the acutest form of personal suffering—then one is very unhappy. (*Secretaries,* 168)

Rodríguez Feo understands the quotidian in terms that resemble Woolf's "cotton wool of daily life"—the soft, dulling effect of routine, guarding against rarer moments of visionary insight. Stevens did not view ordinary experience in this way. His contentment with routine trumped any desire to "live at the peak or 'cumulus' of intensity." While influenced by Paterian aestheticism, Stevens's life and work do not find a model in the "hard, gemlike flame" of Pater's ecstatic burning. More like William James, Stevens makes a choice: he chooses the ordinary, and his poetry recognizes it as a value. In the above letter, Rodríguez Feo comes to terms with the quotidian whereas Stevens never fights against it.

In response to this letter, Stevens describes a book he is reading, the letters of the French writer Romain Rolland, taking pleasure in Rolland's details of daily life:

> Last night one of his letters was full of complaints about a noisy neighbor. Somehow it interested me immensely to know that one has noisy neighbors in Paris. Rolland, apparently, lived in an apartment where his wife, Clothilde, was no more hostile to a little dust than we are at home but the neighbors seemed to have moved the chairs every Thursday and cleaned the windows every Friday, polished the kitchen floor every Saturday, did the laundry on Sunday, dusted on Monday, etc. Rolland thought that this was the last word in being bourgeois. How much more closely that sort of thing brings one to Paris than remarks about the growth of interest in Socialism, the artificiality of Sarah Bernhardt, the facility with which Duse was able to weep on the state, the slightly ironic sneer that D'Annunzio always wore. (*Secretaries,* 171–72)

Although Stevens was drawn to the scholarly European intellectualism found in the foreign literary journals that he regularly bought and read, he nonetheless voices his preference for the banal material facts of how people get through their days, especially in a place like Paris, a city he continually imagined.

Stevens celebrates the idea that one might see the most striking resemblances between seemingly disparate things—between Caribbean mangos and the ruins of Munich, or between the faraway commonplaces of others and one's own local routines. To learn about other people's commonplaces, for Stevens, is to understand the political reality of his times. These ideas are the focus of Stevens's 1947 lecture at Harvard, "Three Academic Pieces." The lecture essentially serves as Stevens's analysis of his own poetic project, an explicit defense of his own poetry, and his profession of faith in himself. It is also perhaps his most complicated exploration of the relationship between the commonplace and postwar politics, a lecture that is more elusive than the earlier "Imagination as Value." Stevens argues that a poet must seek out the most satisfying resemblances in even the most terrifying facts of life. Nothing should be so foreign to a poet that he cannot make it resemble something he knows. The lecture, like "Ordinary Evening," picks up on the cities and places with which Stevens is acquainted from his letters. A striking passage from the essay, one that has received surprisingly little commentary, associates birds from a Viennese hunting scene with the imminence of nuclear warfare:[18]

> The eye does not beget in resemblance. It sees. But the mind begets in resemblance as the painter begets in representation; that is to say, as the painter makes his world within a world; or as the musician begets in music, in the obvious small

> pieces having to do with gardens in the rain or the fountains of Rome and in the obvious larger pieces having to do with the sea, Brazilian night or those woods in the neighborhood of Vienna in which the hunter was accustomed to blow his horn and in which, also, yesterday, the birds sang preludes to the atom bomb. It is not difficult, having once predicated such an activity, to attribute it to a desire for resemblance. (*NA* 76)

"Resemblance," the key word in the passage (and in the essay), allows the artist to understand what "the eye" sees, when what is seen seems impossible to comprehend. Stevens's language in "Three Academic Pieces" draws upon Andrew Marvell's "The Garden" in which "The mind, that Ocean where each kind / Does straight its own resemblance find; / Yet it creates, transcending these, / Far other worlds, and other seas." The "soul," in Marvell's poem, is like a singing bird, whose song transcends "the body's vest" (Gardner, *New Oxford,* 336). Stevens's lecture, in contrast, suggests that the poet does not transcend the world but finds resemblances among its seemingly most disparate elements. Stevens's praise of "resemblance" (versus his critique of metaphor in "Ordinary Evening") hinges on the difference between assimilation and heterogeneity. Whereas metaphor, for Stevens, can be evasive, pulling elements out of context and transforming them, resemblance is a mode of bringing things together, naturalizing elements that "look alike," or that ultimately share the same human origin. Stevens maintains that humans are capable of composing poetry and music but also of creating the atrocities of war, and this is what the power of resemblance helps us to understand. Nothing humans have created can be nonhuman or unnatural, even the atom bomb. To think otherwise is to forgo responsibility. Crimes are essentially human, and it is the poet's role to reveal resemblances among all things.

Stevens's attitude about the war nonetheless seems startlingly blasé, equating an atom bomb with singing birds, or massive destruction with the creation of poetic song. Rather than fundamentally changing his understanding of what poetry should be, Stevens believes that poetry should recognize and absorb radical political changes, that poetry itself should acknowledge its resemblance to other destructive forces. Poetry emerging in a nuclear age must "think about war," but Stevens understands that poetry has always responded to the influences of the times. The "normal" man" with the "normal" job, Stevens envisions himself as part of a world of people who simply carry on, living the kind of life that many others lead in a postwar climate. In a 1954 letter to Barbara Church, he writes:

> Our own days are the days of wind and rain, like today. Yet it is precisely on such days that we give thanks for the office. Sometimes one realizes what an exceeding help work is in anyone's life. What a profound grace it is to have a destiny no

> matter what it is, even the destiny of the postman going the rounds and of the bus driver driving the bus. (*SL* 843)

Stevens's self-conception appears in his description of the red robin in the penultimate stanza of "Notes":

> Red robin, stop in your preludes, practicing
> Mere repetitions. These things at least comprise
> An occupation, an exercise, a work,
>
> A thing final in itself and, therefore, good:
> One of the vast repetitions final in
> Themselves and, therefore, good, the going round
>
> And round and round, the merely going round,
> Until merely going round is a final good,
> The way wine comes at a table in a wood. (*CP* 405)

"Preludes" consist of looking toward what comes next whereas the bird might be happy with the repetitions themselves, satisfied with the present, the "final good." Stevens does not conceive of himself as divided between the prelude of insurance work and his career as a poet. As Peter Brazeau has noted, Stevens always kept the lower right drawer of his office desk open for filing poetry ideas, marking the fluid relationship between his insurance work and writing poetry (*Parts of a World*, 38). His "destiny" was to continue the repetitions of both, relatively unchanged, even as he achieved literary eminence and, in his later years, received the Bollingen Prize for Poetry, the Pulitzer Prize, and the National Book Award. Strikingly, the red robin in "Notes" also harkens back to Stevens's earlier lecture in which the "birds sang preludes to the atom bomb," an image that reverberates with Yeats's "hammered gold" Byzantine bird singing "Of what is past, or passing, or to come," and Kubla Khan's "ancestral voices prophesying war." But Stevens's robin shuns the immortal authority of art's edifice and the romantic pull of apocalypse.

As Stevens grew older, his sense of the normal became even more pronounced. In a January 1953 letter to Rodríguez Feo, Stevens writes:

> We have just had a really winter week-end—snow, sleet, rain. I wanted to stay in bed and make for myself a week-end world far more extraordinary than the one that most people make for themselves. But the habitual, customary, has become, at my age, such a pleasure in itself that it is coming to be that the pleasure is at least as

> great as any. It is a large part of the normality of the normal. And, I suppose, that projecting this idea to its ultimate extension, the time will arrive when just to *be* will take in everything without the least *doing* since even the least doing is irrelevant to pure being. (*SL* 767)

The normal at this point has become the substance of *being*. Stevens cannot separate the pleasures of the normal from other more decadent pleasures. This appreciation for the "habitual, customary" repetitions that compose a life finds full expression in Stevens's last two volumes of poetry, *The Auroras of Autumn* (1950) and *The Rock* (1951), full of figures looking backward and poems that value "the normality of the normal." "An Ordinary Evening in New Haven" stands as Stevens's most important and extended poem on the subject. Contemplating the value of ordinary experiences and finding language a sufficient medium, "Ordinary Evening" exemplifies the most striking feature of Stevens's poetics. Especially against the tendencies of other modernist poets, "Ordinary Evening" marks the commonplace as a source of satisfaction in a world where divinity can be only that which is palpable and of the earth.

## "An Ordinary Evening in New Haven"

> The serious reflection is composed
> Neither of comic nor tragic but of commonplace.

Between comedy and tragedy, self and other, beginnings and endings, and extremes of the weather, the commonplace is Stevens's middle ground. To look at "An Ordinary Evening in New Haven" through the lens of Stevens's complex ideas about the commonplace may seem like an obvious approach to the poem, but this essential feature of Stevens's poetics has not received much consideration—neither as a subject in and of itself nor in conjunction with Stevens's poem.[19] Understanding Stevens's investment in the commonplace opens up the poem's central preoccupations: the good of repetition as a way of living and moving forward, the eschewal of abstraction in favor of the physical earth, the pervasive and elusive quality of the everyday, and the desire to see things for what they are, untransformed by metaphor. The poem also illuminates Stevens's ideas about language's sufficiency, a trust in language that grows out of his reliance on the commonplace, which is unique against the strain of other modernist poets. The commonplace becomes the most distinctive mark of Stevens's modernism and the most resonating influence of his work.

The commonplace materializes as an animating energy in "Ordinary Evening," as the poem repeats beginnings and endings: "Alpha continues to begin. / Omega is refreshed at every end" (*CP* 469). The poem continually returns to "The strength at the centre" (*CP* 477). Although Stevens wants to "achieve the normal," his emphasis remains on the nature of perception as much as on the thing perceived: "not grim / Reality but reality grimly seen," as he writes in canto 14. Stevens does not overcome "reality," but seeks it "grimly," studying the ordinary in and of itself, "with an eye that does not look / Beyond the object" (*CP* 475). He modifies William Carlos Williams's dictum "No ideas but in things," as the last poem in Stevens's *Collected Poems* acknowledges, titled "Not Ideas about the Thing but the Thing Itself" (*CP* 534). For Stevens, to grasp hold of the "thing" requires continued attention, not exacting description. This distinction has marked Stevens's symbolist and romantic inheritance against Williams's marked objectivist aims.[20] The commonplace is not understood through a hard-edged description of objects or images (a wheelbarrow, faces in a crowd), but through an approach to representation itself, eschewing the transformative power of description.

In concept, dwelling on the commonplace may seem to have more transformative potential than objectivism's techniques, but in practice, Stevens's formal strategies in "Ordinary Evening" temper the paradox of representing the unrepresented. The poem might even be called ruminative or reflective, terms that come from Eliot's 1921 essay "The Metaphysical Poets," in which he distinguishes Victorian from metaphysical poets and makes clear that he greatly prefers the latter. The ruminative Victorian poet is distinctly nonmodernist, "disassociated" from his sensibility, whose writing is "refined" but whose feeling is "crude" (64–65). And although Stevens cannot be said to fall into any of the categories Eliot offers in this essay, "Ordinary Evening" does in a sense ruminate rather than yoke together heterogeneous ideas. The poem does not intend to shock or to defamilarize experience, but to inhabit it. It is telling that many of Stevens's titles include the word "of" or begin with "of" ("Of the Surface of Things," "Of Modern Poetry," "Of Mere Being") as his poetry aspires to be a part of, to inhabit, the subject matter it addresses. With leisurely "of-ness," "Ordinary Evening" settles into its subject matter. The poem is meditative and meandering, not compositional or concrete.

Ultimately, Stevens locates the commonplace in a mood and style: the plain mood of New Haven and what the poem recognizes as an "endlessly elaborating" style (*CP* 486). The poem suits itself to the ongoing, open nature of the everyday as defined by Lefebvre, embodying its "regular, unvarying succession" (*Everyday,* 24). "Ordinary Evening" offers an understanding of the ordinary as something satisfying to a businessman traveling to a lackluster city on a midweek winter day, a trip that Stevens himself might have undertaken. Organized in stanzaic triads, a form that Stevens often used for his longer discursive poems, "Ordinary Evening" extends where "Notes toward a Supreme Fiction" (his first poem to use this form) left. The "ephebe," or young poet, reappears to walk alone "In the big X of the returning primitive" (*CP* 474). Professor Eucalyptus of New Haven and the imaginative Spanish hidalgo join all of the playful fables "Notes" contains, illustrating—or perhaps challenging and complicating—Stevens's more doctrinal language. Eleanor Cook suggests that the title puns on "new heaven" and that the poem is "eucalyptic" and not "apocalyptic" (269). Indeed the style of the commonplace, for both "Notes" and "Ordinary Evening," resists revelation. In response to the critic Robert Pack's argument that "Notes" "does not really lead anywhere" which to Stevens is "not quite the same thing as get anywhere," Stevens writes: "I don't mean to try to exercise the slightest restraint on what you say. Say what you will. But we are dealing with poetry, not with philosophy. The last thing in the world that I should want to do would be to formulate a system" (*SL* 863–64).

But "Ordinary Evening" in comparison to "Notes" is marked by a darker, colder climate of solitary meditation. Wintertime cajoles a stark self-analysis, reflected by a barren world. The poem relishes plainness. The memory of spring's ripeness, bawdy and Chaucerian, affronts the cool simplicity of ice:

> So lewd spring comes from winter's chastity
> So, after summer, in the autumn air,
> Comes the cold volume of forgotten ghosts,
>
> But soothingly, with pleasant instruments,
> So that this cold, a children's tale of ice,
> Seems like a sheen of heat romanticized. (*CP* 468)

Like Stevens's snowman, imagining "Nothing that is not there and the nothing that is," the poem strips away the romantic, and yet creates a new romanticism in ordinary experience. "We must somehow cleanse the imagination of the romantic," Stevens writes in "Imagination as Value": "The imagination is one of the great human powers. The romantic belittles it. . . . It is to the imagination what sentimentality is to feeling" (*NA* 138). Stevens's cleansing of romantic sentimentality, like Joyce's, is a disavowal of epiphanic or sublime moments. But Joyce catalogs the particular whereas Stevens meditates upon it. For Stevens, as he writes in "The Course of a Particular," "It is the cry of leaves that do not transcend themselves" (*OP* 123). The commonplace should not remove us from the world, but reconfirm our commitment to it:

> At the centre, the object of the will, this place,
> The things around—the alternate romanza
>
> Out of the surfaces, the windows, the walls,
> The bricks grown brittle in time's poverty,
> The clear. A celestial mode is paramount,
>
> If only in the branches sweeping in the rain:
> The two romanzas, the distant and the near,
> Are a single voice in the boo-ha of the wind. (*CP* 480)

Stevens explores the relationship between "the distant and the near": the things outside and the things within, divided by windows, walls, and bricks. The images that emerge from the poem capture this tension between near and far, what is seen and unseen, like the blowing wind, or "wafts of wakening," or "misted contours, credible day again" (*CP* 473, 470). Recognizing the "celestial" (and emphasizing its necessity), the poem nonetheless cautions against being uprooted, caught up in the purely metaphysical. The "alternate romanza," the primordial "boo-ha" voice, resides in this poem of the earth.

Akin to architects constructing their own town from "windows," "walls," and "bricks," individuals create palpable worlds derived from their inner conceptions. Nothing can exist entirely of the mind, but must be unified with the earth in a "single voice." While this fusion between the ephemeral and the tangible, "a total double-thing," may constitute the "real," to settle on any notion of the real—stable and nontransforming—is to deny life, in the sense of Stevens's conception of change as necessary and invigorating. Achieving definition is death.

> It is fatal in the moon and empty there.
> But, here, allons. The enigmatical
> Beauty of each beautiful enigma
>
> Becomes amassed in a total double-thing.
> We do not know what is real and what is not.
> We say of the moon, it is haunted by the man
>
> Of bronze whose mind was made up and who, therefore, died.
> We are not men of bronze and we are not dead. (*CP* 472)

Refusing to arrive at a static notion of the real, the poem struggles to see clearly; "In a faithfulness as against the lunar light," against the pull of the subjective imagination (*CP* 472). The individual "whose mind was made up" is like a bronze statue, rooted in rigidity, unable to respond to the fluctuations of the weather, of the world. The challenge remains to reject the temptations of lunar light, to reject romanticizing, and to respond to change, a challenge that reengages this poem with the pragmatist principles of Stevens's Harvard years. No wonder the "endlessly elaborating poem" itself is so long and self-effacing, suggesting that "A more severe, / More harassing master would extemporize / Subtler, more urgent proof that the theory / Of poetry is the theory of life" (*CP* 486). But the poem itself renounces the notion of mastery, of theoretical proofs that cannot be challenged.

"Ordinary Evening" will not arrive at a conclusion, but revels in circling round, returning to the subject from various angles so that we even sense the way in which the poem came together as a meditation, an improvisation—or as Stevens suggests in one of his adages about poetry, an experiment. The poem also draws upon proverbial literature—the figure of Ecclesiast appears in the poem to emphasize, as Eleanor Cook has noted, the wisdom that comes from balance and age, a balance that is also reflected in the poem's final chiasmus (274). Unless one counts all five poems of *Owl's Clover* together, "An Ordinary Evening in New Haven" is Stevens's longest poem, partly because Stevens became increasingly fascinated with the subject as he wrote. In a November 17, 1949, unpublished letter to Dorothea Rudnick, secretary of the Connecticut Academy of Arts and Sciences (where Stevens first read a shortened version of the poem), Stevens admits: "When I wrote the poem I liked the subject and continued to work with it as long as it interested me even though it became much longer than I could possibly use in New Haven."[21] And in a May letter, Stevens describes the process of writing the poem, concentrating on the stark nakedness of his subject.

> At the moment I am at work on a thing called An Ordinary Evening In New Haven. This is confidential and I don't want the thing to be spoken of. But here my interest is to try to get as close to the ordinary, the commonplace and the ugly as it is possible for a poet to get. It is not a question of grim reality but of plain reality. The object is of course to purge oneself of anything false. I have been doing this since the beginning of March and intend to keep studying the subject and working on it until I am quite through with it. (*SL* 636–37)

Stripped of "anything false," *l'art brut*, Stevens's long poem strengthened his commitment to the commonplace. The poem surmounted his earlier frustrations to "achieve the normal," a task he once thought impossible.

Stevens's desire to turn away from slack or frivolous poetry that is purely imaginative animates the language of "Ordinary Evening." He wrote the poem after finishing a group of six poems that were not entirely rewarding to him, published as "A Half Dozen Small Pieces" in a Roman magazine.[22] According to Stevens, these poems were concerned with "such things as came into [his] head," as if he himself had been swayed by lunar light (*SL* 642). Stevens's letter to Barbara Church in July 1949 expresses a renewed desire to return to the "normal." The letter describes the very difficulties Stevens faced in writing "Ordinary Evening." He compares the group of six poems with the aim of his longer, more conscientiously written poem:

> I have just sent off a half dozen short poems to *Botteghe Oscure* of Rome. These were on such things as came into my head. They pleased me. But after a round of this sort of thing I always feel the need of getting some different sort of satisfaction out of poetry. Often when I am writing poetry I have in mind an image of reading a page of a large book: I mean the large page of a book. What I read is what I like. The things that I have just sent to Rome are not the sort of things that one would find on such a page. At least what one ought to find is normal life, insight into the commonplace, reconciliation with every-day reality. The things that it makes me happy to do are things of this sort. However, it is not possible to get away from one's own nature. (*SL* 642–43)

James Longenbach argues that in writing "Ordinary Evening," Stevens "return[s] to the easier task of a long meditative poem" rather than push himself "to establish that contact with the ordinary world" (294–95). Stevens's very last poems—the short lyrics like "The Course of a Particular"—were more of a challenge for him, Longenbach argues, and in their stark austerity these poems are more compelling than "Ordinary Evening" (293–306). I am suggesting that "Ordinary Evening" was not easy for Stevens but the culmination of a long-standing search for the commonplace, enacted by the structure of the poem itself. The length of the poem may indeed be a weakness, but a necessary one, as the subject itself resists conclusiveness. The commonplace as a literary style is thus a risky endeavor, allowing for a reader's own affective disinterest. In the above letter, Stevens imagines a reader's perspective; he wants to write poems specifically for the reader's pleasure, and his "large book" conjures up a small child's enjoyment of an oversize picture book. But Stevens's ability to write poems with "insight into the commonplace, reconciliation with the every-day" does not come easily to him, and he is unsure whether a reader will be compelled by this poetic aim. Furthermore, he acknowledges that the everyday cannot easily be represented without being transformed, a point that I emphasize in my epigraph from this letter:

> I am planning to stick to odds and ends until the end of August. I have been making promises right and left and I want to try to fulfill these. At the moment what I have in mind is a group of things which mean a good deal more than they sound like meaning: for instance, airing the house in the morning; the colors of sunlight on the side of the house; people in their familiar aspects. All this is difficult for me. It is possible that pages of insight and of reconciliation, etc. are merely pages of description. The trouble is that poetry is so largely a matter of transformation. To describe a cup of tea without changing it and without concerning oneself with some extreme aspect of it is not at all the easy thing that it seems to be. (*SL* 643)

Stevens seems to reassess his recently written poem in light of his initial intention, unsure whether "Ordinary Evening" successfully describes or changes the nature of the ordinary. How might a poem respect the simplicity of domestic light, the colors of a suburban house, the familiar habit of taking tea, without making any of these moments "extreme"? How might Stevens avoid the transformative power of metaphor, what the poem calls "the intricate evasions of as"?

"Ordinary Evening" considers the changes language effects upon experience itself, proposing that poetry can never exactly pin down, or master, what it is after. In the final canto of the poem ("The less legible meanings of sounds, the little reds"), Stevens composes a catalog of images that embody the elusive quality of the commonplace, the openness of experience in contrast to a "final form" that guides an individual through life:

> These are the edgings and inchings of final form,
> The swarming activities of the formulae
> Of statement, directly and indirectly getting at,
>
> Like an evening evoking the spectrum of violet,
> A philosopher practicing scales on his piano,
> A woman writing a note and tearing it up. (*CP* 488)

In comparison to the exactitude and precision that might characterize an objectivist poem, Stevens's list is revisionary, as if each image revises the one that precedes it, like a woman who tears up her first draft to start on another. The list form is a striking enactment of the elusiveness and democracy of the commonplace, as if items might be added or deleted or repeated later. And like one of Joyce's lists, the list here is a counterweight to the temptations of poetic metaphor. The poem acknowledges the allure of metaphor—the creative power of "like" and "as"—in lines suggestive of Barbara Church's travels:

> As it is, in the intricate evasions of as,
> In things seen and unseen, created from nothingness,
> The heavens, the hells, the worlds, the longed-for lands. (*CP* 486)

Fictions of longing are confronted by the world "As it is," marking a disjunction between romanticized desire (perhaps a certain conception of Europe) and ordinary experience (life in Hartford). The poem works to reveal the "nothingness" that stands behind longing, espousing ordinary experience as the only substantial truth; to crave something else (sublimity, divinity, some other place) constitutes an "evasion" of reality.

And yet language also becomes the power that gives life and makes meaning in a world without a god:

> The dry eucalyptus seeks god in the rainy cloud.
> Professor Eucalyptus of New Haven seeks him
> In New Haven with an eye that does not look
>
> Beyond the object. He sits in his room, beside
> The window, close to the ramshackle spout in which
> The rain falls with a ramshackle sound. He seeks
>
> God in the object itself, without much choice. (*CP* 475)

Desiring rain, the eucalyptus tree finds god in physical things: a rainy cloud, the weather of the world. But this is not divinity that lies "beyond the object"; rather, it exists in the most mundane "ramshackle" objects and sounds. Ordinary things should be the subjects of poems; the poem later explains that it is the "description that makes it divinity" (*CP* 475). This line might be read in a few ways: as a rejection of the kind of description that turns ordinary experience into something sublime, in the sense that metaphor evades reality. Or the poem may be redefining divinity altogether, extending Stevens's notion of divinity from earlier poems such as "Sunday Morning" and "The Idea of Order at Key West." "Divinity must live within herself," Stevens writes in the former poem, turning away from belief in transcendence beyond the physical self, and questioning the existence of heavenly life after death (*CP* 67). The ethos of "Ordinary Evening," however, is more resolute; the death of God leaves Professor Eucalyptus (no doubt a stand-in for Stevens) "without much choice"; his option is to turn to the earth, to commonplace experiences, as the only powerful substitute for the illusions of religious imagining.

"Ordinary Evening," it is clear, does not describe ordinary habits or employ ordinary language to describe the things of this world. Although the poem is ostensibly set on an autumn evening in a plain New Haven hotel, the poem thinks about the ordinary and explains its own preoccupations.

> We keep coming back and coming back
> To the real: to the hotel instead of the hymns
> That fall upon it out of the wind. We seek
>
> The poem of pure reality, untouched
> By trope or deviation, straight to the word,
> Straight to the transfixing object, to the object
>
> At the exactest point at which it is itself,
> Transfixing by being purely what it is,
> A view of New Haven, say, through the certain eye,
>
> The eye made clear of uncertainty, with the sight
> Of simple seeing, without reflection. We seek
> Nothing beyond reality . . . (*CP* 471)

Solace cannot be found in escaping the world through lofty "hymns." Rather, the "real" is located in the most banal, anonymous environments, a "hotel." The poem wants to hone in "straight to the transfixing object," avoiding visionary inspiration. Exactitude is achieved by not transforming experience through adornment, "trope or deviation." The clear eye sees New Haven certainly, in its barrenness. Or at least this is a desire that "We keep coming back and coming back / To."

Stevens's emphasis on the commonplace fundamentally differs from that of other modernist poets whose long poems employ ordinary language or theorize the ordinary, such as Williams's epic of the local, *Paterson,* or Gertrude Stein's celebration of the ordinary as a source of linguistic and domestic pleasure in *Tender Buttons.* While Stevens's work, like Stein's, has been read as reflecting Williams James's notion of perception, the formal diction and conventional syntax of "Ordinary Evening" has a gentler and more mannered effect than Stein's radical experiments with language or Williams's use of American vernacular, and in this sense his work is *closer* to the ordinary. Stevens is concerned less with upsetting grammatical norms than with contemplating commonplace experiences that language describes. Stevens's fabulous wordplay is part of his "never-ending meditation" on the ordinary, a style that shares something with Joyce's shifting styles in *Ulysses.* In fact, "Ordinary Evening" acknowledges that poetic attempts to represent the ordinary may objectify the ordinary, making it "extreme"—a consequence of colloquial language, with its grammatically imperfect or abrupt fragments of speech. This paradox challenges many poets concerned primarily with language's performance, with what language can *do.* As one practitioner of language poetry, Charles Bernstein, has put it, the attempt to represent actual speech through "ordinary" diction is always a move away from the ordinary. Ordinary language is actually a fetishized literary style. Bernstein points to the issue of "representation as objectification" as "the fly in the ointment of transparency," in the sense that objectification removes things from the very "flow of the ordinary, from its location in the everyday" ("Pour une critique," 13).[23] For Bernstein and other language poets, a kind of writing that attempts to break down this objectification of the ordinary becomes a major concern. Stevens circles around the issue. While he does not overtly question language's transparency, his method in the poem is always to move toward something unachievable, as his opening stanza states: "Of this, / A few words, an and yet, and yet, and yet—" (*CP* 465). Stevens avoids the colloquial altogether, crafting fresh phrases: "vulgate of experience," "crude collops," "sepulchral hollows," "perquisites of sanctity," "Paradisal parlance," "gay tournamonde." The last word is simply Stevens's own neologism, suggesting "an image of the world in which things revolve," as he explained (*SL* 699).

Stevens recognizes the paradox of representing ordinary experience but still trusts language as a means of revolving, turning around, exploring the ordinary. To come back again and again to the same idea, but expressed in a new vocabulary, demonstrates how one thinks about the commonplace and comes to understand it. As Cavell argues (through Wittgenstein), we bring words "back home" by trying them out, and this process is one of self-knowledge rather than metaphysics, acquired through new methods, practice, repetition (*Must We Mean,* 61–67). Fittingly, Stevens's satisfaction with the commonplace sustains his trust in language's ability to "transfix" our seeing through the repetitions of the poem itself. In one sense, language itself is a commonplace; we construct words in habitual ways, based on the rules of grammar, or "how to do things with words," in J. L. Austin's phrase.[24] To write poetry that foregrounds language's *in*ability to represent ordinary experience is to write poetry that must defy, above all, grammatical conventions. The modernist poet must do much more than simply respond to Pound's call to "make it new." Though Stevens aspires to dismantle the complacency of poetic observations, neologisms and fresh phrases are not enough to undermine the habits of language. But, it must be noted, this is not Stevens's real objective, as he knew when distancing himself from Eliot's "supreme cry of despair." Stevens finds the language of poetry a dependable medium for this late self-analysis. Language is an instrument of achievement, as declared in canto 12.

> The poem is the cry of its occasion,
> Part of the res itself and not about it.
> The poet speaks the poem as it is,
>
> Not as it was: part of the reverberation
> Of a windy night as it is . . . (*CP* 473–74)

The poem does not signify something; it is *part of* that something. Canto 12 ends: "Together, said words of the world are the life of the world" (*CP* 474). Poetic language is not transformative description but part of the thing it describes, part of experience itself.

Searching for something to fill a "nothingness" or "emptiness," "Ordinary Evening" circles around the commonplace and finds it a sufficient value (*CP* 486, 467). In a world that lacks the direction and order of traditional modes of belief, ordinary experiences become essential to the question, "What am I to believe?" as Stevens asks in "Notes." In "Sunday Morning," the question is phrased differently ("Why should she give her bounty to the dead?"), inspiring a medley of images of the earth: "Passions of rain, or moods in falling snow; / Grievings in loneliness, or unsubdued / Elations when the forest blooms" (*CP* 67). The images in "Ordinary Evening" are less mobile and varied. Color and change come up against a sedentary acceptance of more banal experiences. The power—the overriding conviction of the poem—derives from ordinariness as the sole entity left at the end of life, and a reconciliation with its centrality. There is no doubt that Stevens could imagine a world beyond everyday experience, but Stevens's late poems in particular seem conflicted about the possibility of a world of utter perfection, a world stripped of messy human desire where frailty and pain do not exist. An unknown place "In its permanent cold," as Stevens writes in "The Rock," ultimately lacks the pull of a world marked by constant change, by shifting aims, by the temporality of the everyday (*CP* 526). In "Esthétique du Mal," the poet conceives of "non-physical people, in paradise" who perhaps "experience / The minor of what we feel" (*CP* 325). This "minor" is certainly damning. Whether or not Wallace Stevens finally believed in an idea of heaven, in the last days of his life, the poignant knowledge of "Ordinary Evening" derives from its acknowledgment of the commonplace as the only "major" experience in which humans can fully trust.

If there is a sense of sadness or failure in "Ordinary Evening," it is an inevitable kind of failure if the commonplace is one's subject. As with the other modernist writers who experimented with how best to represent ordinary experience, Stevens finds that there is no final style, no conclusive mode to get at the kinds of experiences in which people live the bulk of their lives. "Diffuse and casual," Stevens called "Ordinary Evening," and "endlessly elaborating"—terms that fit other modernist styles that take a risk to "achieve" the ordinary—Steinian repetition, Joycean lists—as the ordinary is always just out of reach, vulnerable to transfiguration by the language used to describe it. Like Joyce, who does not trust the decontextualizing pull of epiphany, and like Woolf, who sees that heightened moments are always embedded in an ever-present "cotton wool," Stevens treats the commonplace as the steady state to which one will always return. Stevens merges his mode of poetic return with his lifelong dedication to the rhythms of work and home life. But of course, art and life can never be the same. A poem and a novel both come to an end no matter how ambiguous and open modernist endings can be. "It may be a shade that traverses / A dust, a force that traverses a shade," Stevens writes in the tentative, back-and-forth last lines of "Ordinary Evening," suggesting an entity that is both absent and forever felt, the dust of death and an ongoing journey (*CP* 489). Life continues on after the work of art has been made: Stevens's long, late poem motions a reader back to the diffuse, open-ended climate in which one lives.

# CONCLUSION

## Beginnings and Endings: Proust's Temporality and the Everyday

An infinity of things befall that one man, some of which it is impossible to reduce to unity; and in like manner there are many actions of one man which cannot be made to form one action.
—Aristotle, *Poetics*

In the last volume of Proust's *In Search of Lost Time,* a chance incident sparks a revelation that allows the narrator to arrive at a theory of art. The moment is pivotal and certainly one of Proust's most famous. Walking into the courtyard of the Guermantes mansion where a party is being held, the narrator trips against uneven paving stones to dodge an oncoming car and is suddenly unburdened of his present anxieties. Not unlike his earlier taste of the madeleine, this occurrence floods him with memories of the past, but this time he is much older and is "determined not to resign myself to a failure to understand them." Connecting the paving stones to the sensation of stepping on stones in the baptistery of St. Mark's in Venice, the narrator speaks of how atemporality—the simultaneity of past and present—is constructed arbitrarily by memory. He wonders how to capture this atemporality in narrative form, since life is constituted not by big moments but by smaller ones that are rarely remembered.

> At most I noticed cursorily that the differences which exist between every one of our real impressions—differences which explain why a uniform depiction of life

> cannot bear much resemblance to the reality—derive probably from the following cause: the slightest word that we have said, the most insignificant action that we have performed at any one epoch of our life was surrounded by, and coloured by the reflexion of, things which logically had no connexion with it and which later have been separated from it by our intellect which could make nothing of them for its own rational purposes. . . . The simplest act or gesture remains immured as within a thousand sealed vessels, each one of them filled with things of a colour, a scent, a temperature that are absolutely different one from another. (6:260)

The narrator understands that trivial moments are each defined by its own set of circumstances, isolated, and seemingly unrelated to one another (that's what makes them trivial), and yet he knows that he must bring these moments together to create the narrative of his life. "This distinctness of different events," he realizes, "would entail very considerable difficulties" (6:261). One of the difficulties—as the sheer length of *In Search of Lost Time* attempts to resolve—is the disjunction between the length of a novel, with its significant and interrelated events, and a fully lived life. *In Search of Lost Time* amplifies and distends its narrative to fit the temporality of the everyday, and yet the novel also recognizes the fundamental incompatibility of the everyday with narrative form.

Not unlike the narrator's ironic claim in the "Aeolus" chapter of *Ulysses* that the lighting of a cigarette "determined the whole after course of both our lives," the incompatibility of small, everyday events with the "course" of a narrative becomes in Proust's work a central theme. What I will explore in this concluding chapter is how the temporality of the everyday functions with and against narrative form, turning to *In Search of Lost Time* as a case in point but also bearing in mind how this relationship plays out in the modernist texts already discussed. As in the case of *Ulysses*, the everyday is unable to be systematized; by its nature, it is always open. Ordinary experiences do not always "signify" larger meanings, nor do they have Aristotelian beginnings, middles, and ends. Rather, the ordinariness of life is omnipresent and diffuse, so that to embrace the everyday is to embrace our inability to envision life as a narrative, for we cannot know the structure of how it will end.

To construct a work of art out of the everyday raises an essential problem of representation, a problem that animates and defines modernism's stylistic innovations. Despite the abundant resources of language, many modernist writers realized that ordinary experience cannot be rendered without being somewhat altered in the process of literary representation. If the everyday lacks a connective line that leads toward some finality—as Proust's narrator understands—then it is seemingly impossible to construct a work of art in which things are related in a cohesive fashion. "A uniform depiction of life," Proust's narrator notes in the passage above, "cannot bear much resemblance to the reality."[1] In the work of Wallace Stevens, a writer also interested in finding the "resemblance" between seemingly incompatible entities, a long, meandering poem such as "An Ordinary Evening in New Haven" becomes a method of eluding conclusions, of keeping the form of art open, of resisting a moment of summation. The final chiasmus of "Ordinary Evening" ("It may be a shade that traverses / A dust, a force that traverses a shade") suggests revisionary thought, like the back-and-forth movement of the poem itself. Poetry, in this respect, is arguably a more apt genre to represent the ordinary, despite its association, as Woolf argues, with inward and revelatory moments.

The uniformity of the nineteenth-century novel's classic three-volume structure, or six-month to two-year time frame, are the most obvious formal devices that many modernist writers abandoned. But on a more fundamental level, modernist representations of temporality can be viewed not only as a refutation of teleology, but as a response to the everyday's inability to be evened out or organized. The minutes of the day, chiming sixty minutes on the hour, mark time's dependable measure, like Big Ben over Woolf's London. But an individual's experience of time, as represented in *Mrs. Dalloway,* is not defined by this sense of measure. Rather, time contracts and expands based upon an individual's impression of it. As Bergson argued, we do not perceive of time as divided into regular increments. Summarizing the argument he put forth in *Time and Free Will* (1889), Bergson writes: "This imaginary homogenous time is . . . an idol of language, a fiction whose origin is easy to discover. In reality there is no one rhythm of duration; it is possible to imagine many different rhythms which, slower or faster, measure the degree of tension or relaxation of different kinds of consciousness and thereby fix their respective places in the scale of being" (*Matter,* 207). Deeply influenced (if not inspired) by Bergson, Proust's work illustrates the difference between the structural concept and human experience of time. "The time which we have at our disposal every day is elastic," Proust writes in volume 2, *Within a Budding Grove.* "The passions that we feel expand it, those that we inspire contract it; and habit fills up what remains" (2:257). For Proust's narrator, time is always in motion and flux, immeasurable, and eluding a narrative line.

Ordering time and seeing an end to time—measure and teleology—are closely related, in the sense that an end retrospectively allows the imposition of order on what precedes it, as if all events follow toward a particular conclusion. One recurrent strategy of organizing the temporality of the everyday—despite the narrator's ultimate recognition of this impossibility—is the repetition of trivial events into habits that allow for something like a beginning, middle, and end, in a more local manifestation, to occur over and over again. Habit "fills up what remains"; it is the constituent of time that does not expand or contract; it is the individual's *attempt* to regulate time, to control change. As William James sees it, habit embodies the human will acting in the world, imposing a constant system upon temporal flux. Habit lies at the heart of the Jamesian "man of action"; it has the characteristic of necessity in that certain behaviors must be done in a particular way. But habit has also been viewed less positively, as a manifestation of human weakness for order in the face of a much greater power. In his *Confessions,* Augustine most famously describes habits that hold him back from fully embracing God. In Latin, the word for habit is "consuetudo," a euphemism for marital intercourse that Augustine associates with his sin—seeking pleasure and sublimity not in God but in God's creatures (Chadwick, introduction, xvii). This attachment to the physical world of the present moment must be rejected, in Augustinian terms, in order to embrace a God that is defined in terms of eternal time. "You are before all things past and transcend all things future," Augustine writes, directing his address to God, who has no beginning and no end (230). Turning away from this radical and divine openness, habit is a temptation to repeat mini-narratives that bring humans immediate satisfaction.

Not unlike Augustine's battle with habit, Marcel's confession, in volumes five and six, situates Albertine at the center of his comfortable and self-protective domestic life. Living with him at home in Paris, Albertine is associated with "the heavy curtain of habit" that is rarely lifted to allow for the bright novelty of new sensations and fresh memories (5:732). Rather, she conceals the variable world beyond the window. Marcel's initial joy at finding Albertine's hat, coat or umbrella at the door (indicating that she is at home) is replaced after many months of cohabitation by his knowledge that the bars of light at Albertine's window trap both her and him in an "eternal slavery" of domestic everydayness (5:65, 445). And yet, Marcel's comfort with Albertine is also his mode of self-protection, a dynamic similar to how habit is often presented in modernist writing more broadly. The pleasures of habit are both life affirming and life denying, attractive because they are *safe.* The world of the knowable holds the individual back from a "spiritual" realm that Augustine defines as without measure. "We must constantly choose between health and sanity on the one hand, and spiritual pleasure on the other," Proust's narrator explains, "I have always been cowardly enough to choose the former" (5:159). To choose "health and sanity" is to choose a life of habit, protecting one's body and mind from spiritual revelations often catalyzed by change.

Ultimately, control over the vicissitudes of time is the narrator's deepest desire, a desire he feels when quite young. When his father first sanctions his future as a writer (an episode to which I will return), the narrator begins to feel time slipping away; no longer a child, but someone with a projected future, he is "not situated somewhere outside Time, but was subject to its laws" (2:74). Proustian habit—because it stabilizes temporality—quells the narrator's fear of not having enough time to accomplish his goals. Habits of sleep, of consumption, and of place, in particular, become his delusive crutch. But habits, paradoxically, are also the driving force behind temporal fluidity; the narrator is deeply aware that his habits have the double effect of deadening him to the very kinds of experiences that he cherishes. When a habit is broken, the past may flood open into memory and the narrator can move beyond the present tense. He is then finally able to write his life. Indeed, as he steps into the Guermantes courtyard, the narrator is aware that he has been "torn from my habits" and thus "was feeling a lively pleasure" (6: 253). This pleasure—as he commits himself to sustaining and understanding it—becomes his ability to finally pull together the chance, indiscriminate events of his life into narrative form, giving it a structure that both befits and defies the everyday.

Proustian habit is a noteworthy counterpoint to Gertrude Stein's use of habit, which creates "an existence suspended in time," as Stein described the method of her last works (*Transatlantic,* 103). Both Proust and Stein draw upon habit as a means of controlling time's teleology—a point that feminist critics of Stein's work have celebrated as a rejection of male linearity in favor of cyclic or repetitive time. But to live "suspended in time," for Stein, also means to live outside of history, for there is "nothing historical about this book except the state of mind," as the epilogue to *Mrs. Reynolds* claims (331). By sticking to their habits, Stein's characters attempt to live outside the historical moment of the Second World War, or more specifically, the Vichy regime in France. In this sense, Stein's late war writings are less concerned with *endings* than with escaping history, whereas in Proust's novel, habit is foremost a means of iterating and reiterating actions that have a particular necessity, that offer the delusion of controlling time by creating one's own beginning and end. Habits are not necessarily detached from a social and historical context, but as Robert Pippin has argued, the novel's concern with how the narrator arrives at self-knowledge is contingent upon how "one's self-image becomes a social fact through action" (*Persistence,* 318). Pippin argues that Proust's novel is an illustration of how the individual needs to *fail* at "becoming who you are" before knowing that he is on the right track. In this sense, the revelations of involuntary memory—which pull the narrator out of context—should not be valued any more than the narrator's "long experience, profound struggle, and negotiations with others" (*Persistence,* 308, 311). From the telegraph and railway to the Dreyfus Affair and the onset of the First World War, Proustian habits are engaged with a specific historical world. No wonder, then, that the epiphany on the paving-stones at the start of the novel's last volume does not immediately mark a change in Marcel's life. Like Rilke's *you must change your life,* the moment does not clarify, for Marcel, the nature of the necessary change. It takes several hundred pages until Marcel begins to write. During this period, what Marcel has realized about time's atemporality must be integrated into a temporal world—a world in which Marcel must make time to write. In this respect, Proust (like Joyce) disavows the revelations of the epiphanic moment in favor of the social and material context from which the epiphany emerges and must return.

And yet, to construct a narrative of habit, *In Search of Lost Time* often obscures a precise presentation of time and place. A reader may be unaware of Marcel's age during certain "big" experiences mentioned only in passing (his first sexual experience, his first dual, Swann's death); or only in retrospect can events be ordered "before" and "after." Proust's novel recognizes that habits do not really control time: habits are small narratives within a larger narrative of social and historical time. So although the novel offers a sweeping and shrewd depiction of fin-de-siècle French culture and society, it also aims to avoid a clear sense of beginnings and endings, of placement in time in relation to Marcel's own life. As many critics have noted, Proust's sustained use of the *imparfait* creates an aura of changelessness, especially regarding Marcel's childhood. For instance, note the narrator's description of Saturday lunch in Combray, an event that becomes its own "asymmetrical" custom because it takes place an hour earlier than usual:

> C'est ainsi que tous les samedis, comme Françoise allait dans l'après-midi au marché de Roussainville-le-Pin, le déjeuner était pour tout le monde, une heure plus tôt. Et ma tante avait si bien pris l'habitude de cette dérogation hebdomadaire à ses habitudes, qu'elle tenait a cette habitude-là autant qu'aux autres. Elle y était si bien "routinée," comme disait Françoise, que s'il lui avait fallu un samedi, attendre pour déjeuner l'heure habituelle, cela l'eût autant "dérangée" que si elle avait dû, un autre jour, avancer son déjeuner à l'heure du samedi. (95)
>
> Thus, for instance, every Saturday, as Françoise had to go in the afternoon to market at Rousainville-le-Pin, the whole household would have to have lunch an hour earlier. And my aunt had so thoroughly acquired the habit of this weekly exception to her general habits, that she clung to it as much as to the rest. She was so well "routined" to it, as Françoise would say, that if, on a Saturday, she had had to wait for her lunch until the regular hour, it would have "upset" her as much as if on an ordinary day she had had to put her lunch forward to its Saturday hour. (1:153)

In this passage, the *imparfait* appropriately establishes the way that Aunt Leonie depends on the continuity of household habits—they should not change; they should not end. She relies upon habits to organize her week, to repeat familiar beginnings and endings, like grooves in time. Other events that presumably happened with frequency (the nighttime kiss, walks around Combray, playing at the Champs-Elysées) are similarly described in the *imparfait,* but described just once, as the narration assumes that these events happened multiple times—that they were, in fact, habits. As Franco Moretti has noted in his study of nineteenth-century "filler," the *imparfait* is a "tense that promises no surprises; the tense of repetition, ordinariness, the background—but a background that has becomes more significant than the foreground itself" ("Serious," 378). Proust's use of the *imparfait,* despite signaling repetition, is bound up in the paradox of representing the ordinary—it becomes significant.

Gérard Genette calls this type of narration "iterative narration," noting that Proust's "richness and precision of detail" make it hard for any reader to believe that these events happened more than once (121). When habits are narrated with such attention and care, they become the "pseudo-iterative," a prevalent characteristic of the modern novel from Genette's point of view. The pseudo-iterative perhaps most obviously marks the difficulty of describing the ordinary without it seeming like a once-in-a-lifetime phenomenon. Ultimately, in attributing a beginning, middle, and end to habit, the pseudo-iterative imposes a narrative form upon the ordinary, sacrificing the possibility of narrating the ordinary without it seeming extraordinary. The same could be said about *Mrs. Dalloway,* a novel that savors experiences that seemingly happen all of the time (buying flowers, taking a nap), though the English language does not have a verb tense that negotiates a middle ground between the simple past and the progressive past. For Proustian repetition, on occasion, is also signified by a distinctive use of the *passé composé* or *passé simple.* The famous first sentence, describing a habit of going to bed early, is composed conspicuously in the *passé composé:* "Longtemps, je me suis couché de bonne heure." Thus, the claim could also be made that *In Search of Lost Time* offers a reader a profound sense of when experiences begin and end, given the fact that certain habitual events are narrated definitively in the past, and emerge palpably from the long stretches of *imparfait.* The fact that both claims can be made about the novel (Time seems to have no beginning and no end *and* Beginnings and endings are clearly demarcated) underscores the novel's balancing act between small narratives of habit and an acceptance of the everyday's essential openness.

Another modernist literary strategy for representing habit is the repetition of certain phrases and descriptions signifying that an event occurs multiple times. Linguistic repetition enacts a character's physical repetitions, and imparts to the reader the actual feel of an action happening more than once. This representation of habit marks Stein's late wartime writings and is also a defining feature of Beckett's work, which has a fundamental connection back to Proust. Haunted by endings that never occur, many of Beckett's characters exist in a state of self-imposed repetitions, attempting to impose order on a terrifying openness—what the narrator of *How It Is* calls "vast tracts of time" (107). Lying immobile in the mud, this narrator repeats phrases as he repeats the same bodily functions, hoping for an end to his misery. But the final words of the text—"comment c'est," as originally written in French—of course sustain the repetitions all over again, and pun on "commencer" or more likely "commencez," a command to the reader to restart, as if unending suffering cannot be avoided. Suffering is "how it is." Similarly in Beckett's one-act play titled *Play* (1962), the last words spoken in the verbal love-triangle mark the fundamental inability to come to an end. "Repeat, Play," one of the talking heads in an urn utters, and the play is repeated for a second time, identical to the first. *Répétition* is indeed rehearsal, as the French word signifies, making life into a theatrical event, as if life has an aesthetic unity that yet cannot be achieved. Both of these works rest on the premise that human beings cannot control their natural ends—cannot make life into art—though they will not stop trying (and talking), and though they are acutely aware that life *will* end. Both Beckett and Proust, whom Beckett so much admired, suggest that the finality of the artistic work is, in a sense, an affront to the very openness of living.

Proust's narrator knows that his own narrative is uniquely formed by his lack of knowledge of how it will end—so that the ending of *In Search of Lost Time* (if this is indeed the work that the narrator writes) of course folds back upon itself, much like a work of Beckett's. In several instances, the narrator muses upon the futility of trying to locate beginnings and endings, usually in connection with his love for Albertine or with desire more generally. He is critical of the way *The Captive* opens (a description of him lying in bed), calling it "mendacious flimsiness," though he cannot decide how else to begin (5:250). He admits to being "forced to whittle down the facts, and to be[ing] a liar," since the multitude of phenomena that he could narrate ultimately compel him to limit and thus falsify the events of his life (5:250). Indeed, when his father acknowledges, in Volume 2, that his son will most likely become a writer, Marcel feels a terror, caused by the idea of limiting life to narrative form, or more specifically, seeing his *own* life in terms of a narrative. The passage reveals the narrator's precocious and self-deprecating sense of humor about his lifelong preoccupation:

> I was not situated somewhere outside of Time, but was subject to its laws, just like those characters in novels who, for that reason, used to plunge me into such gloom when I read of their lives. . . . Novelists are obliged, by wildly accelerating

> the beat of the pendulum, to transport the reader in a couple of minutes over ten, or twenty, or even thirty years. . . . In saying of me, "he's no longer a child," "his tastes won't change now," and so forth, my father had suddenly made me conscious of myself in Time, and caused me the same kind of depression as if I had been, not yet the enfeebled old pensioner, but one of those heroes of whom the author, in a tone of indifference, which is particularly galling, says to us at the end of a book: "He very seldom comes up from the country now. He has finally decided to end his days there." (2:74–75)

Marcel imagines himself from the point of view of his father, who now regards his son as more of an artist than a future diplomat. Acknowledging this vocation requires seeing himself in terms of a projected narrative, but Marcel cannot align his experiences with those of a literary character. The projection of his life as a narrative precludes the openness of what will come next, and precludes the real uncertainty of how it will end. Thus to imagine his life in narrative terms, he must imagine some sort of death, in this case, the feeble and pathetic death of a character abandoned by his author, or his father. The moment parallels his mother's "first abdication" with the goodnight kiss, in which "the ideal she had formed for me" is relinquished in light of her son's "involuntary ailment" (1:51, 50). Ultimately, to see his life through his parents' prescient eyes does not correspond to Marcel's aesthetic sense. His artistic proclivities, in this respect, are entirely different from the conditions laid out by Norpois, the ex-ambassador and family friend with whom the family has just dined. Norpois disparages the lack of "structure," "action," and "foundation" in Bergotte's writing, which of course is an indictment of the very style of narrative that the young Marcel emulates (2:61). The first to pass judgment on Marcel's early writing (a judgment that makes Marcel feel his "intellectual nullity and that [he] was not cut out for the literary life" [2:63]), Norpois is a powerful cultivating influence, albeit old-fashioned. Ultimately, Marcel comes to understand the limitations of Norpois' point of view and to ridicule the man. Marcel seeks a narrative form that resists the regimented structure Norpois champions.

The emotions, in particular, do not respond to narrative structure. To feel desire, or love (or ambivalence) is not to understand when these feelings begin and end. The narrator nonetheless *tries* to pinpoint moments in time when particular feelings emerge, though he finds this kind of "retrospective arrangement," as Joyce might call it, nearly impossible:

> When one wants to remember in what manner one began to love a woman, one is already in love with her; daydreaming about her beforehand, one did not say to

> oneself: "This is a prelude to love; be careful!"—and one's day-dreams advanced unobstrusively, scarcely noticed by oneself. (5:197)

Continuous, an individual's emotions cannot be divided into units of measure. Clear causes and effects that might explain the constitution of his interior self, or contribute to a *bildungsroman,* seem utterly impossible for Proust's narrator to put together. Of course, it is temporal distance that eases the pain of desire or loss, as he acknowledges when reflecting on the fact that he no longer cares deeply for his childhood love, Gilberte, and fading emotion will no doubt mark his feelings about Albertine. What is so striking, then, is that time and habit are conflated in their ability to deaden the narrator to his most fully felt emotions. In the quest to control the narrative of his life—and to give order to the emotions that seem by nature without beginning or end—time becomes a series of habits. The role of art (particularly the novel), as Proust's narrator explains in the last volume, is to undo these habits, to undo time, and to understand life itself: "When we have arrived at reality, we must, to express it and preserve it, prevent the intrusion of all those extraneous elements which at every moment the gathered speed of habit lays at our feet" (6:302). The paradox is that the narrator has composed his life by means of habit, so to undo habit is to undo his very existence. There is no real possibility of having "arrived at reality," a phrase that implies an endpoint, for reality is bound into time.

But what would happen if we could actually know how and when our lives will end? If an end were in sight, would it be possible to live outside of time? Marcel has the occasion to muse upon this possibility. The letter he receives notifying him of Albertine's death instigates his long meditation on how a foreknowledge of her death (which happens in a sudden riding accident) might have changed her actions. If Albertine knew that she was going to die so soon after she left him, Marcel surmises, then she would not have left him. This conjecture seems to soothe his profound sense of loss (5:690). That is, in thinking about her death, he thinks about the narrative of her life, and how differently that narrative would have been constructed had she known the ending. The artifice of this construction—never mind its perversity—satisfies him, largely because his awareness of life's lack of structure, ultimately, is what keeps him from writing down his life.

Coming to terms with discontinuity and openness, it could be said, is the theme of Proust's grand narrative. Although there is undoubtedly architecture behind Proust's voluminous novel, there is also a radical lack of a guiding order, a feature with which most readers must come to terms.[2] Beckett (in accord with a steady current of criticism about the novel) found the formal elements of

*Swann's Way* strange, if not artificial: "[Proust] has every kind of subtle equilibrium, charming trembling equilibrium and then suddenly a stasis," he wrote, noting that "the arms of the balance wedged in a perfect horizontal line," were "heavily symmetrical" (quoted in Knowlson, *Damned,* 121). Gilles Deleuze, on the far end of another line of thinking about Proust's novel (which is, in many ways, a deconstructionist's dream) argues that *In Search of Lost Time* is conscious of its own incompletion. "When Proust compares his work to a cathedral or to a gown," Deleuze writes, "it is not to identify himself with a Logos as a splendid totality but, on the contrary, to emphasize his right to incompletion, to seams and patches" (161). Alternatively, Roger Shattuck describes the construction of *In Search of Lost Time* as "simple and as sturdy as that of a suspension bridge" (xv). Shattuck emphasizes two sustained features that give shape to the novel: the walking paths in Combray, marking (among other things) two different ways of life that converge in the novel's last volume; and Proust's use of the pronoun "I" to denote both the protagonist (whose name, Marcel, is mentioned twice) and the mature adult who narrates events. The way in which Marcel *becomes* the narrator holds the work together, Shattuck argues, as the "I" "projects a stereoscopic perspective" by which a reader is carried both backward and forward (162).

In my mind, the thematic unities of *In Search of Lost Time* are sustained and developed while the structural unity of the novel remains gorgeously uneven, as if modeling an uncontainable life in which one will never know how much time remains. In this sense, the middle of the novel is crucial, opening up between two points that *must* be arbitrary, spanning a bridge that is far from perfectly arched. While Shattuck finds a symmetry in the way that the novel's perspectives collapse into one (Marcel becoming the narrator of the book we are reading), other critics have rightly suggested that we cannot trust that *In Search of Lost Time* is the book that Marcel sets out to write. Antoine Compagnon describes *In Search of Lost Time* as "the product of an enormous act of procrastination" and suggests that "the book we have is rather the postponement of that other one" (270). Similarly, Joshua Landy argues that *In Search of Lost Time* cannot be the narrator's masterpiece for two reasons: "He is not about to write it because he has already written it," and "what he has already written is not a novel, but only (from his point of view) a memoir" (40). Proust's novel, in this respect, demands that we distinguish between literature and life, as the narrator sets forth to write a work of literature that emerges from his life, but does not (and cannot) contain *all* of it. Despite the narrator's fixation on this point, readers and critics of *In Search of Lost Time* have assumed and argued otherwise, as if life itself can conform to a work of literature.

Alexander Nehamas has argued compellingly that Proust's narrator is the perfect embodiment of the person who fashions his "life as literature," to quote the title of Nehamas's book on Nietzsche.[3] Nehamas connects the Proustian narrator's self-fashioning with Nietzsche's idea of the eternal recurrence, which Nehamas understands neither in terms of history repeating itself nor in terms of the nature of the universe. Rather, eternal recurrence is "not a theory of the world but a view of the ideal life," Nehamas writes. "It holds that a life is justified only if one would want to have again the same life one had already had, since, as the will to power shows, no other life can ever be possible" (*Nietzsche*, 6–7). This interpretation of eternal recurrence is contingent upon the idea that the present moment holds all of the past and future within it. The present could not exist unless everything previous to it happened precisely as it did; the present moment leads to a future that is similarly organic. "Nothing that ever happens to us," Nehamas interprets Nietzsche, "even if it is the result of the most implausible accident and the wildest coincidence, is contingent—once it has occurred" (149). Drawing upon Proust's narrator as an example, Nehamas quotes the narrator's realization in *Time Regained* for the epigraph of his own book: "And I understood that all these materials for a work of literature were simply my past life" (6:304).

As an authority on Nietzsche, Nehamas's interpretation of eternal recurrence is both striking in its originality and convincing in its application to Nietzsche's own life and work, especially as the development of Nietzsche's philosophy can be read as subsequent self-interpretations of his life, which Nietzsche also shaped through his compulsive epistolary correspondence. But in applying this interpretation of eternal recurrence to Proust's novel, Nehamas acknowledges only a part of what the narrator, at the end, has to say about the relationship between indiscriminate events and narrative form. Certainly, the narrator sees the possibility of making his loose and formless life into something with meaning, something that has in fact been *willed.* While "all the materials for a work of literature" come from his past life, the problem nonetheless remains that *all* of his past life cannot make it into his work of literature. Insignificant events—unmemorable, isolated, each with a "colour, a scent, a temperature"—must contribute to a life that is fashioned into a work of art, but this is not how narratives are normally made. That is, insignificant events have been chosen for narration because of their *seeming* insignificance, but they always achieve significance through narrative representation. Ultimately, the everyday exposes the limitations of narrative form; according to Aristotle, "that which makes no perceptible difference by its presence or absence is no real part of the whole" (635).

The narrator does not experience the "distinct" events of his life as wholly connected. Herein lies the difference between art and life: we are unable to view life as an organic shape because we cannot retrospectively assess its completion. Not until we die, if then (and only for others), can life be shaped into an Aristotelian "whole." Proust, more than Nietzsche, is willing to allow for moments in life that are difficult to connect with one another, that do not constitute a perfectly balanced form. While Proust values the way in which literature deepens our experience of life, or the way that "literature establishes the terms in which later events will be met," as Shattuck has suggested (228), Proust nonetheless champions the significance of life—as the narrator comes to understand himself through living it—beyond the model that art offers.

Proust's narrator constructs his life into a narrative of habit as a means of giving temporary shape to a life, like all lives, that changes continually over the course of time. But even as he relies upon habit as a safe repetition of past satisfactions, he knows that his sense of repetition is false. Habit is a curtain, like Albertine's eyes, veiling "almost the whole universe" beyond the window (5:732). If an event can never repeat itself exactly, but is marked by its unique duration in time, then habit's function is to cover up the startling reality of continual change. In this sense, habit is like the balm of envisioning one's life in narrative terms—or imposing a known narrative structure upon one's life. Both, the narrator knows, cannot be trusted. Comparing his grief over Albertine's departure with Swann's grief over Odette, the narrator explains how his grief is different, even as the narrative urges us to draw a symmetrical link, like points on a bridge, between Swann and Marcel. Marcel's bedroom captivity similarly summons up the life of his Aunt Leonie, like two more joined points. But life cannot conform to the parallels we make in literature: "For nothing ever repeats itself exactly, and the most analogous lives which, thanks to kinship of character and similarity of circumstances, we may select in order to represent them as symmetrical, remain in many aspects opposed" (5:673). This sentiment of opposition—that moments in time are antagonistic to unity—chafes against the narrator's real task of pulling all the ordinary moments of his life together into a novel. The organic unity of a work of art not only seems impossible, but untrue. And so Proust's work of art adapts itself to the shape of a life that is, like the paving stones, uneven and unexpected.

# Notes

## Introduction

1. Important accounts of modernism—and modernist realism—describe modernism's "highly subjectivist premises" (Eysteinsson, *Concept of Modernism,* 27) and a turn from the "objective reality" of the nineteenth-century novel to modernism's "decadent" subjective experience" (Lukacs, *Realism* 19). Fredric Jameson similarly characterizes modernism's "strategies of inwardness," including its "personal styles and private languages" (*Fables of Aggression,* 2). Along these lines, the Marxist critique of modernism generally asserts that modernism represents a withdrawal to privacy, a denial of history, and a privileging of subjectivity.

2. One exceptional study is Bryony Randall's recent *Modernism, Daily Time, and Everyday Life,* which dwells particularly on the temporal dimensions of dailiness and its relationship to gender. Randall argues that daily time is a formal *structure* and that the everyday is *content,* or a range of practices to which one pays a particular kind of attention (2). Alternatively, my three categories emphasize the distinction among moments that are treated with heightened attention (the epiphany) from the moments that spark no such revelation—only the latter I treat as "ordinary."

3. See Sianne Ngai's *Ugly Feelings.*

4. I use the terms "ordinary" and "everyday" fairly interchangeably throughout this book. French theorists of the 1950s and 1960s generally tend to speak of the "everyday," and Wittgenstein, J. L. Austin, and Stanley Cavell usually speak of the "ordinary," specifically ordinary language. Although there are considerable differences among all of these thinkers, the everyday and the ordinary are closely connected concepts.

5. For a discussion of lists and catalogs in Joyce, see Senn, "Entering the Lists"; Benstock, "Cataloging"; and Hugh Kenner's *Stoic Comedians.*

6. See Wolfgang Iser's reading of *Marius the Epicurean* in *Walter Pater: The Aesthetic Moment.*

7. Jonathan Levin explores Stevens's "pragmatist imagination" in *The Poetics of Transition: Emerson, Pragmatism, and American Literary Modernism.* Many other critics, including Frank Lentricchia and Richard Poirier, have called attention to Stevens's inheritance of pragmatist thought, though no one specifically discusses the relationship between Stevens's pragmatism and his preoccupation with the ordinary.

8. See Edward Duffy for a sharply critical overview of Cavell's work, particularly the moral fervor behind Cavell's project of "redeeming" the ordinary.

9. There are important differences between the philosophies of James and Bergson. As Randall points out, Bergson views habit less positively than does James (*Modernism,* 44). But both thinkers ultimately believed that habit is fundamental to the promotion of social relations.

10. See *Yale French Studies* 73, a special issue titled "Everyday Life," edited by Alice Kaplan and Kristin Ross, that includes essays by Lefebvre, Blanchot, and Baudrillard. See also Richard Johnson's "What Is Cultural Studies Anyway?" Johnson argues that cultural studies began when its practitioners "turned [their] assessments from literature to everyday life" (38). For a more recent application of everyday life theory to a broad range of fields, see *New Literary History* 33.4. See also the online journal *Modernist Cultures,* which titled its spring 2006 issue "Modernism and the Everyday."

11. Georges Perec attempted to rewrite *Ulysses* in a work titled *Le Portulen,* which would follow two friends as they visited various drinking establishments one night in Paris. But the work of Perec, who knew both Barthes and Lefebvre, best embodies a commitment to the ideas of French everyday life theory. *Les Choses* describes a young couple's desire to have all of the possessions that they associate with good living. *La Vie mode d'emploi* catalogs the interiors of a ten-story building in Paris, recognizing the difficulty of tracking what essentially slips away, what is "practically untellable," as Lefebvre describes it.

12. See Doug Mao's *Solid Objects: Modernism and the Test of Production* for a fuller discussion of how many modernist writers found pleasure in the "objects" of mass production while also demonstrating an essential distrust of capitalism's structures.

13. I thank Nicholas Dames for this striking suggestion.

14. As Rey Chow has argued, appealing to the everyday as either the "bedrock of reality" (as Lefebvre might do) or as "collective false consciousness" is a ploy both predictable and arbitrary; each idea loads the everyday with a predetermined agenda ("Sentimental Returns," 639).

15. See also E. P. Thompson's *Customs in Common* for an exploration of British working-class customs as both deferential and rebellious in the eighteenth and nineteenth centuries.

16. The association between women and the everyday nonetheless persists. Randall revisits the association by looking at how dailiness functions in the work of Richardson, Stein, and Woolf. Randall accounts for the productive aspects of everyday reverie, often associated with the feminine, but this state of dispersed attention, in my account, constitutes men's everyday lives as well.

17. See Victoria Rosner's *Modernism and the Architecture of Private Life* for a compelling analysis of the generative value of interior spaces for modernism.

18. See Franco Moretti's essay "Serious Century," included in the English version of his anthology *The Novel.* See also his "The Moment of Truth" in *Signs Taken for Wonder,* and "The Comfort of Civilization" in *The Way of the World.*

19. For a further discussion of these ideas, see Auerbach's "Figura" in *Scenes from the Drama of European Literature* and the first chapter of *Mimesis.*

20. Woolf specifically cites Biffen's manifesto in her review of Gissing's *oeuvre.* See "The Novels of George Gissing."

21. See Naomi Schor's *Reading in Detail* for the argument that "detail" has been historically associated with the feminine.

22. For an extended discussion of Eliot's defense of Dutch painting, especially in opposition to Ruskin, see Ruth Yeazell's *Art of the Everyday: Dutch Painting and the Realist Novel.*

23. See Alexander Nemerov's "The Flight of Form" for a trenchant reading of how Auden's poem remakes Bruegel's painting. According to Nemerov, the self-absorbed plowman depicted in the painting, oblivious to the sufferings of others, is for Auden "the modern intellectual at the end of the 1930s" (793).

24. See Glen MacLeod's *Wallace Stevens and Modern Art* for a catalog of paintings in Stevens's personal art collection.

25. See, in particular, Stevens's 1935 essay on Moore, "A Poet That Matters."

26. Recent critical studies have rightly looked at the immanence of objects as they appear not just in modern poetry, but also in fiction. See Doug Mao's *Solid Objects: Modernism and the Test of Production,* Bill Brown's *A Sense of Things: The Object Matter of American Literature,* and John Erikson's *The Fate of the Object: From Modern Object to Postmodern Sign in Performance, Art, and Poetry.* For a discussion of "things" as they first emerged in eighteenth-century fiction, see Cynthia Wall's *The Prose of Things: Transformations of Description in the Eighteenth Century.*

27. World Wars I and II play a prominent role in most of Stein's works from the mid-1920s until her death, including *The Autobiography of Alice B. Toklas, Everybody's Autobiography, Paris France, Wars I Have Seen, Brewsie and Willie,* and *Mrs. Reynolds.*

28. Stein also seems to hope that the young students listening to her lecture might receive her work with an appreciative understanding of its relevance and meaning. See John Whittier-Ferguson's "The Liberation of Gertrude Stein: War and Writing."

29. See Sandra Gilbert and Susan Gubar's three-volume work on modernism and gender, *No Man's Land,* which extends Paul Fussell's paradigm of the "binary deadlock" of trench warfare by arguing that war aggravates gender binaries. See also Modris Eksteins's *Rites of Spring: The Great War and the Birth of the Modern Age,* which emphasizes the energy of the avant-garde movements in Germany at the turn of the century and after in contrast with England's desire for peace and order. More recently, Vincent Sherry's *The Great War and the Language of Modernism* widens Fussell's and Eksteins's accounts by looking at how British Liberalism responded to the First World War and impacted the writers of the period.

30. See "The Camp as Biopolitical Paradigm of the Modern," part 3 of Giorgio Agamben's *Homo Sacer: Sovereign Power and Bare Life.*

31. See Koenraad Geldolf's "The Unbearable Literariness of Literature: Spectral Marxism and Metaphysical Realism in Charles Taylor's *Sources of the Self.*"

32. See Stevens's statement on the front flap of the dust jacket for *The Man with the Blue Guitar and Other Poems,* reprinted in *Opus Posthumous.*

33. See Dominic Manganiello's *Joyce's Politics* for a discussion of the extent of Joyce's pacifism and anarchism. See Robert Spoo, "'Nestor' and the Nightmare," for

an extended discussion of how the chapter "Nestor" resonates in context of the First World War.

## Chapter One

1. It is possible to draw upon a line of thinking exemplified by Jean Baudrillard—and extended by Fredric Jameson in his work on *Ulysses*—to understand Joyce's objects as detached from their function, proliferating into pure signs. But my argument, here, upholds Joyce's continuity with naturalism.

2. For a thorough study of the nature and extent of Ibsen's influence upon Joyce, see B. J. Tysdahl's *Joyce and Ibsen.* See Schenker for a discussion of the nature of Joyce's irony as indebted to Ibsen. Also see Hugh Kenner's "Joyce and Ibsen's Naturalism."

3. *Ulysses* qualifies as an "encyclopedic narrative," according to Edward Mendelson's definition of the genre. See his "Encyclopedic Narrative: From Dante to Pynchon."

4. Pater's influence on Joyce's style and on modernist writing more generally is addressed by Denis Donoghue in *Walter Pater: Lover of Strange Souls* and by Perry Meisel in *The Myth of the Modern.* See also Frank Moliterno's *The Dialectics of Sense and Spirit in Pater and Joyce* for a more specific account of what Joyce read and responded to in Pater.

5. Stephen draws upon Flaubert's image of the artist as a "god," but the passage also echoes the second aphorism at the start of *The Picture of Dorian Gray:* "To reveal art and conceal the artist is art's aim" (138).

6. Joyce's lectures in Trieste are the constant reference in commentaries on his politics, but, as Derek Attridge points out, they have been read as both strongly supportive of Irish nationalism and highly critical of it. See Attridge's introduction to *Semicolonial Joyce.* Also see G. J. Watson's argument that *Ulysses* specifically deconstructs the mythology of "romantic Ireland."

7. See Toril Moi's *Henrik Ibsen and the Birth of Modernism* for a discussion of how *The Wild Duck* questions the role of idealism in everyday life and examines the utility of ordinary language.

8. See, for instance, Zack Bowen's "Joyce and the Epiphany Concept" and Theodore Spencer, who understands the theory of epiphany as the guiding principle throughout Joyce's entire *oeuvre,* arguing that Joyce "shows forth" in degrees of magnitude (introduction to *Stephen Hero,* 16–17).

9. See Hugh Kenner's *The Stoic Comedians.*

10. Kenner argues that Joyce never believed in the "myth" of Ulysses, but was primarily interested in "a man who lived and fought and voyaged," as contemporary archeological scholarship was revealing (65). See "Beyond Objectivity" in Kenner's *Joyce's Voices* (1978). See also Michael Seidel's *Epic Geography,* which traces Joyce's use of Victor Bérard's *Les Phéniciens et l'Odyssée,* the source Joyce depended upon for mapping the movements in *Ulysses.* Seidel suggests that Joyce was particularly attracted to Bérard's claim that *Odysseus* was a Semitic-Greek wanderer.

11. See Jennifer Levine's "Ulysses" and chapter 4 of Kenner's *Joyce's Voices* for arguments against Joyce's privileging of myth in *Ulysses.*

12. See Derek Attridge's "The Postmodernity of Joyce: Chance, Coincidence, and the Reader" in his *Joyce Effects.*

13. Kenner points out that the budget omits any mention of transactions from "Circe" which Bloom would want to keep from Molly, including tram fare to the red light district. See Kenner's "Circe."

14. See Colin MacCabe's *James Joyce and the Revolution of the World* and Phillip Herring's *Joyce's Uncertainty Principle.* Margot Norris's recent work on *Dubliners* and *Ulysses* relies less on the purely structuralist approach that she took to *Finnegans Wake;* see her "Joyce's Heliotrope" and *Suspicious Readings of Joyce's* Dubliners.

15. As he was composing the first chapters of *Ulysses,* Joyce tried his hand at writing an Ibsen-like drama, *Exiles*—a fact that suggests how Joyce found Ibsen's genre a suitable form for the commonplace, even as he was experimenting with remarkably different styles in *Ulysses.* The physical nature of drama, however, does not solve the paradox of the ordinary: the mass of represented details in *Ulysses,* for instance, corresponds to the clutter of the naturalist stage. A tactile "reality" is yet "de-realized" by its representative nature.

16. See chapter 7 in Kenner's monograph on *Ulysses* for a discussion of the novel's narration as produced by at least three different voices, including a voice generated by the text itself. David Hayman, in *Ulysses: The Mechanics of Meaning,* coined the name "the Arranger," and Christopher Butler has more recently argued that in *Ulysses* we are reminded "not of the author's disappearance but of his varying status, and of the cunning ways in which his hand may be hidden" (71). Karen Lawrence refers to the novel's "consciousness or mind of the text," especially prominent in the second half of *Ulysses,* as the third-person narrative style is abandoned and "style goes 'public,' as language is flooded by the memory of its prior use" (*Odyssey of Style,* 184, 8).

17. See Julia Kristeva's, "Joyce's 'The Gracehoper' or Orpheus' Return" and Barthes' *The Pleasure of the Text.*

18. See Arthur Power, *Conversations,* 44–46.

19. See Frank Kermode's *Sense of an Ending.*

## Chapter Two

1. "So that is her problem. She is a poet, who wants to write something as near to a novel as possible," Forster writes in *Virginia Woolf,* his somewhat hesitant tribute to her, after her death (23).

2. I follow recent scholarship that assumes Woolf's work is deeply engaged with a world beyond the inner workings of "the mind," including Woolf as a public intellectual (Melba Cuddy-Keane, *Virginia Woolf, the Intellectual*), Woolf's response to war and politics (Vincent Sherry, *The Great War;* Christine Froula, *Virginia Woolf and the Bloomsbury Avant-Garde*), and Woolf's anti-imperialism and racial attitudes (Jane Marcus, *Hearts of Darkness*). See also Victoria Rosner's *Modernism and the Architecture of Private Life,* in which the idea of the modernist "interior" is considered as both a physical space and a nonmaterial reality.

3. "A Letter to a Young Poet" was specifically addressed to Lehmann, who showed it to Auden, Spender, and Day Lewis. The examples Woolf chooses are not the poets' best. She noticeably ignores Auden, no doubt the finest poet in the group. See Cuddy-Keane (*Virginia Woolf, the Intellectual,* 96–114) for an analysis of the essay's rhetoric and its reception.

4. In "Mr. Bennett and Mrs. Brown," Woolf writes: "Mr. Joyce's indecency in *Ulysses* seems to me the conscious and calculated indecency of a desperate man who feels that in order to breathe he must break the windows. At moments, when the window is broken, he is magnificent. But what a waste of energy! And, after all, how dull indecency is, when it is not the overflowing of a superabundant energy or savagery, but the determined and public-spirited act of a man who needs fresh air!" (116). In her diary, Woolf described Joyce as "a queasy undergraduate scratching his pimples" (*WD* 2:188–89).

5. See Hermione Lee's chapter "Young Poets" in *Virginia Woolf.*

6. For a fuller discussion of this idea, see Hegel's *Aesthetics* 1090–93. See also Naomi Schor, who argues that Hegel disdains everyday domestic details—which he associates with the feminine—and that this disdain reveals his limited interest in the rising art of his time, the novel (*Reading in Detail,* 23–41). For a discussion of the Victorian "series" novel as a genre suited to the everyday, see Laurie Langbauer's *Novels of Everyday Life.* In comparison, the novel of just "one day," as Bryony Randall argues in *Modernism,* is particularly suited to the everyday's temporality. Ella Ophir argues along these same lines in "Modernist Fiction" that literary representations of ordinary life are explicitly tied to the history of the novel and the particularities of the novel's form.

7. Ramsay Macdonald's Labor government collapsed in August, on the heels of the general strike in England and the stock market crash in America. Rapid inflation threatened to follow. The summer was marked by "violent political argument," Woolf noted (*WL* 4:373).

8. Contrast Harvena Richter's study of Woolf's subjectivity, *Virginia Woolf: The Inward Voyage,* with Susan Squier's analysis of London's exteriority, *Virginia Woolf and London: Sexual Politics of the City.* Also see Alex Zwerdling's *Virginia Woolf and the Real World* and Alice van Buren Kelley's *The Novels of Virginia Woolf: Fact and Vision,* analyses of Woolf's fiction that pivot on these binaries. Compelling exceptions to this trend are Mark Hussey's *The Singing of the Real World: The Philosophy of Virginia Woolf's Fiction* and Victoria Rosner's *Modernism and the Architecture of Private Life.*

9. Christopher Reed notes: "Lytton Strachey, writing under the imprimatur of the National Council Against Conscription, like Bell, produced a controversial pacifist pamphlet (M. Holroyd, *Lytton Strachey,* 614–15); Roger Fry helped refugees with agricultural reclamation on the French front during World War I; Duncan Grant volunteered time to suffrage groups and designed a poster (color plate 1 in L. Tickner, *Spectacle of Woman*); Virginia Woolf, in addition to her well known feminist writings, helped with Labour Party political organizing, ran meetings of the Women's Cooperative Guild in her home, and served on numerous left-leaning committees; Vanessa Bell, at the onset of the first World War, volunteered at the National Council for Civil Liberties" (*Bloomsbury Rooms,* 279n).

10. Woolf read and reread Proust from 1922 onward. She wrote to Roger Fry: "Proust so titillates my own desire for expression that I can hardly set out the sentence.

Oh, if I could write like that! I cry. And at the moment such is the astonishing vibration and saturation and intensification that he procures—theres [*sic*] something sexual in it—that I feel I can write like that, and seize my pen and then I can't write like that. Scarcely anyone so stimulates the nerves of language in me: it becomes an obsession" (*WL* 2:525).

11. See Miller's "*Mrs. Dalloway:* Repetition as the Raising of the Dead" in *Fiction and Repetition.*

12. Elsie is introduced early in a long paragraph: "Elsie was a strongly-built wench, plump, fairly tall, with the striking free, powerful carriage of one bred to various and hard manual labour. Her arms and bust were superb. She had blue-black hair and dark blue eyes, and a pretty curve of the lips. The face was square but soft" (29). Though Bennett's novel takes Elsie's plight as a central subject, the narrator often assumes that he knows more about her, objectively, than she knows about herself.

13. For a fuller discussion of the procession of the unknown warrior, see Sarah Cole's *Modernism, Male Friendship, and the First World War.*

14. Woolf heard sparrows speaking Greek during one of her illnesses, according to Leonard Woolf's account (*Beginning Again,* 77). See the chapter titled "Madness" in Hermione Lee's *Virginia Woolf* for a balanced and insightful examination of the nature of her illness.

15. See, in particular, Karen DeMeester's "Trauma and Recovery in Virginia Woolf's *Mrs. Dalloway.*" DeMeester draws upon recent work in the field of trauma studies by Kali Tal, Judith Herman, Elaine Scarry, and Cathy Caruth. Her argument is echoed in many other readings of *Mrs. Dalloway;* see, for instance, Jane Lilienfeld's "Accident, Incident, and Meaning: Traces of Trauma in Virginia Woolf's Narrativity"; and Marlene Briggs's "Veterans and Civilians: Traumatic Knowledge and Cultural Appropriation in *Mrs. Dalloway.*"

16. Woolf was closely connected to the British psychoanalytical movement and frequently drew upon the language of psychoanalysis in her own writing. Leonard Woolf reviewed *The Psychopathology of Everyday Life* in 1914, and Hogarth Press began publishing translations of the International Psycho-Analytical Library Series—including James and Alix Strachey's translations of Freud—in the 1920s. But Woolf was skeptical of Freud and did not read his works seriously until 1939, specifically *Moses and Monotheism, Civilisation and Its Discontents, Group Psychology and the Analysis of the Ego,* "Thoughts for the Time on War and Death," and *Why War?* (Lee, *Virginia Woolf,* 197, 472, 722–27).

17. See *Virginia Woolf, The Waves,* transcribed and edited by J. W. Graham. For a thorough and even-handed examination of Woolf's attitude toward working-class women, see Mary M. Childers's "Virginia Woolf on the Outside Looking Down."

18. See Michael Tratner's *Modernism and Mass Politics* for a discussion of how the "Time Passes" section enacts radical cultural and artistic changes wrought by war, particularly through the characters of Mrs. McNab and Mrs. Bast.

19. See James M. Haule's "*To the Lighthouse* and the Great War: The Evidence of Virginia Woolf's Revisions of 'Time Passes.'"

20. See note 4. Also see Peter Schwenger, who argues that Woolf's conception of "things" (in relationship to Perec) hinges on how they generate narrative, not how they deny human subjects or stories.

21. As Ben Highmore has observed, De Certeau's conception of resistance is what hinders and dissipates the energy flow of domination, but it is not wholly oppositional (*Everyday Life*, 152–53).

## Chapter Three

1. See *The Autobiography of Alice B. Toklas* for Stein's account of James's important influence upon her. See Rosalind Miller for how Stein's early Radcliffe manuscripts reveal that Stein thought highly not only of James's philosophy but also his commitment to living a life of action.

2. Stein's "politics," especially as they are disclosed in her World War II texts, have been a subject of great debate recently, as critics try to come to terms with Stein's seeming passivity in the face of war. See, in particular, John Whittier-Ferguson, Phoebe Stein Davis, Wanda Van Dusen, Barbara Will, Zofia Lesinska, Maria Diedrich, and Janet Malcolm.

3. For a study of the influence of Jamesian habit upon early literary modernists, see Renée Tursi's *The Force of Habit at the Turn of the Century.* Also see Tursi's mention (70) of the Reade aphorism that opens this section. James wrote this aphorism in his own copy of the *Briefer Course*, the shortened version of *Principles of Psychology*, across the top of the first recto page of the chapter on habit. For a broad examination of James's pragmatism and its influence on Stein's modernism, see Jonathan Levin's *The Poetics of Transition.* For the argument that Stein eventually rejects James's intellectual influence and unconsciously accepts Freudian thinking, see Lisa Ruddick's *Reading Gertrude Stein.*

4. See Louis Menand's *The Metaphysical Club.* Menand suggests that James's philosophy was particularly compelling at a time in America when another civil war did not seem unlikely: it was a philosophy that warned against the importance of ideas (the intractable ideologies of North and South).

5. James's opposition to strict ideologies and static notions of "truth" draws its strength from Emerson's anti-foundational nonconformism rather than from the mystical and religious elements of his transcendentalism. For a discussion of the interconnections between Transcendentalism and pragmatism in Emerson's thought, see the chapter titled "Divine Overflowings" in Jonathan Levin's *The Poetics of Transition* (17–44).

6. Menand entertainingly recounts James's indecision—about what profession to pursue, whether to marry, and where he ought to live. James's sister Alice called him a "blob of mercury" (*Metaphysical Club*, 76).

7. See Ann Douglas's *Terrible Honesty: Mongrel Manhattan in the 1920s.* Douglas pits James and Stein's "pluralistic optimism" against Freud's "elitist pessimism" to explain the dual nature of 1920s New York, a decade marked by rapid changes in technology, transportation, news media, and entertainment (191–93).

8. "Melanctha" is likely based on Stein's early romantic experience with May Bookstaver, whom she met while studying medicine at Johns Hopkins. Tellingly, Stein imagines her role in the relationship in terms of Jeff's middle-class stoicism; she sides with his desire for "regular living" instead of Melanctha's moodier passions.

9. See Wolfgang Iser's *The Aesthetic Moment* for a critique of Pater's "moment" as an experience without manifest consequences. Alternatively, Heather Love ("Forced Exile") reads Pater's affinity for Botticelli's "middle ground"—the turn away from social obligation, the failure to choose good or evil—as stemming from Pater's own experience of social exclusion as a homosexual.

10. See Philip Fischer's "The Failure of Habit."

11. See Lisi Schoenbach's "'Peaceful and Exciting,'" an essay that squares with my argument about the centrality of habit in Stein's work, though Schoenbach links Stein's "pragmatic modernism" with a possibility of progressive social change that I believe Stein's World War II writings do not sustain.

12. See, for instance, Jayne Walker's *The Making of a Modernist.*

13. William James's response to Henry's late prose style marks the difference between them. After reading *The Golden Bowl,* William complained to his brother that he enjoyed neither "the kind of 'problem'" in the book nor the "method of narration by interminable elaboration of suggestive reference." He suggested that Henry's method and his own "seem the reverse, the one of the other." To drive home this point, he asked Henry to write a book "with no mustiness in the plot, with great vigor and decisiveness in the action, no fencing in the dialogue, no psychological commentaries, and absolute straightness in style"—and then good-naturedly suggested that he publish it in William's name (Perry, *Thought and Character,* 1:423–24).

14. Stein wrote *Mrs. Reynolds* between 1940 and 1943, while she was living in occupied France, but at the time Bennett Cerf was the head of Random House, and he considered the novel too experimental to sell. In contrast, *Wars I Have Seen* achieved bestseller status shortly after publication in autumn 1945.

15. This period has been called France's "phoney war" for the reason that France entered the war slowly and reluctantly. Because of the Franco-British guarantee to Poland, France was forced to act when Germany invaded Poland. The French army, geared for defense, mobilized very slowly, waiting for the British to mobilize with more modern weaponry, especially airplanes. See James McMillan's *Twentieth-Century France.*

16. Janet Malcolm notes that Stein and Toklas never acknowledged that Bernard Faÿ was their protector; rather, in Faÿ's memoir "Les Précieux" he recounts a visit with Pétain in which he secured the women's safety.

17. The original typescript, included in the Random House Papers at Columbia University, is marked by Bennett Cerf's note at the top of the first page: "For the records. This disgusting piece was mailed from Belley on Jan. 19, 1942."

18. See Stein, "Composition as Explanation."

19. *Mrs. Reynolds* has received sustained critical attention only in the last several years. See, in particular, Phoebe Stein Davis, Zofia Lesinska, and John Whittier-Ferguson.

20. Beckett joined a Résistance cell of the British Special Operations Executive, translating, typing and helping to deliver information reports. He narrowly escaped the Gestapo and hid out in Roussillon for two years, subsisting as a manual laborer. After the war, he worked with the Irish Red Cross in Normandy, where he witnessed the war's real devastations. See Knowlson, *Damned to Fame,* 273–322.

21. In "'A Book in Translation about Eggs and Butter,'" Maria Diedrich argues that Stein's emphasis on the temporal present represents a rejection of masculine values of violence as well as "rationality, linearity, and hierarchical order" (92).

22. See "Gertrude Stein's Unpublished Works."

## Chapter Four

1. For both arguments, see Albert Gelpi's *Wallace Stevens: The Poetics of Modernism.*

2. Christian Wiman made this claim at the 2004 Wallace Stevens conference in a panel discussion about how Stevens's *Collected Poems* might fare over the next fifty years. Susan Howe, also on the panel, strongly disagreed with Wiman, having already claimed that Stevens "is our American Coleridge," and later in conversation, that Stevens is indeed *the* greatest American poet. See *The Wallace Stevens Journal* (Fall 2004) for written versions of their talks.

3. See Cavell, Lentricchia, Poirier and Kermode, all of whom treat Stevens within the realm of ordinary language theory, the first three specifically in relation to American pragmatism. Recent contributions to *The Wallace Stevens Journal* suggest that Stevens's work continues to avail itself to approaches that draw heavily from philosophy.

4. See Helen Vendler's *Words Chosen Out of Desire;* Alan Filreis's *Wallace Stevens and the Actual World* and *Modernism from Right to Left;* and James Longenbach's *Wallace Stevens: The Plain Sense of Things.* In addition, see Jacqueline Vaught Brogan's *The Violence Within The Violence Without: Wallace Stevens and the Emergence of a Revolutionary Poetics,* which also calls attention to a poetic shift in Stevens's work that more readily addresses women.

5. For instance, "Earthy Anecdote," the first poem in *Harmonium,* and "Ploughing on Sunday"—poems marked by short lines, exact repetition and simple rhymes—both enact the primitivism they celebrate (*CP* 3, 20).

6. See Cavell's *In Quest of the Ordinary,* in which he argues that apprehending the ordinary is a performative rather than constative task.

7. Helen Vendler argues that *Owl's Clover* revealed to Stevens "the limits of his rhetoric and the limits of the topical" (*On Extended,* 118). Angus Cleghorn argues precisely the opposite in *Wallace Stevens' Poetics,* a rare exception to Vendler's assessment, suggesting that *Owl's Clover* in fact reveals Stevens's extensive polemical underpinnings.

8. Ronald Lane Latimer. Papers, Box 1, Folder 17, Special Collections Research Center. University of Chicago Library.

9. Stevens's salary during the Great Depression was altered only by a modest pay cut during 1932–33 (Brazeau, *Parts of a World,* 231–32).

10. Stevens's "suject" is not a misspelling of the French, but most likely taken from a late-sixteenth-century manuscript, Guillaume Legangneur's *Epigrammes anciens sur plusieurs beaux sujects: Extraicts de l'anthologie des epigrammes grecs par Henry Estienne,* from which Stevens quotes in his commonplace book (Bates, *Sur Plusieurs,* 18).

11. Stevens quotes from A. R. Powys's review of *The Revival of Christian Architecture,* by A. Welby Pugin, *London Mercury* 28 (May 1933): 63–64.

12. Stevens's comments on *The Waste Land* are part of a November 11, 1922, letter to Alice Corbin Henderson: "Eliot's poem is, of course, the rage. As poetry it is surely

negligible. What it may be in other respects is a large subject on which one could talk for a month. If it is the supreme cry of despair it is Eliot's and not his generation's. Personally, I think it's a bore" (Filreis, "Stevens' Letters to Alice Corbin Henderson," 19). In a much later letter to William Van O'Connor, Stevens writes: "Eliot and I are dead opposites and I have been doing about everything that he would not be likely to do" (*SL* 677).

13. For an extended discussion of the relationship between these two poets, see Olson's "Stevens and Auden: Antimythological Meetings."

14. See Filreis for an extended analysis of the postwar political context, particularly the 1952 presidential campaign, when the positive political rhetoric of reconstruction dramatically contrasted with the accounts that Barbara Church sent Stevens of the continued misery of Europe (*Actual,* 231–41).

15. This section of "Esthétique du Mal" was reprinted as "The Soldier's Wound" in Richard Eberhart and Selden Rodman's 1945 volume *War and the Poet,* and in Oscar Williams's *The War Poets of 1945* (Filreis, *Actual,* 137).

16. See Frank Lentricchia, *Ariel and the Police,* for the association Stevens makes between poetry and femininity. That Stevens could title one of his lectures "The Figure of the Youth as a Virile Poet"—in earnest—testifies to his attempt to imagine poetic success as something suitable to his masculine nature.

17. Other frequent correspondents include Leonard C. van Geyzel, who lived in Ceylon and often sent Stevens tea; Thomas McGreevy, the Irish Catholic poet in Dublin; Paule Vidal, the Parisian bookseller; Peter Lee, the young Korean poet and scholar; Walter Pach, the art collector and critic who often traveled through Europe; and Marianne Moore.

18. One exception is Barbara Estrin's *The American Love Lyric after Auschwitz and Hiroshima,* which takes Stevens's statement in "Three Academic Pieces" as its directive. According to Estrin, Stevens identifies how poetry and destruction emerge from the same vital source (2).

19. Filreis and Longenbach place Stevens's work in a social, historical, and political context, but both suggest that Stevens loses touch with these elements in his later, longer, meditative work, including "Ordinary Evening." Eleanor Cook, in *Poetry, Word-Play, and Word-War in Wallace Stevens,* provides the most thorough reading of "Ordinary Evening" and "Esthétique du Mal" in connection with Stevens's ideas about the commonplace. Also see Siobhan Phillips's "Wallace Stevens and the Mode of the Ordinary" for a discussion of Stevens's ordinary in relation to diurnal time.

20. For a further consideration of the relationship between Stevens and Williams, see "Stevens and Williams: The Epistemology of Modernism" in Albert Gelpi's *Wallace Stevens: The Poetics of Modernism,* 3–23. For a discussion of the aims of objectivist (versus symbolist) poetry, see Charles Altieri's "The Objectivist Tradition."

21. Huntington Library WAS 468, Box 40. See the carbon copy of the shorter version in WAS 2997, which consists of eleven sections (of the longer thirty-one) in the following order: 1, 6, 9, 11, 12, 16, 22, 28, 30, 31, 39 (*SL* 662n).

22. The poems published in *Botteghe Oscure* (Autumn 1949) include "What We See Is What We Think," "A Golden Woman in a Silver Mirror," "The Old Lutheran Bells

at Home," "Questions Are Remarks," "Study of Images I," and "Study of Images II" (*SL* 642).

23. Translations from the French are Bernstein's (e-mail to author, May 8, 2002).

24. See J. L. Austin's *How to Do Things with Words* (1962).

## Conclusion

1. I use the word "narrator" to demarcate the central character of *In Search of Lost Time* though this convention overlooks the distinctions among Proust's use of *je*, or "I." See Marcel Muller (*Les Voix narratives*), who describes seven distinct "I's" in the novel, and Roger Shattuck (*Proust's Way*), who narrows these down to an essential three: Marcel, the boy who grows up and does not know what the future holds; the narrator, who is Marcel grown old and become a writer; and the author, who on a few occasions comments upon his novel (33). I take Shattuck's lead by referring to the narrator or to Marcel depending upon the moment at hand.

2. In an August 1919 letter, Proust compares his novel to a cathedral although he did not keep the architectural titles that were to assert the novel's solidity (*Correspondance* 18:359). See Luc Fraisse's *L'Oeuvre cathédrale* for a larger discussion of how the novel takes the cathedral as its inspiration.

3. As Nehamas, Landy, and Duncan Large have argued, the connections between Proust and Nietzsche (whose work Proust barely knew) are perhaps closer than Proust's connections to any other modern philosopher.

# Bibliography

Abel, Elizabeth. *Virginia Woolf and the Fictions of Psychoanalysis.* Chicago: University of Chicago Press, 1989.

Adorno, Theodor. *Prisms.* Translated by Samuel and Shierry Weber. Cambridge, MA: MIT, 1988.

Agamben, Giorgio. *Homo Sacer: Sovereign Power and Bare Life.* Translated by Daniel Heller-Roazen. Stanford, CA: Stanford University Press, 1998.

Altieri, Charles. "The Objectivist Tradition." *Chicago Review* 30, no. 3 (Winter 1979): 5–22.

Arendt, Hannah. *The Human Condition.* Chicago: University of Chicago Press, 1998.

Ashbery, John. *Self-Portrait in a Convex Mirror.* New York: Penguin, 1975.

Attridge, Derek. *Joyce Effects: On Language, Theory, and History.* Cambridge: Cambridge University Press, 2000.

Attridge, Derek, and Marjorie Howes, eds. *Semicolonial Joyce.* Cambridge: Cambridge University Press, 2000.

Auden, W. H. *Collected Poems.* Edited by Edward Mendelson. London: Faber and Faber, 1976.

———. *Selected Poems.* Edited by Edward Mendelson. New York: Vintage, 1989.

———. "Writing." *The Dyer's Hand,* 12–27. New York: Vintage, 1989.

Auerbach, Eric. *Mimesis: The Representation of Reality in Western Literature.* Translated by Willard Trask. New York: Doubleday Anchor Books, 1957.

———. *Scenes from the Drama of European Literature.* Minneapolis: University of Minnesota Press, 1984.

Augustine. *Confessions.* Translated by Henry Chadwick. Oxford: Oxford World's Classics, 1998.

Austin, J. L. *How to Do Things with Words.* Cambridge, MA: Harvard University Press, 1967.

Barthes, Roland. *The Pleasure of the Text.* Translated by Richard Miller. New York: Farrar, Straus, and Giroux, 1975.

———. *Mythologies.* Translated by Annette Lavers. New York: Noonday, 1993.

———. "The Reality Effect." In *The Rustle of Language,* trans. Richard Howard, 141–48. Berkeley: University of California Press, 1989.

Barthes, Roland. "Writing the Event." In *The Rustle of Language,* trans. Richard Howard, 149–54. Berkeley: University of California Press, 1989.

Bates, Milton, ed. *Sur Plusieurs Beaux Sujects: Wallace Stevens' Commonplace Book, A Facsimile and Transcription.* Stanford, CA: Stanford University Press and Henry E. Huntington Library, 1989.

Baudrillard, Jean. *Simulacra and Simulation.* Translated by Sheila Faria Glaser. Ann Arbor: University of Michigan Press, 1994.

———. *The System of Objects.* Translated by James Benedict. London: Verso, 1996.

———. *Symbolic Exchange and Death.* Translated by Iain Hamilton Grant. London: Sage, 1993.

———. *The Vital Illusion.* Edited by Julia Witwer. New York: Columbia University Press, 2000.

Beckett, Samuel. *Endgame.* Translated by Samuel Beckett. New York: Grove, 1958.

———. *How It Is.* Translated by Samuel Beckett. New York: Grove, 1964.

———. *Malone Dies.* New York: Grove, 1956.

———. *Molloy.* New York: Grove, 1955.

———. *Our Exagmination Round His Factification for Incamination of Work in Progress* (1929). London: Faber, 1984.

———. "Play." *Collected Shorter Plays of Samuel Beckett.* New York: Grove, 1984.

———. *Proust and Three Dialogues with George Duthuit.* London: John Calder, 1999.

———. *The Unnamable.* New York: Grove, 1958.

Beer, Gillian. *Virginia Woolf: The Common Ground.* Ann Arbor: University of Michigan Press, 1996.

Beja, Morris, and Shari Benstock, eds. *Coping with Joyce.* Columbus: Ohio State University Press, 1988.

Bellos, David. *Georges Perec: A Life in Words.* London: Harvill, 1993.

Bennett, Arnold. *Riceyman Steps.* London: Collins, 1956.

Benstock, Bernard. "Cataloguing in *Finnegans Wake:* Counting Counties." In *Joyce in Context,* ed. Vincent J. Cheng and Timothy Martin, 259–69. Cambridge: Cambridge University Press, 1992.

Bergson, Henri. *Creative Evolution.* Translated by Arthur Mitchell. Mineola, NY: Dover, 1998.

———. *Matter and Memory.* Translated by N. M. Paul and W. S. Palmer. New York: Zone, 1991.

Bernstein, Charles. "Pour une critique de l'ordinaire. Entretien avec Charles Bernstein." *Etudes Francaises* 33, no. 2 (Autumn 1992): 7–20.

Berry, Ellen E. *Curved Thought and Textual Wandering: Gertrude Stein's Postmodernism.* Ann Arbor: University of Michigan Press, 1992.

Blanchot, Maurice. "Everyday Speech." *Yale French Studies* 73 (1987): 12–20.

Bloom, Harold. *Wallace Stevens: The Poems of Our Climate.* Ithaca, NY: Cornell University Press, 1977.

Braudel, Fernand. *The Structure of Everyday Life.* Vol. 1 of *Civilization and Capitalism, 15th–18th Century.* Translated by Siân Reynolds. Berkeley: University of California Press, 1992.

———. *The Mediterranean: And the Mediterranean World in the Age of Phillip II.* Translated by Siân Reynolds. 2 vols. Berkeley: University of California Press, 1995.

Bowen, Zach. "Joyce and the Epiphany Concept: A New Approach." *Journal of Modern Literature* 9, no. 1 (1981/82): 103–14.

Bowles, Paul. "Desultory Correspondence: An Interview with Paul Bowles on Gertrude Stein." Conducted by Florian Vetsch. *Modern Fiction Studies* 42, no. 3 (Fall 1996): 627–45.

Brazeau, Peter. *Parts of a World: Wallace Stevens Remembered.* New York: Random House, 1977.

Breal, Michel. *Melanges de Mythologie et de Linguistique.* Paris: Hachette, 1877.

Bridgman, Richard. *Gertrude Stein in Pieces.* New York: Oxford University Press, 1970.

Briggs, Julia. *Virginia Woolf: An Inner Life.* London: Allen Lane, 2005.

Briggs, Marlene. "Veterans and Civilians: Traumatic Knowledge and Cultural Appropriation in *Mrs. Dalloway.*" In *Virginia Woolf and Communities: Selected Papers from the Eighth Annual Conference on Virginia Woolf,* 43–49. New York: Pace University Press, 1999.

Brogan, Jacqueline Vaught. *The Violence Within The Violence Without: Wallace Stevens and the Emergence of a Revolutionary Poetics.* Athens: University of Georgia Press, 2003.

Brown, Bill. *A Sense of Things: The Object Matter of American Literature.* Chicago: University of Chicago Press, 2003.

Budgen, Frank. *James Joyce and the Making of Ulysses.* Oxford: Oxford University Press, 1989.

Bürger, Peter. *Theory of the Avant-Garde.* Translated by Michael Shaw. Minneapolis: University of Minnesota Press, 1984.

Burns, Edward, and Ulla E. Dydo. "Gertrude Stein: September 1942 to September 1944." *The Letters of Gertrude Stein and Thornton Wilder,* 401–21. New Haven, CT: Yale University Press, 1996.

Burnshaw, Stanley. "Turmoil in the Middle Ground." In *Critical Essays on Wallace Stevens,* ed. Steven Gould Axelrod and Helen Deese, 36–38. Boston: G. K. Hall, 1988.

Burrin, Philippe. *France under the Germans.* Translated by Janet Lloyd. New York: New Press, 1996.

Butler, Christopher. "Joyce and the Displaced Author." In *James Joyce and Modern Literature,* ed. W. J. McCormack and Alistair Stead, 56–73. London: Routledge and Kegan Paul, 1982.

Caruth, Cathy. *Unclaimed Experience: Trauma, Narrative, and History.* Baltimore: Johns Hopkins University Press, 1996.

Cavell, Stanley. *In Quest of the Ordinary: Lines of Skepticism and Romanticism.* Chicago: University of Chicago Press, 1988.

———. *Must We Mean What We Say?* Cambridge: Cambridge University Press, 2002.

———. *This New Yet Unapproachable America.* Albuquerque, NM: Living Batch Press, 1989.

———. "What's the Use of Calling Emerson a Pragmatist?" In *The Revival of Pragmatism: New Essays on Social Thought, Law, and Culture,* ed. Morris Dickstein, 72–80. Durham, NC: Duke University Press, 1998.

Certeau, Michel de. *The Practice of Everyday Life.* Translated by Steven F. Rendall. Berkeley: University of California Press, 1984.

Chadwick, Henry. Introduction to Augustine's *Confessions,* ix–xxvi. Oxford: Oxford World's Classics, 1998.

Charters, Ann. Introduction to Gertrude Stein's *Three Lives,* vii–xxii. New York: Penguin, 1990.

Cheng, Vincent J., and Timothy Martin, eds. *Joyce in Context.* Cambridge: Cambridge University Press, 1992.

Childers, Mary M. "Virginia Woolf on the Outside Looking Down: Reflections on the Class of Women." *Modern Fiction Studies* 38, no. 1 (Spring 1992): 61–79.

Chow, Rey. "Sentimental Returns: On the Uses of the Everyday in the Recent Films of Zhang Yimou and Wong Kar-Wai." *New Literary History* 33 (2002): 639–54.

Cleghorn, Angus. *Wallace Stevens' Poetics: The Neglected Rhetoric.* New York: Palgrave, 2000.

Cole, Sarah. *Modernism, Male Friendship, and the First World War.* Cambridge: Cambridge University Press, 2003.

Compagnon, Antoine. *Proust between Two Centuries.* Translated by Richard E. Goodkin. New York: Columbia University Press, 1992.

Cook, Eleanor. *Poetry, Word-Play, and Word-War in Wallace Stevens.* Princeton, NJ: Princeton, University Press, 1988.

Copeland, Carolyn Faunce. *Language and Time and Gertrude Stein.* Iowa City: University of Iowa Press, 1976.

Cuddy-Keane, Melba. *Virginia Woolf, the Intellectual, and the Public Sphere.* New York: Cambridge University Press, 2003.

Danto, Arthur C. *After the End of Art: Contemporary Art and the Pale of History.* Princeton, NJ: Princeton University Press, 1997.

———. *The Transfiguration of the Commonplace.* Cambridge, MA: Harvard University Press, 1981.

Davidson, Michael. "Notes beyond the Notes: Wallace Stevens and Contemporary Poetics." In *Wallace Stevens: The Poetics of Modernism,* ed. Albert Gelpi, 141–60. Cambridge: Cambridge University Press.

Davis, Phoebe Stein. "'Even Cake Gets to Have Another Meaning': History, Narrative, and 'Daily Living' in Gertrude Stein's World War II Writings." *Modern Fiction Studies* 44, no. 3 (Fall 1998): 569–607.

Debord, Guy-Ernest. *The Society of the Spectacle.* Paris, 1967. *The Situationist International Text Library.* http://library.nothingness.org/articles/all/all/pub_contents/4.

Defoe, Daniel. *Robinson Crusoe.* New York: Dodd, Mead, 1946.

DeKoven, Marianne. *A Different Language: Gertrude Stein's Experimental Writing.* Madison: University of Wisconsin Press, 1983.

Deleuze, Gilles. *Proust and Signs: The Complete Text.* Translated by Richard Howard. Minneapolis: University of Minnesota Press, 2000.

DeMeester, Karen. "Trauma and Recovery in Virginia Woolf's *Mrs. Dalloway.*" *Modern Fiction Studies* 44, no. 3 (Fall 1998): 649–73.

Des Pres, Terrence. *The Survivor: An Anatomy of Life in the Death Camps.* Oxford: Oxford University Press, 1976.

Dettmar, Kevin J. H. *The Illicit Joyce of Postmodernism.* Madison: University of Wisconsin Press, 1996.

Dickstein, Morris, ed. *The Revival of Pragmatism: New Essays on Social Thought, Law, and Culture.* Durham, NC: Duke University Press, 1998.

Diedrich, Maria. "'A Book in Translation about Eggs and Butter': Gertrude Stein's World War II." In *Women and War: The Changing Status of American Women from the 1930s to the 1950s,* 87–106, ed. Maria Diedrich and Dorothea Fischer-Hornung. New York: St. Martin's, 1990.

Donoghue, Denis. *Walter Pater: Lover of Strange Souls.* New York: Alfred A. Knopf, 1995.

Douglas, Ann. *Terrible Honesty: Mongrel Manhattan in the 1920s.* New York: Farrar, Straus, and Giroux, 1995.

Duffy, Edward. "Stanley Cavell's Redemptive Reading: A Philosophical Labor in Progress." In *Ordinary Language Criticism: Literary Thinking after Cavell after Wittgenstein,* ed. Kenneth Dauber and Walter Jost. Evanston, IL: Northwestern University Press, 2003.

Eksteins, Modris. *Rites of Spring: The Great War and the Birth of the Modern Age.* Boston: Houghton Mifflin, 1989.

Eliot, George. *Adam Bede.* London: Penguin, 1985.

———. *Middlemarch.* Oxford: Oxford University Press World's Classics, 1988.

Eliot, T. S. *The Complete Poems and Plays: 1909–1950.* New York: Harcourt Brace, 1980.

———. *Four Quartets.* San Diego: Harcourt Brace Jovanovich, 1971.

———. Introduction to *Nightwood,* by Djuna Barnes, xi–xvi. New York: New Directions, 1961.

———. "The Metaphysical Poets." In *Selected Prose of T. S. Eliot,* ed. Frank Kermode, 59–67. New York: Harcourt Brace, 1975.

———. "Tradition and the Individual Talent." In *Selected Prose of T. S. Eliot,* ed. Frank Kermode, 37–44. New York: Harcourt Brace, 1975.

———. "*Ulysses,* Order and Myth." In *Selected Prose of T. S. Eliot,* ed. Frank Kermode, 175–78. New York: Harcourt Brace, 1975.

Ellmann, Richard. *James Joyce.* New York: Oxford University Press, 1965.

Emerson, Ralph Waldo. *Essays and Lectures.* Edited by Joel Porte. New York: Library of America, 1983.

Erikson, Jon. *The Fate of the Object: From Modern Object to Postmodern Sign in Performance, Art, and Poetry.* Ann Arbor: University of Michigan Press, 1995.

Estrin, Barbara L. *The American Love Lyric after Auschwitz and Hiroshima.* New York: Palgrave, 2001.

Eysteinsson, Astradur. *The Concept of Modernism.* Ithaca, NY: Cornell University Press, 1990.

Faÿ, Bernard. *Les Précieux.* Paris: Librairie Académique Perrin, 1966.

Felski, Rita. Introduction. "Everyday Life." *New Literary History* 3 (2002): 607–22.

———. "The Invention of Everyday Life." In *Doing Time: Feminist Theory and Postmodern Culture,* 77–98. New York: New York University Press, 2000.

Filreis, Alan. *Modernism from Right to Left: Wallace Stevens, the Thirties, and Literary Radicalism.* Cambridge: Cambridge University Press, 1994.

———. "Voicing the Desert of Silence: Stevens' Letters to Alice Corbin Henderson." *Wallace Stevens Journal* 12, no. 1 (Spring 1988): 3–20.

Felski, Rita. *Wallace Stevens and the Actual World.* Princeton, NJ: Princeton University Press, 1991.

Fischer, Philip. "The Failure of Habit." In *Uses of Literature,* ed. Monroe Engel, 3–18. Cambridge, MA: Harvard University Press, 1973.

Flaubert, Gustav. *Bouvard and Pécuchet.* Translated by A. J. Krailsheimer. London: Penguin, 1976.

Forster, E. M. *Virginia Woolf.* New York: Harcourt, Brace, 1942.

Fraisse, Luc. *L'Oeuvre cathédrale: Proust et l'architecture médiévale.* Paris: Corti, 1990.

Freud, Sigmund. *Beyond the Pleasure Principle.* Translated by James Strachey. New York: W.W. Norton, 1989.

Froula, Christine. *Virginia Woolf and the Bloomsbury Avant-Garde: War, Civilization, Modernity.* New York: Columbia University Press, 2005.

Fussell, Paul. *The Great War and Modern Memory.* New York: Oxford University Press, 1975.

Gardner, Helen. *The New Oxford Book of English Verse: 1250–1950.* Oxford: Oxford University Press, 1992.

Geldof, Koenraad. "The Unbearable Literariness of Literature: Spectral Marxism and Metaphysical Realism in Charles Taylor's *Sources of the Self.*" *New Literary History* 30, no. 2 (1999): 325–49.

Gelpi, Albert, ed. *Wallace Stevens: The Poetics of Modernism.* Cambridge: Cambridge University Press, 1985.

Genette, Gérard. *Narrative Discourse: An Essay in Method.* Translated by Jane E. Levin. Ithaca, NY: Cornell University Press, 1980.

"Gertrude Stein's Unpublished Works." *Times Literary Supplement,* Feb. 5, 1954, 90.

Gifford, Don, with Robert J. Seidman. *Ulysses Annotated.* 2nd ed. Los Angeles. University of California Press, 1988.

Gilbert, Sandra, and Susan Gubar. *No Man's Land.* 3 vols. New Haven, CT: Yale University Press, 1994.

Gissing, George. *New Grub Street.* Edited by D. J. Taylor. London: Everyman, 1997.

Graham, J. W., ed. *Virginia Woolf: The Waves: The Two Holograph Drafts.* Toronto: University of Toronto Press, 1976.

Gramsci, Antonio. *An Antonio Gramsci Reader: Selected Writings 1916–1935.* Edited by David Forgacs. London: Lawrence and Wishart, 1999.

Hart, Clive, and Leo Knuth. *A Topographical Guide to James Joyce's* Ulysses. Colchester, England: Wake Newslitter Press, 1981.

Haule, James M. "*To the Lighthouse* and the Great War: The Evidence of Virginia Woolf's Revisions of 'Time Passes.'" In *Virginia Woolf and War: Fiction, Reality, and Myth,* ed. Mark Hussey. Syracuse, NY: Syracuse University Press, 1991: 164–79.

Hayman, David. *Ulysses: The Mechanics of Meaning.* Englewood Cliffs, NJ: Prentice Hall, 1970.

Hegel, G. W. F. *Aesthetics: Lectures on Fine Art.* Translated by T. M. Knox. 2 vols. Oxford: Clarendon, 1988.

Hemingway, Ernest. *A Farewell to Arms.* New York: Scribner Classics, 1986; New York: Macmillan, 1987.

Herman, Judith Lewis. *Trauma and Recovery.* New York: Basic Books, 1992.

Herring, Phillip. *Joyce's Uncertainty Principle.* Princeton, NJ: Princeton University Press, 1987.
Highmore, Ben. *Everyday Life and Cultural Theory.* London: Routledge, 2002.
Howe, Susan. "*The Collected Poems:* The Next Fifty Years." *Wallace Stevens Journal* 28 (Fall 2004): 231–34.
———. *Souls of the Labadie Tract.* New York: New Directions, 2007.
Hussey, Mark. *The Singing of the Real World: The Philosophy of Woolf's Fiction.* Columbus: Ohio State University Press, 1986.
———, ed. *Virginia Woolf and War: Fiction, Reality, and Myth.* Syracuse, NY: Syracuse University Press, 1991.
Ibsen, Henrik. *The Complete Major Prose Plays.* Translated by Rolf Fjelde. New York: Plume, 1978.
Iser, Wolfgang. *Walter Pater: The Aesthetic Moment.* Translated by David Henry Wilson. Cambridge: Cambridge University Press, 1987
Jakobson, Roman. "The Metaphoric and Metonymic Poles." In *Critical Theory Since Plato,* ed. Hazard Adams, 1113–16. New York: Harcourt Brace Jovanovich, 1971.
James, William. *The Writings of William James. A Comprehensive Edition.* Edited by John J. McDermott. New York: Random House, 1967.
Jameson, Fredric. *Fables of Aggression: Wyndham Lewis, the Modernist as Fascist.* Berkeley: University of California Press, 1979.
———. "*Ulysses* in History." In *James Joyce and Modern Literature,* ed. W. J. McCormack and Alistair Stead, 126–41. London: Routledge and Kegan Paul, 1982.
Jay, Paul. *Contingency Blues: The Search for Foundations in American Criticism.* Madison: University of Wisconsin Press, 1997.
Johnson, Richard. "What Is Cultural Studies Anyway?" *Social Text* 16 (1986/87): 38–80.
Johnson, Samuel. "Rambler No. 4" and "Rambler No. 60." In *The Norton Anthology of English Literature, The Major Authors.* 7th ed. New York: W.W. Norton, 2001.
Joyce, James. *A Portrait of the Artist as a Young Man.* New York: Bantam, 1992.
———. "Drama and Life." *The Critical Writings.* Edited by Ellsworth Mason and Richard Ellmann, 38–46. Ithaca, NY: Cornell University Press, 1989.
———. *Dubliners.* Edited by Hans Walter Gabler with Walter Hettche. New York: Vintage, 1993.
———. *Finnegans Wake.* New York: Viking Penguin, 1984.
———. "Ibsen's New Drama." *The Critical Writings.* Edited by Ellsworth Mason and Richard Ellmann, 47–67. Ithaca, NY: Cornell University Press, 1989.
———. *Letters of James Joyce.* Edited by Stuart Gilbert. Vol. 1. New York: Viking, 1957.
———. *Letters of James Joyce.* Vols. 2 and 3. Edited by Richard Ellmann. New York: Viking, 1966.
———. *Poems and Shorter Writings.* Edited by Richard Ellmann, A. Walton Litz, and John Whittier-Ferguson. London: Faber, 1991.
———. *Stephen Hero.* Edited by John J. Slocum and Herbert Cahoon. New York: New Directions, 1963.
———. *Ulysses.* New York: Random House, 1961.
Kaplan, Alice. "Puzzle Man." *Modern Language Notes* 111, no. 4 (1996): 797–803.
———, and Kristin Ross, eds. Introduction. *Everyday Life: Yale French Studies* 73 (1987): 1–4.

Kelley, Alice van Buren. *The Novels of Virginia Woolf: Fact and Vision.* Chicago: University of Chicago Press, 1971.

Kenner, Hugh. "Circe." In *James Joyce's* Ulysses: *Critical Essays,* 359–51. Berkeley: University of California Press, 1974.

———. "Joyce and Ibsen's Naturalism." *Sewanee Review* 59, no. 1 (Winter 1951): 75–96.

———. *Joyce's Voices.* Berkeley: University of California Press, 1978.

———. *The Stoic Comedians: Flaubert, Joyce, and Beckett.* Berkeley: University of California Press, 1974.

———. *Ulysses.* 1980. Rev. ed. Baltimore: Johns Hopkins University Press, 1987.

Kermode, Frank. *Sense of an Ending: Studies in the Theory of Fiction.* New York: Oxford University Press, 1966.

———. *Wallace Stevens.* London: Faber, 1960.

Knowlson, James. *Damned to Fame: The Life of Samuel Beckett.* New York: Simon and Schuster, 1996.

Kristeva, Julia. "Joyce's 'The Gracehoper' or Orpheus's Return." In *New Maladies of the Soul, 172–88.* Translated by Ross Guberman. New York: Columbia University Press, 1995.

Landy, Joshua. *Philosophy as Fiction: Self, Deception, and Knowledge in Proust.* Oxford: Oxford University Press, 2004.

Langbauer, Laurie. "Cultural Studies and the Politics of the Everyday." *Diacritics* 22 (1992): 47–65.

———. *Novels of Everyday Life: The Series in English Fiction, 1850–1930.* Ithaca, NY: Cornell University Press, 1999.

Large, Duncan. *Nietzsche and Proust: A Comparative Study.* Oxford: Oxford University Press, 2001.

Law, Jules David. "Simulation, Pluralism, and the Politics of Everyday Life." In *Coping with Joyce,* ed. Morris Beja and Shari Benstock, 195–205. Columbus: Ohio State University Press, 1989.

Lawrence, Karen. *The Odyssey of Style in* Ulysses. Princeton, NJ: Princeton University Press, 1981.

Lee, Hermione. *Virginia Woolf.* London: Chattus and Windus, 1996.

Lefebvre, Henri. *Critique of Everyday Life.* Translated by John Moore. 3 vols. London: Verso, 1946–82.

———. *Everyday Life and the Modern World.* Translated by Sacha Rabinovitch. London: Penguin, 1971.

———. *The Production of Space.* Translated by Donald Nicholson-Smith. Oxford: Blackwell, 2000.

Lentricchia, Frank. *Ariel and the Police: Michel Foucault, William James, Wallace Stevens.* Madison: University of Wisconsin Press, 1988.

Lesinska, Zofia. "Gertrude Stein's War Autobiographies: Reception, History, and Dialogue." *Literature Interpretation Theory* 9, no. 4 (1999): 313–43.

Levin, Jonathan. *The Poetics of Transition: Emerson, Pragmatism, and American Literary Modernism.* Durham, NC: Duke University Press, 1999.

Levine, Jennifer. "Ulysses." In *The Cambridge Companion to James Joyce,* ed. Derek Attridge, 131–59. Cambridge: Cambridge University Press, 1997.

Lewis, Pericles. "Churchgoing in the Modern Novel." *Modernism/Modernity* 11, no. 4 (2004): 669–94.

Lilienfeld, Jane. "Accident, Incident, and Meaning: Traces of Trauma in Virginia Woolf's Narrativity." In *Virginia Woolf: Turning the Century, Selected Papers From the Ninth Annual Conference on Virginia Woolf,* 153–58. New York: Pace University Press, 2000.

Litz, A. Walton, and Robert Scholes. Introduction to *Dubliners,* by James Joyce. New York: Penguin, 1996.

Lodge, David. "The Language of Modernist Fiction: Metaphor and Metonymy." In *Modernism 1890–1930,* ed. Malcolm Bradbury and James McFarlane, 481–96. Harmondsworth, England: Penguin, 1976.

Longenbach, James. *Wallace Stevens: The Plain Sense of Things.* New York: Oxford University Press, 1991.

Lotman, Jurii M. *The Structure of the Artistic Text.* Translated by Gail Lenhoff and Ronald Vroon. Ann Arbor: University of Michigan Press, 1977.

Love, Heather. "Forced Exile: Walter Pater's Queer Modernism." In *Bad Modernisms,* ed. Douglas Mao and Rebecca L. Walkowitz, 19–43. Durham, NC: Duke University Press, 2006.

Lukács, Georg. *Realism in Our Time: Literature and the Class Struggle.* New York: Harper and Row, 1971.

MacCabe, Colin. *James Joyce and the Revolution of the World.* London: Macmillan, 1978.

MacLeod, Glen. *Wallace Stevens and Modern Art.* New Haven, CT: Yale University Press, 1993.

Malcolm, Janet. *Two Lives: Gertrude and Alice.* New Haven, CT: Yale University Press, 2007.

Manganiello, Dominic. *Joyce's Politics.* Boston: Routledge and Kegan Paul, 1980.

Mann, Thomas. *Buddenbrooks.* Translated by H. T. Lowe-Porter. New York: Vintage-Random House, 1952.

———. *The Magic Mountain.* Translated by H. T. Lowe-Porter. New York: Alfred A. Knopf, 1975.

Mao, Douglas. *Solid Objects: Modernism and the Test of Production.* Princeton, NJ: Princeton University Press, 1998.

Mao, Douglas, and Rebecca L. Walkowitz, eds. *Bad Modernisms.* Durham, NC: Duke University Press, 2006.

Marcus, Jane. *Hearts of Darkness: White Women Write Race.* New Brunswick, NJ: Rutgers University Press, 2004.

McCormack, W. J. "Nightmares of History: James Joyce and the Phenomenon of Anglo-Irish Literature." In *James Joyce and Modern Literature,* ed. W. J. McCormack and Alistair Stead, 77–107. London: Routledge and Kegan Paul, 1982.

McCormack, W. J., and Alistair Stead, eds. *James Joyce and Modern Literature.* London: Routledge and Kegan Paul, 1982.

McDermott, John J. *Streams of Experience: Reflections on the History and Philosophy of American Culture.* Amherst: University of Massachusetts Press, 1986.

McFarlane, James, ed. *Henrik Ibsen: A Critical Anthology.* Middlesex, England: Penguin, 1970.

McMillan, James. *Twentieth-Century France: Politics and Society 1898–1991.* New York: Routledge, 1992.

Meisel, Perry. *The Myth of the Modern: A Study of British Literature and Criticism after 1850.* New Haven, CT: Yale University Press, 1987.

Menand, Louis. *The Metaphysical Club: A Story of Ideas in America.* New York: Farrar, Straus, and Giroux, 2001.

Mendelson, Edward. "Encyclopedic Narrative: From Dante to Pynchon." *Modern Language Notes* 91 (1976): 1267–75.

Miller, J. Hillis. *Fiction and Repetition: Seven English Novels.* Cambridge, MA: Harvard University Press, 1982.

Miller, Rosalind S. *Gertrude Stein: Form and Intelligibility.* New York: Exposition Press, 1949.

Mitchell, Charles E. *Individualism and Its Discontents: Appropriations of Emerson, 1880–1950.* Amherst: University of Massachusetts Press, 1997.

Moi, Toril. *Henrik Ibsen and the Birth of Modernism: Art, Theater, Philosophy.* Oxford: Oxford University Press, 2006.

Moliterno, Frank. *The Dialectics of Sense and Spirit in Pater and Joyce.* Greensboro, NC: ELT, 1988.

Montaigne, Michel de. "On Repentance." In *Essays,* 235–50. Translated by J. M. Cohen. New York: Penguin, 1993.

Moretti, Franco. "Serious Century." In *History, Geography, and Culture,* Vol. 1 of *The Novel.* Edited by Franco Moretti. Princeton, NJ: Princeton University Press, 2006.

———. *Signs Taken for Wonders.* London: Verso, 1988.

———. *The Way of the World: The* Bildungsroman *in European Culture.* London, Verso, 1987.

Muller, Marcel. *Les Voix narratives dans la Recherche du temps perdu.* Geneva: Droz, 1965.

Musil, Robert. *The Man Without Qualities.* Translated by Sophie Wilkins and Burton Pike. 2 vols. New York: Vintage, 1996.

Nehamas, Alexander. *Nietzsche: Life as Literature.* Cambridge, MA: Harvard University Press, 1985.

Nemerov, Alexander. "The Flight of Form: Auden, Bruegel, and the Turn to Abstraction in the 1940s. *Critical Inquiry* 31 (Summer 2005): 780–810.

Ngai, Sianne. *Ugly Feelings.* Cambridge, MA: Harvard University Press, 2005.

Norris, Margot. "Joyce's Heliotrope." In *Coping with Joyce,* ed. Morris Beja and Shari Benstock, 3–24. Columbus: Ohio State University Press, 1989.

———. *Suspicious Readings of Joyce's* Dubliners. Philadelphia: University of Pennsylvania Press, 2003.

North, Michael. *Reading 1922: A Return to the Scene of the Modern.* New York: Oxford University Press, 1999.

Olson, Liesl M. "Stevens and Auden: Antimythological Meetings." *Wallace Stevens Journal* 27 (Fall 2003): 240–54.

Ophir, Ella. "Modernist Fiction and 'the accumulation of unrecorded life." *Modernist Cultures* 2, no. 10: 6–20. http://www.js-modcult.bham.ac.uk/fetch.asp?article=Issue3_ophir.pdf

Pater, Walter. *Selected Writings of Walter Pater.* Edited by Harold Bloom. New York: Columbia University Press, 1974.

Perec, Georges. *La vie mode d'emploi.* Paris: Hachette, 1978.

———. *Les choses: une histoire des années soixante.* Paris: Juillard, 1965.

Perry, Ralph Barton. *The Thought and Character of William James.* 2 vols. Boston: Little, 1935.

Phillips, Siobhan. "Wallace Stevens and the Mode of the Ordinary." *Twentieth Century Literature* 54.1 (Spring 2008): 1–30.

Pippin, Robert. *The Persistence of Subjectivity: On the Kantian Aftermath.* Cambridge: Cambridge University Press, 2005.

Poggioli, Renato. *The Theory of the Avant-Garde.* Translated by Gerald Fitzgerald. Cambridge, MA: Belknap, 1997.

Poirier, Richard. *Poetry and Pragmatism.* Cambridge: Harvard University Press, 1992.

———. *The Renewal of Literature: Emersonian Reflections.* New Haven, CT: Yale University Press, 1987.

Pound, Ezra. *Literary Essays.* Edited by T. S. Eliot. New York: New Directions, 1968.

Power, Arthur. *Conversations with James Joyce.* Edited by Clive Hart. Dublin: Cahill, 1974.

Proust, Marcel. *À la recherche du temps perdu.* Texte établi sous la direction de Jean-Yves Tadié. Paris: Gallimard, 1999.

———. *Correspondance de Marcel Proust.* Edited by Philip Kolb. 21 vols. Paris: Plon, 1970–1993.

———. *In Search of Lost Time.* Translated by C. K. Scott Moncrieff and Terence Kilmartin. Revised by D. J. Enright. New York: Modern Library, 1993.

Pynchon, Thomas. *Gravity's Rainbow.* New York: Penguin, 1973.

Randall, Bryony. *Modernism, Daily Time, and Everyday Life.* Cambridge: Cambridge University Press, 2008.

Reed, Christopher. *Bloomsbury Rooms: Modernism, Subculture, and Domesticity.* New Haven, CT: Yale University Press, 2004.

Richter, Harvena. Virginia Woolf: *The Inward Voyage.* Princeton, NJ: Princeton University Press, 1970.

Rilke, Rainer Maria. *The Selected Poetry of Rainer Maria Rilke.* Translated by Stephen Mitchell. New York: Vintage, 1989.

Rorty, Richard. *Contingency, Irony, and Solidarity.* Cambridge: Cambridge University Press, 1989.

Ross, Kristin. *Fast Cars, Clean Bodies: The Decolonization and the Reordering of French Culture.* Cambridge, MA: MIT, 1995.

Rosner, Victoria. *Modernism and the Architecture of Private Life.* New York: Columbia University Press, 2005.

Ruddick, Lisa. *Reading Gertrude Stein: Body, Text Gnosis.* Ithaca, NY: Cornell University Press, 1990.

Rushdie, Salmon. *Midnight's Children.* London: Jonathan Cape, 1981.

Russell. F. A. "Who Was the Author of . . ." *Notes and Queries,* 9th ser., 12 (Oct. 17, 1903): 309.

Scarry, Elaine. *The Body in Pain: The Making and Unmaking of the World.* New York: Oxford University Press, 1985.

Schenker, Daniel. "Stalking the Invisible Hero: Ibsen, Joyce, Kierkegaard, and the Failure of Modern Irony," *English Literary History* 51, no. 1 (Spring 1984): 153–83.

Schoenbach, Lisi. "'Peaceful and Exciting': Habit, Shock, and Gertrude Stein's Pragmatic Modernism." *Modernism/Modernity* 11, no. 2 (2004): 239–59.

Schor, Naomi. *Reading in Detail: Aesthetics and the Feminine.* New York: Methuen, 1987.

Schulkind, Jeanne. Introduction to *Moments of Being,* by Virginia Woolf, 11–24. New York: Harcourt Brace Jovanovich, 1985.

Schwenger, Peter. "Still Life: A User's Manual." *Narrative* 10, 2 (May 2002): 140–55.

Seidel, Michael. *Epic Geography.* Princeton, NJ: Princeton University Press, 1976.

Senn, Fritz. "Entering the Lists: Sampling Early Catalogues." In *Joyce in Context,* ed. Vincent J. Cheng and Timothy Martin, 241–58. Cambridge: Cambridge University Press, 1992.

Shattuck, Roger. *Proust's Way: A Field Guide to "In Search of Lost Time."* New York: W.W. Norton, 2000.

Sherry, Vincent. *The Great War and the Language of Modernism.* New York: Oxford University Press, 2003.

Shklovsky, Victor. "Art as Technique." In *Russian Formalist Criticism: Four Essays.* Translated by Lee T. Lemon and Marion J. Reis, 5–22. Lincoln: University of Nebraska Press, 1965.

Showalter, Elaine. Introduction to *Mrs. Dalloway,* by Virginia Woolf, xi–xlviii. London: Penguin, 1992.

Smidt, Kristian. "Joyce's Norwegian Teachers." *English Studies* 44, no. 2 (April 1963): 121–22.

Spencer, Theodore. Introduction to *Stephen Hero,* by James Joyce, 7–19. Edited by John J. Slocum and Herbert Cahoon. New York: New Directions, 1963.

Spoo, Robert. "'Nestor' and the Nightmare: The Presence of the Great War in *Ulysses.*" In *Joyce and the Subject of History,* ed. Mark A. Wollaeger, Victor Luftig, and Robert Spoo, 105–24. Ann Arbor: University of Michigan Press, 1996.

Squier, Susan. *Virginia Woolf and London: Sexual Politics of the City.* Chapel Hill: University of North Carolina Press, 1985.

Stein, Gertrude. "An American and France." *What Are Masterpieces,* ed. Robert Bartlett Haas, 59–70. New York: Pitman.

———. *The Autobiography of Alice B. Toklas.* London: Penguin, 1966.

———. *Brewsie and Willie.* London: Brilliance Books, 1988.

———. "Composition as Explanation." In *Selected Writings of Gertrude Stein,* ed. Carl Van Vechten, 511–23. New York: Vintage, 1990.

———. *Everybody's Autobiography.* Cambridge, MA: Exact Change, 1993.

———. *Lectures in America.* Boston: Beacon, 1935.

———. *The Making of Americans.* In *Selected Writings of Gertrude Stein,* ed. Carl Van Vechten, 259–326. New York: Vintage, 1990.

———. *Mrs. Reynolds.* Los Angeles: Sun and Moon, 1980.

———. *Narration.* Chicago: University of Chicago Press, 1935.

———. *Paris France.* New York: Liveright, 1996.

———. "Poetry and Grammar." In *Lectures in America,* 209–46. Boston: Beacon, 1935.

———. "Portraits and Repetitions." In *Lectures in America,* 165–206. Boston: Beacon, 1935.

———. *Selected Writings of Gertrude Stein.* Edited by Carl Van Vechten. New York: Vintage, 1990.

———. *Tender Buttons.* Mineola, NY: Dover, 1997.
———. *Three Lives.* London: Penguin, 1990.
———. "A Transatlantic Interview." In *What Are Masterpieces,* ed. Robert Bartlett Haas, 97–104. New York: Pitman, 1970.
———. *Wars I Have Seen.* New York: Random House, 1945.
———. "What Is English Literature." In *Lectures in America,* 11–55. Boston: Beacon, 1935.
Stevens, Wallace. The *Collected Poems of Wallace Stevens.* New York: Random House, 1954.
———. *Letters of Wallace Stevens.* Edited by Holly Stevens. Berkeley: University of California Press, 1966.
———. *The Necessary Angel: Essays on Reality and the Imagination.* New York: Random House, 1951.
———. *Opus Posthumous.* Edited by Milton J. Bates. New York: Random House, 1989.
———. *Sur Plusieurs Beaux Sujects: Wallace Stevens' Commonplace Book.* Edited by Milton J. Bates. Stanford, CA: Stanford University Press and Huntington Library, 1989.
Stevens, Wallace, and José Rodríguez Feo. *Secretaries to the Moon: The Letters of Wallace Stevens and José Rodríguez Feo.* Edited by Beverly Coyle and Alan Filreis. Durham, NC: Duke University Press, 1986.
Tal, Kali. *Worlds of Hurt: Reading the Literatures of Trauma.* Cambridge; New York: Cambridge University Press, 1996.
Taylor, Charles. *Sources of the Self: The Making of Modern Identity.* Cambridge: Harvard University Press, 1989.
Thomas, Joseph J. "Figures of Habit in William James." *New England Quarterly* 66, no. 1 (1993): 3–26.
Thompson, E. P. *Customs in Common.* New York: New Press, 1991.
Toklas, Alice B. *The Alice B. Toklas Cookbook.* London: Serif, 2004.
Tratner, Michael. *Modernism and Mass Politics: Joyce, Woolf, Eliot, Yeats.* Stanford, CA: Stanford University Press, 1995.
Trilling, Lionel. "The Fate of Pleasure: Wordsworth to Dostoevsky." In *Literary Views: Critical and Historical Essays,* ed. Carroll Camden, 93–114. Chicago: University of Chicago Press, 1964.
Tursi, Renée. *The Force of Habit at the Turn of the Century: William James, Henry James, Edith Wharton, W. E. B. Dubois.* PhD diss., Columbia University, 2000.
Tysdahl, B. J. *Joyce and Ibsen.* Oslo: Norwegian University Press, 1968.
Van Dusen, Wanda. "Portrait of a National Fetish: Gertrude Stein's 'Introduction to the Speeches of Maréchal Pétain.'" *Modernism/Modernity* 3, no. 1 (1996): 69–92.
Vaneigem, Raoul. *The Revolution of Everyday Life.* Translated by Donald Nicholson-Smith. Paris, 1967. *The Situationist International Text Library.* http://library.nothingness.org/articles/SI/en/pub_contents/5.
Vendler, Helen. *On Extended Wings: Wallace Stevens' Longer Poems.* Cambridge, MA: Harvard University Press, 1969.
———. *Wallace Stevens: Words Chosen Out of Desire.* Knoxville: University of Tennessee Press, 1984.
Walker, Jayne L. *The Making of a Modernist: Gertrude Stein from Three Lives to Tender Buttons.* Amherst: University of Massachusetts Press, 1984.

Wall, Cynthia. *The Prose of Things: Transformations of Description in the Eighteenth Century.* Chicago: University of Chicago Press, 2006.

Watson, G.J. "The Politics of *Ulysses.*" In *Joyce's* Ulysses: *The Larger Perspective,* ed. Robert D. Newman and Weldon Thornton, 39–58. Newark: University of Delaware Press, 1987.

Watt, Ian. *The Rise of the Novel: Studies in Defoe, Richardson, and Fielding.* Berkeley: University of California Press, 1962.

Whittier-Ferguson, John. "The Liberation of Gertrude Stein: War and Writing." *Modernism/Modernity* 8, no. 3 (2001): 405–28.

———. "Stein in Time: History, Manuscripts, and Memory." *Modernism/Modernity* 6, no. 1 (1999): 115–51.

Wilde, Oscar. *The Picture of Dorian Gray. The Portable Oscar Wilde.* Edited by Richard Aldington and Stanley Weintraub, 138–391. New York: Penguin, 1981.

Will, Barbara. "Lost in Translation: Stein's Vichy Collaboration," *Modernism/Modernity* 11, no. 4 (2004): 651–68.

Williams, Raymond. "Culture Is Ordinary." In *Resources of Hope: Culture, Democracy, Socialism,* 3–18. London: Verso, 1989.

———. *Keywords: A Vocabulary of Culture and Society.* Rev. ed. Oxford: Oxford University Press, 1983.

Williams, William Carlos. *Paterson.* New York: New Directions, 1992.

Wiman, Christian. "Position Paper: Wallace Stevens." *Wallace Stevens Journal* 28 (Fall 2004): 240–41.

Wittgenstein, Ludwig. *The Blue and Brown Books.* New York: Harper and Row, 1965.

———. *Philosophical Investigations.* Translated by G. E. M. Anscombe. Oxford: Basil Blackwell, 1968.

Wollaeger, Mark A., Victor Luftig, and Robert Spoo, eds. *Joyce and the Subject of History.* Ann Arbor: University of Michigan Press, 1996.

Woolf, Leonard. *Beginning Again: An Autobiography of the Years 1911 to 1918.* New York: Harcourt Brace and World, 1964.

Woolf, Virginia. "Aurora Leigh." In *Women and Writing,* ed. Michèle Barrett, 133–44. San Diego: Harvest/Harcourt Brace Jovanovich, 1979.

———. *Between the Acts.* London: Penguin Books, 1992.

———. *The Diary of Virginia Woolf.* Edited by Anne Olivier Bell and Andrew McNeillie. 5 vols. New York: Harcourt Brace Jovanovich, 1977–1984.

———. *The Essays of Virginia Woolf.* Edited by Andrew McNeillie. 6 vols. San Diego, CA: Harcourt Brace Jovanovich, 1986.

———. "Jane Austen." In *The Common Reader,* 1st ser., 134–45. New York: Harcourt Brace Jovanovich, 1984.

———. *Jacob's Room.* London: Penguin Books, 1992.

———. "The Leaning Tower." In *Collected Essays,* Vol. 2., 162–81. New York: Harcourt Brace and World, 1966.

———. "A Letter to a Young Poet." In *The Death of the Moth and Other Essays,* 208–26. New York: Harcourt Brace Jovanovich, 1942.

———. *The Letters of Virginia Woolf.* Edited by Nigel Nicolson and Joanne Trautmann. 5 vols. New York: Harcourt Brace Jovanovich, 1975–1980.

———. "A Mark on the Wall." In *The Complete Shorter Fiction of Virginia Woolf*, ed. Susan Dick, 83–89. 2nd ed. San Diego: Harcourt Brace, 1989.

———. "Mr. Bennett and Mrs. Brown." In *The Captain's Death Bed and Other Essays*, 94–119. New York: Harcourt Brace Jovanovich, 1978.

———. *Mrs. Dalloway.* London: Penguin Books, 1992.

———. "Modern Fiction." In *The Essays of Virginia Woolf*, ed. Andrew McNeillie, Vol. 4, 157–65. San Diego, CA: Harcourt Brace Jovanovich, 1994.

———. "Montaigne." In *The Common Reader*, 1st ser., ed. Andrew McNeillie, 58–68. New York: Harcourt Brace Jovanovich, 1984.

———. "The Narrow Bridge of Art." In *Collected Essays*, Vol. 2, 218–29. New York: Harcourt Brace and World, 1966.

———. "The Novels of George Gissing." In *The Essays of Virginia Woolf*, ed. Andrew McNeillie, Vol. 1, 355–62. San Diego, CA: Harcourt Brace Jovanovich, 1986.

———. "On Being Ill." In *The Moment and Other Essays.* New York: Harcourt Brace, 1948.

———. *The Pargiters.* Edited by Mitchell A. Leaska. New York: Harcourt Brace Jovanovich, 1977.

———. "Phases of Fiction." In *Collected Essays*, Vol. 2, 56–102. New York: Harcourt Brace and World, 1966.

———. "A Sketch of the Past." In *Moments of Being*, ed. Jeanne Schulkind, 64–159. New York: Harcourt Brace Jovanovich, 1985.

———. *To the Lighthouse.* London: Penguin, 1992.

———. *The Years.* London: Penguin Books, 1992.

———. *Three Guineas.* New York: Harvest/Harcourt Brace, 1966.

———. "Women and Fiction." In *Collected Essays*, Vol. 2, 141–48. New York: Harcourt Brace and World, 1966.

Wordsworth, William. *Selected Poems and Prefaces.* Edited by Jack Stillinger. Boston: Houghton Mifflin, 1965.

Yeats, William Butler. *The Collected Works of W. B. Yeats.* Vol. 1: *The Poems.* Edited by Richard J. Finneran. New York: Macmillan, 1989.

Yeazell, Ruth. *Art of the Everyday: Dutch Painting and the Realist Novel.* Princeton, NJ: Princeton University Press, 2008.

Zwerdling, Alex. *Virginia Woolf and the Real World.* Berkeley: University of California Press, 1986.

# Index

absentmindedness, ordinary, 6
abstraction, Stevens's, 116
accidents, real life, vs. literature, 54
action and memory, habit, 92–93
activities and things, ordinary, 6
actual world, term, 117
aesthetic order, modernism, 5
affective experience, ordinary, 6, 19
Agamben, Giorgio, 30, 165
"A Letter to a Young Poet," Virginia Woolf, 57, 60–61
*Alice B.*
  cookbook, 90, 100
  Stein and Alice B. Toklas, 89, 102
America, modernism in Europe and, 11
Americanization, everyday life, 13
animating energy, commonplace, 138, 142
"An Ordinary Evening in New Haven," Stevens, 137–148
*A Portrait of the Artist as a Young Man*
  artist becoming divine, 38
  epiphany, 41
Aristotle
  public and private life, 130–131
  real life events, 54–55
art
  connection to humanity, 63
  constructing work of everyday, 150–151
  defamiliarization, 4–5
  habitualization and, 4
  normal as perfect subject for, 122
  shock, 25
"A Sketch of the Past," Virginia Woolf, 62, 74–75, 86
A Topographical Guide to James Joyce's *Ulysses*, 48
Auden
  "In Memory of W. B. Yeats," 128
  "Lullaby," 27
  "Musée des Beaux-Arts," 24
  Stevens difference from, 124–125, 128
  and Woolf, 60
  "Writing," 62
Auerbach, Eric, 18, 19, 22, 77, 78, 80, 164
Augustine, describing habits, 152
avante-garde, Gertrude Stein, 89, 105

balance, wisdom from, 141
Barnes, Djuna, 20
Barthes, Roland, 21, 50, 53, 164, 167
beauty, balance with realism, 60–61
Beckett, Samuel
  choice, 110
  comparison between Stein and, 109–110
  day-to-day existence, 66–67
  *Endgame*, 109–110
  *How It Is*, 110, 156
  on Joyce, 38, 52
  *Krapp's Last Tape*, 69, 108
  *Molloy*, 108, 110
  "Play," 156
  postwar creation of characters, 108
  and Proust, 5, 10, 66, 68, 156, 158–159
  representation of habit, 155–156
  Waiting for Godot, 109–110
  and Woolf, 67
being
  moments of, vs. nonbeing, 64–65
  normal, 137

beingness, modernism, 4
believability, ordinary experience and character, 65
Bennett, Arnold, 7, 71, 169, 171
Bergson, Henri
  *Creative Evolution*, 66
  man of action, 96
  *Matter and Memory*, 90, 92, 96, 151
  theory of intuitive action, 92
  time, 151
  and William James, 11–12, 92–93, 96
Bernstein, Charles, 146, 174
*Between the Acts*, Virginia Woolf, 70, 84–85
Blanchot, Maurice, 12, 54, 79, 164
Bloom, Leopold, list of items eaten, 46–47
Bowles, Paul, 89, 90
Bürger, Peter, 8

calendar, texts without plots, 46
capitalism, everyday life, 14
Cavell, Stanley, 10, 118, 146, 163, 164, 172
Certeau, Michel de, 12, 15, 16, 85, 86, 111, 170
*Chamber Music*, poetry collection, 37
chance incidents, Proust, 149
change
  *Mrs. Dalloway* and response to, 66
  Stevens's conception, 140, 141
chaos, modernism, 5
character forming, habit, 93, 94
characters
  believability of, 65
  desire to pin down, 77
  habit revealing, 68–69
  nature of perception and overlooking, 70–71
  relationship and experience, 71–72
  sympathy for, 22–23
childhood, serving as base for life, 62–63
choice, Samuel Beckett's work, 110
Christian sense, ordinary, 18–19
citizenship, Bloom's definition, 47
class, 9, 15–16, 19, 23
  determining ordinary tasks, 77–78
  everyday moments and upper, 79
  and Stevens, 121
  and William James, 94
  and Woolf, 71, 77–81
coherence, modernism, 5
Cole, Sarah, 169
colonization, everyday life, 13
common objects, lists, 7
commonplace
  animating energy, 138
  mood and style, 138–139
  Stevens's middle ground, 137
  Stevens vs. other modernists, 145–146
  *Ulysses* examining, 33–34
  Wallace Stevens, 115, 119, 129, 130–131, 141–142
Compagnon, Antoine, 159
*Confessions*, habits by Augustine, 152
connectedness
  human beings, 23
  theory of human, 72
conversations, modernist novels, 22
Cook, Eleanor, 139, 141, 173
cotton wool, daily life by Woolf, 73, 86–87, 96, 133
cracked looking glass, Irish art, 38–39
crudeness, Joyce, 43
Cuddy-Keane, Melba, 167, 168
cultural studies, everyday life, 13–14
culture, ordinary, 15–16

daily island life
  American writing, 99
  European and American, 11
  ordinariness of culture, 15–16
  peace and repetition, 29
  Stein writing, 97, 101
daily life, *Mrs. Dalloway*, 67
Danto, Arthur, 5
Debord, Guy-Ernest, 12
defamiliarization, 4–5, 6, 25, 50, 95, 100, 138
defiance, notion of everyday life, 78
Deleuze, Gilles, 159
Des Pres, Terrence, 20, 30
discontinuity, Proust, 158–159
distance and near, relationship by Stevens, 140
divinity, Stevens's notion of, 144–145
domestic habit. *See also* habit
  ordinary, 16
domestic isolation, Stevens, 129
Douglas, Ann, Stein's love of popular, 100
"Drama and Life," reading essay, 37–38

dramatic notations, epiphany style, 41
*Dubliners*, epiphany, 41
Dutch paintings, ordinary life, 23–25

Eliot, George, 19, 21, 23
Eliot, T. S.
  Stevens difference from, 123–125
  "The Metaphysical Poets," 138
Ellmann, Richard, 7, 33, 36, 37
Emerson, Ralph Waldo, 10, 90, 92, 163, 170
*Endgame*, Samuel Beckett, 109–110
England, literature describing things, 97–98
Englishness, importance and hegemony, 97
epic hero, Odysseus, 47–48
epiphany
  experience, 7–8
  fragmentary pieces, 39–40
  Ibsen and, 37–45
  interpreting Joyce's work, 35
  Stephen Hero, 40–41, 43
  styles, 41
errors, everyday, 48–49
ethical system, modern realism, 22
Europe, modernism in, and America, 11
events
  lists, 7
  significance and real life, 53–54
everyday
  constructing work of art, 150–151
  eruption in literature, 36
  limitations, 36
  mishaps, 48–49
  nineteenth century and, 17–27
  poetics of, 44
  repetition of, actions, 66
everyday life
  affirmation of ordinary, 75
  Aristotle, 54–55
  feminist theory of, 80
  Joyce exacting representation of, 38
  potentially defiant or rebellious, 78
  power to trump trauma, 76
  "procession" of people, 72–73
  range of philosophies, 11–12
  significance of events, 53–54
  theory, 12–17
  *Ulysses* celebrating, 45–46
  upper class, 79
  war and, in Stein's writings, 100–101
  writers attempting to replicate, 86
external reality, abandonment of, in *The Waves*, 84
external world, denying, by routine, 73–74

facts
  "Phases of Fiction," 59
  resistance to narrative effect, 7
facts of war, *Mrs. Reynolds*, 109
Faÿ, Bernard, 102, 171
Felski, Rita, 4, 17, 19, 79, 80
feminine style, ordinary, 16–17
Filreis, Alan, 116, 125, 172, 173
*Finnegans Wake*
  Beckett, 38
  real life, 54
flashbacks, *Mrs. Reynolds*, 107–108
flawed mirror, Irish art, 38–39
fly-wheel, metaphor for habit, 94
Forster, E. M., 57, 69, 167
Freud
  and Stein, 96–97, 114
  understanding of repetition, 96–97
  and Woolf, 76
Fussell, Paul, 30, 104, 165

genre, ordinary as, 6, 19
Gissing, George, 20, 22, 165
grammar, list vs. sentence, 53
*Gravity's Rainbow*, crudeness, 43

habit
  character forming, 93, 94
  fly-wheel of society, 91–101
  functions during time of war, 113
  life as narrative of, 161
  memory and action, 92–93
  philosophy of James, 92–93
  Proustian, 153–154
  reality, 158
  repetition, 93
  repetition presenting, 155–156
  revealing characters, 68–69
  Stein's life and work, 90, 97, 102, 153
  substance of life, 68
  time and, 151–152
  Walter Pater disparaging, 94–95

habit (*continued*)
  William James, 91–92, 95–96, 112–113
  working-class individuals, 94
habitualization, art and, 4
*Hedda Gabler*, epiphany, 40
Hegel, G. W. F., 16, 23, 24, 61, 168
hegemony
  Englishness, 97
  habit, 94
heightened experience
  epiphany, 7–8
  every day things, 96
Hemingway, Ernest, 30, 31, 89
Highmore, Ben, 19, 170
history
  influence on poetry, 126
  lists, 47–48
  Mrs. Reynolds, 106–107
history lessons, *Ulysses*, 42

Ibsen
  epiphany, 37–45
  inspiring Joyce, 34–35
imagination
  cleansing the, of romantic, 139–140
  commonplace even in severe circumstances, 125–126
  power, 25
  romantic, 25–26
"Imagination as Value," Stevens, 125, 139
*imparfait*
  Moretti on, 155
  Proust's use of, 154–155
  Stevens allusion to, 127
imperfect, Stevens's repetition, 127
inattention, ordinary, 6
inattentive reading, ordinary, 6
individuality, everyday, 80
inferiority, connotation of ordinary, 9
*In Search of Lost Time*
  chance incident in Proust's, 149–150
  ending, 156–157
  narrative of habit, 154
  thematic unities, 159
insignificant events, significance through narrative, 160
internal states, Woolf's interest in, 58
interpretations, *Ulysses*, 45–46
Irish art, flawed mirror, 38–39
Irish culture, mythology and folklore, 37
iterative narration, Proust, 155
"Ithaca"
  catechistic prose, 50
  lists, 49–50, 52
  *Ulysses* chapter, 35

*Jacob's Room*, Virginia Woolf, 76
James, Henry, linguistic abstraction, 100
James, William
  habit, 90, 91–92, 92–93, 95–96, 112–113
  Henry James vs., 100
  Stevens's work vs., 145
  "a world of pure experience," 92
Jewish sense, ordinary, 18–19
Johnson, Samuel, 86
Joyce, James
  *Dubliners*, 39, 41, 111
  epiphanies, 35
  *Exiles*, 51
  *Finnegans Wake*, 38, 45, 54
  Ibsen inspiring, 34–35
  lists, 35, 45–55, 143–144, 148
  literary inspiration, 38–39
  Odysseus, 47–48
  *A Portrait of the Artist as a Young Man*, 38, 41, 43–44
  realism and romanticism, 37
  scrupulous meanness, 39
  *Stephen Hero*, 40–41, 43
  Stevens's work vs., 146
  *Ulysses*, 5, 6, 7, 16, 21, 26, 27, 31–32, 33–36, 44–55, 146, 150
  vulgarity, 41, 42
  and Woolf, 60, 68, 83, 84

Kenner, Hugh, 46, 47, 163, 166, 167
Kermode, Frank, 55, 125, 126, 167, 172

Landy, Joshua, 159, 174
Langbauer, Laurie, 17, 168
language
  changing experience, 143
  "Ithaca," 50
  novel employing, 19–20
  ordinary to "literary," 52
  power that gives life, 144

Stevens's concept of, 118, 122, 137
Stevens's "normal" animating, 142
Stevens trusting, 146–147
style in *Ulysses*, 51–52
The Waste Land, 123–124
Ulysses, 45
*Lectures in America*, Gertrude Stein, 97
Lefebvre, Henri
*Critique of Everyday Life*, 36, 64, 138
*Everyday Life and the Modern World*, 12, 16, 36
theory of everyday life, 12–17
Levin, Jonathan, 100, 163
Lewis, Pericles, 61
life
childhood as base, 62–63
distinction between public and private, 130–131
events as wholly connected by Proust, 161
"life as literature," 160
narrative of habit, 161
preserving ordinary tasks, 72
Proust distinguishing literature and, 159
lists
ability to go on and on, 49–50
events and objects, 7
grammar, 53
items eaten by Bloom, 46–47
"Ithaca," 49–50, 52
materialism of, 41–42
objects in *Ulysses*, 52–53
Stevens, 143–144
texts without plots, 46
turning, into symbols, 44
*Ulysses*, 35, 45–55
literary character, habit representing, 94
literary values, nineteenth century, 20–21
literature
accidents in real life vs., 54
eruption of everyday, 36
"life as literature," 160
Proust distinguishing, and life, 159
Longenbach, James, 116, 125, 142, 172, 173
looking glass, Joyce, 38–39

MacLeod, Glen, 165
man of action, Bergson defining, 96
Mann, Thomas, 27, 28
Mao, Douglas, 164, 165
masculinity, femininity vs., and everyday life, 16–17
materialism
emphasis by Woolf for building character, 82–83
fabric of things, 66
lists, 41–42
Ulysses, 43
*Matter and Memory*, Henri Bergson, 92, 96
memory, clinging to mundane, 62–63
memory and action, habit, 92–93
*Midnight's Children*, crudeness, 43
mishaps, everyday, 48–49
modernist fiction, heightened experience, 74
modernist novel, inaction and action, 21
modernists, representing temporality, 151
modern realism, Virginia Woolf, 85–86
modern war, ordinary life and, 27–32
money, poetry and Stevens, 121
mood, commonplace, 138–139
Moretti, Franco, 18, 27, 28, 46, 51, 155, 164
"Mr. Bennett and Mrs. Brown," Virginia Woolf, 61
*Mrs. Dalloway*
daily life, 67
experience of time, 151
ordinary task and heightened events, 67
response to change, 66
Virginia Woolf, 66–77
*Mrs. Reynolds*
obscurity and sheer length of, 107–109
routine during war, 101–104
"shadow" of war, 104
treatment of history, 106–107
World War II, 108, 153
mundane, memory and thought, 62–63
mundane activities
everyday by Woolf, 79
housework of women, 80–82
"Myth," *Ulysses*, 34

*Narration*, Gertrude Stein, 94, 99
narrative. *See also* Proust
everydayness, 18
inaction and action, 21

Nazi death camps, imagination and poetry, 126
Nehamas, Alexander, 160
Nemerov, Alexander, 165
Nietzsche, Friedrich, 160, 161, 174
nineteenth century
 everyday, 17–27
 literary values, 20–21
nineteenth-century novel, everydayness, 18
nonbeing
 building literary traditions, 86
 moments of being vs., 64–65
 significance, 64
 traumatic experience, 74–75
normal
 differing for everyone, 121
 perfect subject for art, 122
 substance of being, 137
novel
 hetero-directed form of life, 27–28
 language, 19–20
novelistic realism, lacking delusions of romantic idealism, 34

objects, attention to, 98–99
Odysseus, interest by Joyce, 47–48
"Of Modern Poetry," Stevens's poetry, 123–124
old-fashioned living, Gertrude Stein, 90
openness, Proust, 158–159
Oppen, George, 124
order
 patterns to life, 63, 64
 time, 151–152
ordinary
 affirmation in Woolf's *Mrs. Dalloway*, 75
 central subject by Woolf, 69–70
 commitment of Stevens to, 116
 culture, 15–16
 defining feature of Woolf, 86
 everyday world, 3–4
 giving form to shock, 8–9
 internal and external phenomenon, 65
 modernist attention to, 26–27
 poetry satisfying, 122–123
 pragmatism affirming, 10
 prose vs. poetry, 59
 realism and how, becomes literary, 52
 taking risks to achieve, 148
 *Ulysses* examining, 33–34
 valuing, 5–7
 writers defining primacy of, 10–11
ordinary days, desire for continuation, 76
"Ordinary Evening," Wallace Stevens, 117–118, 121, 122, 131, 138–148
ordinary experiences
 believability of character, 65
 denying external world, 73–74
 life, 72
 Stevens trusting language, 146–147
 Woolf's writings, 58
ordinary life
 Dutch paintings, 23–25
 and modern war, 27–32
ordinary mind, ordinary day, 59
ordinary people, habits of, 100
ordinary things, subjects of poems, 144
organizing life, ordinary, 6–7
ostranenie
 defamiliarization, 4
 inattention vs., 6
overlooking, ordinary things, 70–71

paintings, ordinary life in Dutch, 23–25
*Paris France*, Gertrude Stein, 101
Pater, Walter
 disparaging habits, 94–96
 habit as unconscious action, 95
 and Freud, 96–97
 and Joyce, 37
 and Stevens, 133
 and William James, 11, 90
patterns
 meaning in life, 63
 order, 64
perception
 characters, 70–71
 nature of, in commonplace, 138
Perec, Georges, 13, 164, 169
perspective of reader, Stevens imagining, 142–143
"Phases of Fiction," Virginia Woolf, 59, 83, 85–86
philosophies, everyday life, 11–12

Pippin, Robert, 153
poetics
  everyday, 44
  term, 57
  *The Waves* by Woolf, 83–84
poetry
  everyday, 20
  history's influence on, 126
  money is, and Stevens, 121
  ordinary satisfying, 122–123
  political work, 31
  romantic, 31
  Stevens's approach, 119–120
  Stevens trusting language, 146–147
  subjectivity, interiority, and, 61–62
  vs. prose, 60–77
politics, daily life and, of World War II, 112
positivism, Stein and James, 90
Pound, Ezra, 3, 10, 37, 122, 123, 146
pragmatic modernism, Gertrude Stein, 98
pragmatism, affirming ordinary, 10
*Principles of Psychology*, James' "Habit," 91
private life, distinguishing public and, 130–131
procession
  commemorating life, 72–73
  shadows, 77
prophecy, role in Stein's novel, 112
prose
  epiphany style in, poems, 41
  everyday, 20
  poetry vs., 60–77
  Virginia Woolf's, 57
Proust
  chance incident, 149
  discontinuity and openness, 158–159
  iterative narration, 155
  "life as literature," 160
  life as narrative of habit, 161
  literature and life, 159
  use of *imparfait*, 154–155
public life, distinguishing private and, 130–131
purebred prose, *The Waves* by Woolf, 84

quotidian. *See also* everyday; ordinary
  commonplace, 121
  everyday life theory, 12–17
  Stevens imagining, 142–143
  modernist writers, 19, 27
  realist styles, 34
  Stevens's attention to, 132–134
  Wars I Have Seen, 102
  Woolf's representation, 79, 80

Rabelaisian realism, Joyce, 42
Randall, Bryony, 163, 164, 168
reader's perspective, Stevens imagining, 142–143
real
  locating, 145
  movement of shadow to, 77
  redefining, 62
realism
  balance with "beauty," 60–61
  everyday life, 14
  Joyce, 37
  mirrorlike reflection of world, 54
  modernism, 5
  modernism and, 18–19
  modernist novels, 21–22
  ordinary becomes literary, 52
  recording fact, 35
reality
  evasion of, 144
  familiar through comparison, 132
  habit and time, 158
reality effect, ordinary, 21
real things, denying external world, 73–74
rebellion, notion of everyday life, 78
Reed, Christopher, 65, 168
religion, modernity's relationship to, 61
repetition
  any day moments, 69–70
  everyday actions, 66
  Freud's understanding, 96–97
  habit, 93
  insurance and poetry of Stevens, 136
  living during war, 103–104
  representing habit, 155–156
  Samuel Beckett's postwar characters, 108
  Stein, 103, 148
resemblances
  disparate things, 134–135
  praise of, 135
  Stevens finding, 134–135, 151

resistance to change, Gertrude Stein, 102
Rilke, Rainer Maria, 8, 154
romantic
cleansing imagination of, 139–140
imagination, 25–26
poetry, 31
romantic idealism, experience without delusions of, 34
romanticism
Joyce, 37
Joyce and Ibsen examining deluded, 39
"Villanelle of the Temptress," 43
war years, 28–29
Rorty, Richard, 123
Rosner, Victoria, 69, 164, 167, 168
routines
denying external world, 73–74
domestic, during wartime, 104
self-maintenance, 78
routinization, ordinary, 19
ruminative or reflective, terms, 138
Russian Formalists, ostranenie, 4
Russian structuralist, texts without plots, 46

scatology, realism, 42–43
Schoenbach, Lisi, 98, 171
scrupulous meanness, Joyce's style, 39
self-consciousness, modernist preoccupation, 3
self-mockery, Stevens, 129–130
sensory perception, environment, 44–45
servants
mundane housework, 81–82
routines of, in Woolf's novels, 70
shadow, movement to real, 77
Shattuck, Roger, 159, 161, 174
Shklovsky, Victor, 4, 5, 6, 25, 50, 95, 100
shock
art, 25
modern wartime, 9
ordinary giving form to, 8–9
significance, real life events, 53–54
social status, connotation of ordinary, 9
society, habit as "fly-wheel of society," 91–101
solitary meditation, plainness of poem, 139
Spender, Stephen, 60, 124, 168
status quo, everyday life, 15
Stein, Gertrude
avant-garde, 89, 105
celebrating habit, 90, 97, 102, 153
comparison to Samuel Beckett, 109–110
daily island life, 97, 101
forwardness of time, 111
France during occupation, 102–106
modern, 89–90
Mrs. Reynolds, 106–109
Narration, 94, 99
Paris France, 101
"Poetry and Grammar," 98
"Portraits and Repetition," 6
Stevens's work vs., 145
Tender Buttons, 98, 99, 100
The Making of Americans, 91
*Three Lives,* 94, 106, 111
treatment of history in *Mrs. Reynolds,* 106–107
war and everyday life, 100–101
*Wars I Have Seen,* 100–101, 102, 105, 113
"What Is English Literature," 97, 99
World War II writings, 90, 91, 98, 100, 101, 113–114
*Stephen Hero,* epiphany, 40–41, 43
Stevens, Wallace
"Academic Discourses in Havana," 133
"The Comedian as the Letter C," 120, 127–128
commitment to "sufficiency" of ordinary, 116
commonplace, 115, 119, 129, 130–131, 141–142
conception of change, 140–141
concept of language, 118, 122, 137
conflict between abstract and actual world, 117
"The Course of a Particular," 117, 139
difference from Auden and Eliot, 124–125
divinity, 144–145
domestic isolation, 129
"Esthétique de Mal," 120, 123, 130
finding resemblance, 151
"The Idea of Order at Key West," 144
"Imagination as Value," 125, 139
imagining reader's perspective, 142–143
"The Man on the Dump," 26

*The Man With the Blue Guitar,* 119
"The Noble Rider and the Sound of Words," 126
normal in place of regularly, 120
normal is "activity," 122
"Not Ideas About the Thing but the Thing Itself," 138
"Notes Toward a Supreme Fiction," 24, 115, 116, 130, 136, 139
"Of Modern Poetry," 123–124
"ordinary" and "normal," 115–116
"Ordinary Evening in New Haven," 117–118, 121, 122, 131–132, 137–148
*Owl's Clover,* 119, 120, 141
"The Pleasures of Merely Circulating," 115
"The Poems of Our Climate," 127
resemblances between disparate things, 134–135
response of poems to war, 119–120
self-conception, 136
"The Snow Man," 139
"Sunday Morning," 12, 47, 144
"Three Academic Pieces," 134–135
trusting language, 146–147
"Waving Adieu, Adieu, Adieu," 127
style
commonplace, 138–139
plurality in *Ulysses,* 50–51, 146

Taylor, Charles, 22, 30, 61, 165
telephone directory, texts without plots, 46
temporality
day-to-day experience, 66–67
modernist representations of, 151
*Tender Buttons,* Gertrude Stein, 98, 99, 100
*The Auroras of Autumn,* Stevens, 137
"The Leaning Tower," Virginia Woolf, 60
*The Making of Americans,* Gertrude Stein, 91
themes, Virginia Woolf, 77
"The Narrow Bridge of Art," Virginia Woolf, 60
theory, everyday life, 12–17
*The Rock,* Stevens, 137
*The Waste Land,* language, 123–124
*The Waves,* Virginia Woolf, 83–84
*The Wild Duck,* Ibsen's everyday, 38
*The Years,* Virginia Woolf, 84
things, literature of England describing, 97–98
*Thom's Official Directory,* Joyce's reliance, 48
thought, memory and, 62–63
*Three Lives,* obtuse narration, 111
time
desire to control, 152–153
forwardness of, in Stein's novel, 111
habit filling, 151–152
ordering of, 151–152
reality, 158
*Time and Free Will,* Henri Bergson, 151
"Time Passes," Virginia Woolf, 80–82
Transcendentalism, Ralph Waldo Emerson, 92
trauma
facts by Woolf against force of, 78
power of everyday over, 76
traumatic experience, nonbeing and memorable event, 74–75
trivial moments, Proust, 149–150

*Ulysses*
history, 42
interpretations, 45–46
language, 45, 51–52
limitations of everyday, 36
lists, 35, 45–55, 143–144
materialism, 43
ordinary functions, 33–34
plurality of styles, 50–51, 146
unconscious action, habit as, 95
universality, everyday, 80
unselfconscious routines, ordinary things, 67–68

valuation, ordinary, 5–7, 9
vulgarity, Joyce's material, 41, 42
vulgarity of speech, epiphany, 8

*Waiting for Godot,* Samuel Beckett, 109–110
war. *See also* World War II
before and after, 28, 29
commonplace events, 125
habits during, 100, 113
horrors of humanity, 74
Mrs. Reynolds, 108–109

war. *See also* World War II (*continued*)
ordinary experiences during twentieth century, 30–32
ordinary life and modern, 27–32
response of Stevens's poems to, 119–120
Stein in France during occupation, 102–106
Stevens's attitude about, 135
Stevens's desire for humanist ending, 130
writings of Stein, 100–101
*Wars I Have Seen*, Stein, 100–101, 102, 105, 113
wartime, shock of modern, 9
Watt, Ian, 17, 20, 47, 48
weather, recurrent metaphor, 25
weather of war
observations of Stevens, 126–128
ordinary, 10
"What Is English Literature," Stein celebrating habit, 97, 99
Whittier-Ferguson, John, 105, 165, 170, 171
Will, Barbara, 105, 170
Williams, Raymond, 15, 16
Williams, William Carlos, 26, 27, 123, 129, 138
wisdom, balance and age, 141
women, ordinary, 16–17
Wordsworth, William, 25, 27, 34, 62, 63
Woolf, Leonard, 169
Woolf, Virginia
"A Letter to a Young Poet," 57, 60–61
Between the Acts, 70, 84–85
biography, 58
catchword "ordinary," 69
"cotton wool of daily life," 73, 86–87, 96, 133
facts and things, 77–87
inclusion of prosaic, 82–83
*Jacob's Room*, 76–77
"Jane Austen," 69–70
"The Leaning Tower," 60
"Modern Fiction," 58, 59,63, 66
moments of being vs. nonbeing, 64–65
"Mr. Bennett and Mrs. Brown," 61, 66, 71
*Mrs. Dalloway*, 66–77, 82
"The Narrow Bridge of Art," 65
"On Being Ill," 87
ordinary as defining feature, 86–87
patterns in life, 63
perception and overlooking, 70–71
"Phases of Fiction," 59, 83, 85–86
"poetic" prose, 57
poetry vs., prose, 60–77
significance of nonbeing, 64
"A Sketch of the Past," 62–65
subjectivity, interiority, and poetry, 61–62
themes, 77
"The Narrow Bridge of Art," 65–66
"Time Passes," 80–82
*To The Lighthouse*, 77, 78, 80–82
*The Waves*, 79, 83–84, 87
*The Years*, 84, 87
"world of pure experience," term, 92
World War II. *See also* war
connection of daily life and politics, 112
Mrs. Reynolds, 108, 153
poetic power, 128
poetic thought, 128–129
Stein's writings, 74, 90, 91, 98, 100, 101, 113–114
Stevens's abstraction, 116

Yeats, W. B., 10, 37, 61, 96, 128, 136
Yeazell, Ruth, 165